Lecture Notes in Computer Scie

Commenced Publication in 1973
Founding and Former Series Editors:
Gerhard Goos, Juris Hartmanis, and Jan van Leeuwen

James Odell   Paolo Giorgini
Jörg P. Müller (Eds.)

Agent-Oriented
Software
Engineering V

5th International Workshop, AOSE 2004
New York, NY, USA, July 19, 2004
Revised Selected Papers

 Springer

Volume Editors

James Odell
Agentis
3646 West Huron River Drive, Ann Arbor, MI 48103, USA
E-mail: email@jamesodell.com

Paolo Giorgini
University of Trento, Department of Information and Communication Technology
Via Somamrive, 14, 38050 Provo, Italy
E-mail: paolo.giorgini@dit.unitn.it

Jörg P. Müller
Siemens AG, Corporate Technology, Intelligent Autonomous Systems
Otto-Hahn-Ring 6, 81730 Munich, Germany
E-mail: joerg.p.mueller@siemens.com

Library of Congress Control Number: 2004117070

CR Subject Classification (1998): D.2, I.2.11, F.3, D.1, C.2.4, D.3

ISSN 0302-9743
ISBN 3-540-24286-4 Springer Berlin Heidelberg New York

Springer is a part of Springer Science+Business Media

springeronline.com

© Springer-Verlag Berlin Heidelberg 2005
Printed in Germany

Typesetting: Camera-ready by author, data conversion by PTP-Berlin, Protago-TeX-Production GmbH
Printed on acid-free paper   SPIN: 11375104   06/3142   5 4 3 2 1 0

Preface

The explosive growth of application areas such as electronic commerce, enterprise resource planning and mobile computing has profoundly and irreversibly changed our views on software systems. Nowadays, software is to be based on open architectures that continuously change and evolve to accommodate new components and meet new requirements. Software must also operate on different platforms, without recompilation, and with minimal assumptions about its operating environment and its users. Furthermore, software must be robust and autonomous, capable of serving a naïve user with a minimum of overhead and interference.

Agent concepts hold great promise for responding to the new realities of software systems. They offer higher-level abstractions and mechanisms which address issues such as knowledge representation and reasoning, communication, coordination, cooperation among heterogeneous and autonomous parties, perception, commitments, goals, beliefs, and intentions, all of which need conceptual modelling. On the one hand, the concrete implementation of these concepts can lead to advanced functionalities, e.g., in inference-based query answering, transaction control, adaptive workflows, brokering and integration of disparate information sources, and automated communication processes. On the other hand, their rich representational capabilities allow more faithful and flexible treatments of complex organizational processes, leading to more effective requirements analysis and architectural/detailed design.

As its very successful predecessors, AOSE 2000, AOSE 2001, AOSE 2002, and AOSE 2003 (Lecture Notes in Computer Science, Volumes 1957, 2222, 2585, and 2935), the AOSE 2004 workshop sought to examine the credentials of agent-based approaches as a software engineering paradigm, and to gain an insight into what agent-oriented software engineering will look like.

AOSE 2004 was hosted by the 3rd International Joint Conference on Autonomous Agents and Multiagent Systems (AAMAS 2004) held in New York, USA on July 2004. The workshop received 57 submissions, and 15 of them were accepted for presentation (which is an acceptance rate of 26%). These papers were reviewed by at least two members of an international program committee composed of 29 researchers. The submissions followed a call for papers on all aspects of agent-oriented software engineering and showed the range of results achieved in several areas such as methodologies, modeling, architectures, and tools.

The workshop program included an invited talk, a technical session in which the accepted papers were presented and discussed, and a closing plenary session. It congregated more than 50 attendees among researchers, students and practitioners, who contributed to the discussion of research problems related to the main topics in AOSE.

This volume contains revised and improved versions of the 15 papers presented at the workshop, organized in three sections: *Modeling*, *Design*, and *Reuse and Platforms*. We believe that this thoroughly prepared volume is of particular value to all readers interested in key topics and the most recent developments in the very exciting field of agent-oriented software engineering.

We thank the authors, the participants, and the reviewers for making AOSE 2004 a high-quality scientific event.

November 2004

Paolo Giorgini
Jörg P. Müller
James Odell

Organization

Organizing Committee

Paolo Giorgini (Co-chair)
Department of Information and Communication Technology
University of Trento, Italy
Email: paolo.giorgini@dit.unitn.it

Jörg P. Müller (Co-chair)
Siemens AG, Germany
Email: joerg.p.mueller@siemens.de

James Odell (Co-chair)
James Odell Associates, Ann Arbor, MI, USA
Email: email@jamesodell.com

Steering Committee

Paolo Ciancarini, University of Bologna, Italy
Gerhard Weiss, Technische Universitaet Muenchen, Germany
Michael Wooldridge, University of Liverpool, UK

Program Committee

Bernard Bauer (Germany)
Federico Bergenti (Italy)
Paolo Ciancarini (Italy)
Scott DeLoach (USA)
Marie-Pierre Gervais (France)
Olivier Gutknecht (France)
Brian Henderson-Sellers (Australia)
Michael Huhns (USA)
Carlos Iglesias (Spain)
Nicholas Jennings (UK)
Catholijn Jonker (Netherlands)
David Kinny (Australia)
Manuel Kolp (Belgium)
Yannis Labrou (USA)
Juergen Lind (Germany)

Haralambos Mouratidis (UK)
Matthias Nickles (Germany)
Andrea Omicini (Italy)
Van Parunak (USA)
Juan Pavon (Spain)
Anna Perini (Italy)
Marco Pistore (Italy)
Onn Shehory (Israel)
Paola Turci (Italy)
Gerd Wagner (Germany)
Gerhard Weiss (Germany)
Mike Wooldridge (UK)
Eric Yu (Canada)
Franco Zambonelli (Italy)

Auxiliary Reviewers: Paolo Busetta, Giancarlo Guizzardi, Savas Konur, Viara
Popova, Michael Rovatsos, Alexei Sharpanskykh, Arnon Sturm, Angelo Susi,
Vera Werneck

Table of Contents

Modeling

Design

Reuse and Platforms

Organizational and Social Concepts in Agent Oriented Software Engineering

Xinjun Mao[1] and Eric Yu[2]

[1] Department of Computer Science, National University of Defense Technology, China
xjmao21@21cn.com
[2] Faculty of Information Studies, University of Toronto, Canada
eric.yu@utoronto.ca

Abstract. AOSE methodologies and models borrow abstractions and concepts from organizational and social disciplines. Although they all view multi-agent systems as organized society, the organizational abstractions, assumptions, concepts, and models in them are actually used in different ways. It is therefore desirable to have a systematic way of analyzing and comparing the organizational and social concepts in AOSE. The contribution of this paper is threefold. Firstly, we identify some premises behind the social conceptions adopted in multi-agent systems. Secondly, we define levels of modeling constructs and classify organizational and social concepts in the AOSE literature into categories according to their organizational abstractions. Finally, we analyze two representative AOSE methodologies and their models, explaining how they use organizational and social concepts to analyze and specify multi-agent system, reflecting various social premises at different levels.

1 Introduction

Multi-agent systems (MAS) are rapidly emerging as a powerful paradigm for developing complex system. However, if we want the paradigm to be successfully applied in the development of complex system, the models, technologies and even the methodologies should be developed to support the developers to engineer such systems in a robust, reliable, and repeatable fashion.

MAS research often draws on concepts from other disciplines such as psychology, economic, cognitive science, linguistics, artificial intelligence, etc. For example, we often analyze interaction protocols and communication actions among agents based on the speech acts theory, which comes from philosophy and linguistics. The abstraction of the intentional stance has been borrowed from cognitive science to reason about and analyze the autonomous behaviors of agents. Recently, many methodologies and models borrowing the abstractions and concepts from the organization and sociology disciplines have been put forward for modeling, analyzing and designing MAS. Although these methodologies all view multi-agent systems as organized society in a broad sense, the organization abstractions, concepts, assumptions and models that they adopt are actually varied. The proposed methodologies may vary in the stages of

---

[1] This research was conducted while the first author was visiting the University of Toronto.

J. Odell et al. (Eds.): AOSE 2004, LNCS 3382, pp. 1 – 15, 2005.

software engineering life cycle that they support, thus adopting different assumptions about organizations, and different levels of abstraction in their models. In addition, some of the organizational and social concepts, while using different terminology, may have similar meaning and purpose. Conversely, a given term may have different interpretations and definitions in various models and methodologies.

Many papers have provided comparisons and evaluations of the methodologies in agent oriented software engineering (AOSE), such as [23, 24, 34, 26, 27, 28]. However, there are few efforts to compare them from the standpoint of organizational and social abstractions, especially to analyze the organizational and social concepts in AOSE literature. Since organizational and social abstractions are playing central roles in the design of AOSE methodologies and the development of multi-agent systems, it is important to have a map of the research on organizational and social concepts in AOSE. The rest of this paper is structured as follows. Section 2 analyzes the assumptions in social abstractions. Section 3 defines the modeling construct levels of MAS, identify and classify the organizational and social concepts in AOSE literature and explain in detail how they are used to specify and analyze the MAS. Section 4 analyzes a number of AOSE methodologies that are influential in AOSE. Finally, conclusions and future work are discussed in section 5.

2   Simplifying Assumptions in Social Abstractions

In adopting concepts from the social and organizational sciences, AOSE methodologies are not attempting to capture the full richness of human social phenomena. The borrowed concepts are selected abstractions that are considered to be useful for the purpose of conceiving and designing multi-agent software systems. Thus, each methodology selects a set of concepts and modeling constructs appropriate for its intended purposes, and possibly for a specialized application area or context. In doing so, a methodology incorporates assumptions and premises about organizations and societies, either implicitly or explicitly. Typically, these are simplifying assumptions which reduce the complexity of social phenomena. Despite simplifications and restrictions, through these social and organizational concepts, AOSE methodologies offer higher level abstractions than conventional software engineering paradigms. Thus agent orientation can be seen as the latest step in the progression towards better modeling abstractions that are closer to the real world, shortening the conceptual distance between the full richness of the application domain and the models offered by the software methodology to describe the world.

In analyzing a variety of AOSE methodologies, we note that their premises may vary with regard to at least the following characteristics.

• **Open or Closed.** A system is open if it has no definite boundary, thus allowing new, possibly unknown agents to enter or leave from time to time in the life cycle of the system. Therefore, the collection of entities (e.g., agents) in an open system may change and cannot be completely defined at design time. For instance, the Internet is such an open system. For closed systems, the population of system elements does not vary at run time. Therefore, they can be defined at design time by the software developers. Clearly, open systems present design challenges that are not found in closed ones.

- **Dynamic or Static.** A system is dynamic if the system elements, especially the abilities of agents in the system and the services they provide and/or the inter-agent relationships, can change at run-time. For example, the roles that an agent plays may vary in different contexts and situations, and therefore the inter-agent relationships (e.g., the interactions and/or dependencies) may also change. For a static system, all of the system elements are invariable. Typically, dynamic systems are more complicated and more difficult to develop than static ones.
- **Cooperative or Self-Interested.** The agents in some system may be cooperative in certain social context. They share some common goals and interact with each other in a cooperatively way to willingly provide resources and services. Conversely, the self-interested agent does for itself, and may refuse to provide services or resources for other agents. In addition, conflicts are more likely to occur between self-interested agents, especially when scarce resources need to be shared.
- **Hierarchic.** Many systems are hierarchic, i.e., composed of interrelated sub-systems, each of which is in turn hierarchic in structure, until the lowest level of elementary sub-system is reached [9]. There can be various relationships among the sub-systems. In contrast, the hierarchic systems evolve more quickly than non-hierarchic ones of comparable size, which make them more difficult to deal with [9]. Hierarchic structures are used extensively in software engineering to reduce system complexity. However, many social structures are not hierarchic.
- **Global Constraint.** In some systems, there are global constraints that are respected by all agents in the system and thus govern the relationships and interactions among them. For example, a social law constrains the behavior of agents in the organization. The explicit identification of the global constraints is of particular importance in the context of open system with self-interested agents. Such constraints can simplify system analysis and design.

3 Analyzing Organizational and Social Concepts in AOSE

In this section, we identify several levels of modeling constructs that are used in modeling MAS. We then classify the organizational and social concepts found in the AOSE literature, explaining how they can be used to model MAS.

3.1 Modeling Construct Levels

For the purpose of analysis, we organize the modeling constructs into a number of levels.

- **Single Agent.** In this level, the autonomous behaviors of agents are specified and analyzed in an abstract way. Generally, the functionalities and activities of agents are the most important aspects that should be modeled. For example, what are the functionalities of agents? what the resources and/or activities should they have in order to accomplish their functionalities? etc. The models describing the single agent are important constituents of the system requirement specification to guide the design of software agents.
- **Two Agents.** Agents in MAS are not isolated from one to another. Two agents may have various relationships between them like structural ones and behavioral ones. For example, one agent depends on another agent to get the resources required

to accomplish its tasks, or should explicitly interacts with other agent by some interaction protocol (e.g., contract net) to acquire the resources or the assigned tasks; one agent may be the supervisor of another one and has the authority to assign the tasks to it. The information about the relationships between agents should be explicitly specified and analyzed in support of the requirement specification and analysis and further guide the software architecture design.

• **Two or More Agents Acting in a Coordinated Way.** In some MASs, two or more agents are organized together as a group and act in a coordinated way in order to achieve some common purposes. Agents in one group are often cooperative and have some common goals and joint behaviors. For such MASs, it is necessary in the analysis and design phase to identify and define the groups in the system, specify them in detail about the structural information (e.g., how agents in the group are organized) and the behavioral information (e.g., what the common goals of agents in the group) of them.

• **All Agents.** In this level, all agents in the system are treated as one organization, which should be specified and analyzed. For example, what is the organization structure of the system? Are there any global constraints in the organization that govern all agents in it?

3.2 Modeling Concepts

Now we turn to analyzing what the social premises mean in different modeling construct levels, what the organizational and social concepts are required to model MAS in these levels, and how they are used to specify and analyze the systems with various social premises. Although the organizational and social concepts are diverse in AOSE literature, a clear taxonomy of these concepts can be made according to their modeling purpose and the system construct level that they intend to deal with. In each category, the organizational and social concepts can be further divided into a number of groups. The concepts in each group often have similar semantics and modeling purpose (see Table 1).

Table 1. A taxonomy of organizational and social concepts in AOSE literature

Construct Levels	Organizational and Social Concepts
Single agent	role, position, actor
	responsibility, goal
	permission, right, resource
	activities, plan, task
Two agents	dependency, interaction
Two or more agents acting in a coordinated way	group, group structure
	common goal, joint intention(commitment)
All agents	organization
	organization rule, social law, interaction rule
	organization structure, organization pattern

3.2.1 Concepts for Modeling Single Agent

The organizational and social concepts in this level are used to specify and model the individuals (i.e., agent) in MAS and relatively in a low and micro abstraction level. In general, the functionalities, activities and resources of agents should be specified and analyzed independently of their concrete details.

In addition, according to the social premises described in section 2, agents in MAS may be dynamic or static, cooperative or self-interested. Dynamic agents may have different functionalities and activities in their life cycles. For self-interested agents, their functionalities, activities and resources may conflict with each other. Therefore, these social premises about agents also should be explicitly modeled and analyzed if the target system has these social properties.

- **Role, Position and Actor.** A *role* is an abstract characterization of the behaviors of agents within some specified context of organization. Generally, an agent can play multiple roles and a role can be played by a number of agents in MAS. Other concepts similar to role are *position* and *actor* used in *i** and Tropos. *Position* is a collection of roles that are occupied by one agent and *actor* is a generic concept to denote the intentional entity that may be an agent or role or position.

These concepts are important to abstractly model the agents in MAS, and helpful to manage the complexity of MAS without considering the concrete details of agents (e.g., implementation architectures and technologies). They present an effective way to naturally model the entities in the system. In general, the system's roles that agents play are specified in the role model like ones in Gaia, MaSE, etc. Therefore, the *role* concept, we can find, has been integrated into almost all of the AOSE methodologies based on the organizational and social abstractions.

The dynamic properties of agent can be viewed as that agent plays different roles in different context and situation, which will facilitate to model the dynamic MAS. However, we believe, the traditional role models like ones in MaSE, Gaia, etc., are unable to model such dynamic information. Therefore, other system model based on the role concept should be developed like one in [36] to show how agents dynamically enter or leave roles in different social situations.

- **Responsibility and Goal.** These concepts are used to specify and analyze the functionalities of a role. In Gaia, *responsibilities* are divided into two types; *liveness properties* and *safety properties*. *Liveness properties* describe those states of affairs that an agent must bring about given certain environment conditions. In contrast, *safety properties* correspond to the invariants in multi-agent system that agent must maintain. The *goal* of a *role* represents its strategic interests or intentions. In *i** and Tropos, two kinds of *goals* can be distinguished: *HardGoal* and *SoftGoal*. The latter denotes the goal that has no clear-cut definition or criteria for decision whether it is satisfied or not, and is typically used to specify the non-functional requirements.

Generally the functionalities of roles should be specified and analyzed in requirement phase in order to understand the behaviors of roles and guide the software design that implements the roles' functionalities. In contrast to the tasks, actions and plans of roles, the responsibilities or goals of roles are relatively high-level and stable, even in open and dynamic system, and therefore easy to elicit and specify. In addition, roles are typically goal-driven, therefore the goals or responsibilities of roles are related with their tasks, plans and interactions. The explicit identification and specification of the goals or responsibilities of roles will facilitate to elicit and model the tasks or plans that roles have, the resources and interactions that roles need, the rule it should obey in order to achieve its goals or responsibilities. Moreover, they are also helpful to analyze the potential goals conflict between the self-interested agents.

• **Permission, Right and Resource.** These concepts are used to specify and analyze what the roles require in order to realize their functionalities. *Permissions* in Gaia are the "rights" associated with a *role*. The *permission* of a role identifies the *resources* that are available to that role in order to realize its *responsibilities*. In the information system, the *permission* tends to be the information *resources* [8]. Other analogous concepts are *rights* in [3] and *resource* representing a physical or an informational unintentional entity in *i**, Tropos, and SODA.

Usually the resources are needed when agents intend to achieve their goals or responsibilities. In most cases, they are distributed in the environments that agents situate and may be dynamic. The resources in the environment are often limited and shared by a number of agents. To explicitly specify permission or resource of roles and model the environment that agents situate is significant to analyze how agent interacts with the environment, and the dependency between roles (e.g., some agents need resources while others produce resources). It is of particular importance to investigate the resource or "right" conflicts that may occur between the self-interested agents in dynamic system with limited resources.

• **Activity, Plan, Task.** These concepts are used to specify and analyze the behaviors that roles should have in order to accomplish their functionalities. The *activity* of a role in Gaia is actually the "private" action that may be carried out by the agent without interacting with other agents in order to realize its *responsibilities*. The *plan* concept in Tropos (analogous to the concept *task* in *i** framework) represents, in an abstract level, a way of doing something. The execution of the *plan* can be a means for satisfying a goal [16]. The *tasks* in SODA, however, can be classified as individual ones and social ones and expressed in term of the *responsibilities* they involve, of the competence they require, and of the *resources* they depend on. Typical, *social tasks* are those that require a number of different competences and the access to several different *resources*, whereas *individual tasks* are more likely to require well-delimited competence and limited *resources* [29].

These concepts describe in more detail the behaviors of roles and are necessary in the requirement analysis phase to show how to accomplish the roles' goals or responsibilities, and guide the software design that naturally encapsulate and implement these behaviors. Therefore most of the methodologies in AOSE support to model the role's activity, plan, or task to some extent.

3.2.2 Concepts for Modeling Two Agents

The organizational and social concepts in this level are used to model the relationships between individual agents. In general, the structural relationship and the behavioral relationship between two agents should be modeled when developing MAS. The relationships between agents may change for the dynamic system when the roles that agents play vary. Therefore, such dynamic relationships between agents also should be specified and analyzed if the target systems are dynamic.

- **Dependency and Interaction Protocol.** One of the most important relationships between agents may be the interactions, which describe the behavioral relationship between agents, and are often specified by *interaction protocol* which defines the ways that agents can interact with each other. Most of AOSE methodologies, we can find, have developed various models to explicitly specify the interactions between agents, e.g., the interaction model in Gaia, communication model in MaSE. The *dependencies* between agents mainly describe the structural relationships between agents. They, in the *i** and Tropos, are used to indicate that one role depends, for some reason, on the other in order to attain some goal, execute some plan, or deliver a resource. The dependencies between roles can be classified as four kinds: *HardGoal dependency*, *SoftGoal dependency, task dependency*, *resource dependency*.

Both the structural relationship and the behavior relationship between agents should be modeled when developing MAS. They are also helpful to define the acquaintance model to show what agents or components in MAS are related with each other, which is important to analyze the system requirements and design the software architecture. The explicit specification and analysis of the dependencies between agents are also of particular importance to elicit and define the organization structure and the organization pattern. For dynamic MAS, there are still few works and efforts to model the dynamic relationships between gents. However, one possible way to deal with it is to define multiple models, for example the dependency model and/or interaction model, for agents with dynamic relationship in different organization context and situation.

3.2.3 Concepts for Modeling Two or More Agents Acting in a Coordinated Way

The organizational and social concepts in this level are used to specify and model the groups of MAS, in which agents act in a coordinated way. Group is an effective tool for partitioning and decomposing the organization, and organizing the agents with some common goals or purposes together, which is of particular importance for the hierarchic MAS. As for the dynamic system, the groups of MAS can also change from time to time. For example, the new group is created, agents dynamically leave the on-going groups and enter into a new one, the common characteristics (e.g., goals) of the agents in the group are formed. Therefore, in this level, the dynamic and hierarchic properties of the groups should be explicitly modeled if the target system has these social properties.

- **Group and Group Structure.** A *group* is a set of agents sharing some common characteristics and used as a context for a pattern activities and for partitioning organizations [35, 36, 37]. It is actually a special organization and similar to the concepts of *sub-organization* in [6,9] to decompose the system. Therefore, the *group* concept defines the atomic sets of agent aggregation. The *group structure* is the abstract description of a *group*. It actually identifies and specifies the structural information of groups such as all the *roles* and the *relationships* that can appear with a *group* [35].
- **Common Goal, Joint Intention, Commitment.** The behavioral information of group is another important part that should be specified and analyzed when developing MAS with groups. The common characteristic of agents in group that will govern the behaviors of them is often specified by such concept as *common goal*. In

addition, the concepts such as *joint intention and joint commitment*, are often used to describe how agents in group behave in a coordinated way to accomplish their common goals.

The group concept is useful to analyze, decompose and partition the hierarchic organization with clear group boundary, which is helpful to control the system complexity. The group structure can be used to instantiate various groups that can be created dynamically in the organization. However, additional models should be developed based on the concepts such as group and role in order to specify and analyze the whole dynamic information in this level. For example, [36] develops a model called an organization sequence diagram to specify and analyze how the groups are created and abolished dynamically, how agents in the organization dynamically enter or leave the groups in different organization context and situation.

3.2.4 Concepts for Modeling All Agents

The organizational and social concepts in this level are used to specify and model the macro organization information in MAS, especially for representing and analyzing the organization structure and the global constrains in the organization. The organization composed of all agents in the system may be open, which means that new, maybe unknown agents are allowed to enter into the organization. It is believed that such a system is difficult to develop. In addition, some organization has the global constraints such as social laws to govern the running of the agents (especially self-interested ones) in the organization. Therefore, in this level, the open and global constraint premises of the organization should be modeled if the target system has these social premises.

- **Organization.** An *organization* is viewed as a collection of roles that stand in certain relationships to one another and take part in systematic institutionalized patterns of interactions with other roles [8]. However, Ferber pointed out such a definition lacks a very important feature of organization, i.e., partitioning, a tool to partition the system. Organizations are structured as aggregates of several partitions which may overlap and each partition may itself be decomposed into sub-partitions [36].
- **Organization Rule, Social Rule and Interaction Rule.** These concepts define the global constraint information in the organization that will govern the running of the whole organization or society of MAS. *Organization rule* defines the general and global (supra-role) constraints requirements for the proper instantiation and execution of MAS that the actual organization will have to respect and expresses the information about how the organization is expected to work [4, 5, 6]. Generally, it will restrict the behaviors of agents and the interactions among them in MAS, and should have such properties as global, mutual consistent, satisfiable, stable and persistent, etc. Some methodologies such as Gaia [6] and MaSE [11] have introduced the concept as a fundamental element to model and analyze the MAS. Another analogous concept is *social law* in [1, 2], which is actually for the artificial agent societies and guarantees the successful coexistence of multiple programs and programmers. The *interaction rule* in SODA, however, is a special kind of organization rule which will governs the interactions among the social role and resources so as to make the group accomplish its social task [29].

- **Organization Structure and Organization Pattern.** *Organization structure* defines the specific class of organization and control regime to which agents/roles have to conform in order for the whole MAS to work efficiently and according to its specified requirements. It is a design choice that expresses which kind of organization best fits requirements [4, 5]. The structural organizational relationships are the most important parts that should be specified when defining the organization structure, such as control, peer, benevolence, dependency, and ownership, etc. The *organization pattern* defines and expresses pre-defined and widely used organizational structures that can be reused from system to system [6].

The concepts such as organization rule, social law, etc, are the natural abstraction to the global constraints in the organization. The explicit identification and specification of the *organizational rules* is of particular importance in the context of open systems. With the arrival of new, previously unknown, and possible self-interested agents, the overall organization must somehow enforce its internal coherency despite the dynamic and untrustworthy environment. The identification of global organizational rules allows the system designer to explicitly define: whether and when to allow newly arrived agents to enter the organization , and once accepted, what their position in the organization should be; which behaviors should be considered as an expression of self-interest, and which among them should be prevented [6]. The organization rule is also useful to develop the system with self-interested agents and limited resources in order to govern the autonomous behaviors of agents and the interactions among them to some extents and prevent systems from falling into chaos. Furthermore, the explicit definition of the *organization structure* is also helpful to the open system as the structure of the organization should persist when components or individual enter or leave an organization, and characterize the organization in the abstract or organization level. To reuse organization structure is an effective way to improve the software quality and development efficiency. Therefore, the specification and analysis of the organization structure and pattern are of particular importance not only for defining the structural information of system in the requirement specification and analysis phase, but also for promoting the software reuse.

4 Analyzing AOSE Methodologies and Models

Up to now, there are many methodologies and models based on the organizational and social abstractions. A list of methodologies and their evaluations can be found in [23, 24, 34]. In this section, we only analyze two of them, which are influential in AOSE literature.

4.1 Gaia

Gaia is a complete methodology based on the organization metaphor for the development of MAS and views the process of analyzing and designing MAS as one of constructing computational organizations. It is, to our knowledge, the first AOSE methodology that explicitly takes into account organization as a first-class abstraction. Gaia was originally proposed by Wooldridge et al [8]. An extended version was proposed recently by Zambonelli et al [6]. As the two versions are different in organization assumptions, abstractions, concepts and models, we will refer to the original version as Gaia1, the later version as Gaia2, or simply Gaia when we do not need to make a distinction.

Table 2. The modeling concepts and system models of Gaia

Construct Levels	Organizational and Social concepts	System Models
Single agent	*role, activity, permission, responsibility*	*role model environment model*
Two agents	*interaction*	*interaction model*
Level of two or more agents acting in a coordinated way	*sub-organization*	–
All agents	*organization, organization rule, structure and pattern*	*organizational rule model organization structure model*

Gaia1 views MAS as an organization composed of a collection of *roles* standing in certain relationships to one another and taking part in systematic patterns of *interaction* with other *roles*. It explicitly assumes that the systems to be developed should be static (i.e., the inter-agent relationships do not change at run-time) and closed, the agents in the system also should be static (i.e., the abilities of agents and the services they provide do not change at run-time), there is no true conflict in the system and therefore the agents in the system are cooperative with each other.

In order to analyze and design such kind of systems, Gaia1 presents the role models and interaction models in the analysis phase, and agent model, service model and acquaintance model in the design phase. Each *role* in the role model is defined by four attributes: *responsibility*, *permission*, *activity* and *protocol*, which respectively define the functionalities, resources, private actions and interactions of roles. The relationships among roles are simply defined as the *interactions* specified as the *interaction protocols* defined in the interaction model. The role model and interaction model specified in the analysis phase will guide the software architecture design specified by the agent model, service model and acquaintance model.

Apparently, Gaia1 has rich expression to model MAS in the single agent level and two agents level, but it is weak in the all agents level and level of two or more agents acting in a coordinated way. According to organization assumptions, obviously Gaia1 is just appropriate to the close and static system, e.g., business process management, etc. A complete criticism on the limitations of the Gaia1 methodology can be found in [20].

Gaia2 is an extension to Gaia1. The purposes of Gaia2 are to introduce more organization abstractions into methodology and provide clear guidelines for the analysis and design of complex and open system. It assumes that the organization to be developed has global constraints that are represented by organization rule and hierarchic structure that can be divided into a number of sub-organizations. The system can be open or closed, dynamic or static. Agents in the system can be cooperative or self-interested. The extensions are mainly based on three high-level organization abstractions and concepts such as *organization rule* to represent the global organization constraints that is beneficial to model the open system with self-interested agents, *organization structure* and *organizational pattern* that are helpful to specify and analyze the dynamic system and can be reused from system to system. It also explicitly models the environment information and extends the development process.

These extensions, while preserving the simplicity of Gaia2, enable it to be used in the analysis and design of the open MASs with self-interested agents to some extent, e.g., manufacturing pipeline, conference management, etc. Apparently, Gaia2 enriches the modeling capability in the all agents level by introducing new organizational and social concepts and their related system models in order to deal with the complex open MAS. However, it is still weak in the level of two or more agents acting in a coordinated way. Table 2 lists the organizational and social concepts and related system models in various construct levels of Gaia. Figure 1 shows the meta-model of Gaia.

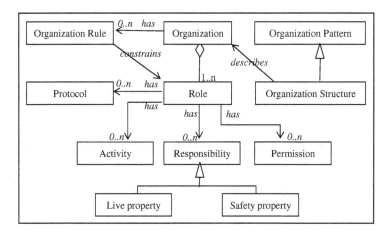

Fig. 1. The meta-model of Gaia

4.2   AALAADIN

AALAADIN [35] is actually an abstraction and generic MAS model and particularly focuses on the organization-centered MAS modeling in order to resolve the drawbacks of classical agent-centered technologies.

AALAADIN assumes that systems to be developed are closed and have hierarchic structure that can be decomposed as a number of interrelated groups, and agents in the system are cooperative. The groups in the organization can be dynamically created, and agent can dynamically enter or leave the group. In order to model such systems, AALAADIN introduces organizational concepts such as *group*, *role* and *structure*. In AALAADIN, an *organization* is composed of a number of overlapping

Table 3. The modeling concepts and system models of AALAADIN

Construct Levels	Organizational and Social concepts	System Models
Single agent	*role*	*organization structure model,*
Two agents	*interaction*	
Level of two or more agents acting in a coordinated way	*group* *group Structure*	*organization sequence model*
All agents	*organization, organization structure*	

groups, each of them aggregates a number of agents that is an active entity playing *roles* within the *group.* An agent can be a member of multiple groups at the same time. AALAADIN place no constraints on the internal architecture of agents and does not assume any formalism for individual agent. *Group and group structure* are introduced to partition *organization* and specify the group information. The *group structure* defines the *roles* and the *interactions* between the roles that can appear within the group. The concept of *organization structure* is also introduced, which defines the *group structure* in the organization and the correspondences between them. A recent work in [36] extended the AALAADIN: the organization description consists in two aspects: a structural aspect and a dynamic aspect. The structure aspect of an organization is made of two parts: a partitioning structure and a role structure. The dynamic aspect of an organization is related to the institutionalized patterns of interactions that are defined within the roles, such as the creation of groups, the entering and leaving of a group by an agent, or acquisition of a role in relation, which can be specified by Organizational Sequence Diagram, an extension of sequence diagram in UML. Although AALAADIN is just an abstract MAS model, it is useful to support the analysis and specification of the system requirements and further guide the design of MASs.

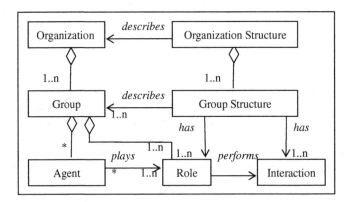

Fig. 2. The meta-model of AALAADIN

Table 3 shows the organizational and social concepts and related system models in AALAADIN. It is obvious that AALAADIN has rich expression to model MAS in the two agents level, all agents level and especially level of two or more agents acting in a coordinated way. But it is weak in the single agent level. This is because that AALAADIN pays more attentions to modeling MAS in an organization-centered way. Such an abstract MAS model is suitable for the closed system with cooperative agents, and especially with the hierarchic structure, e.g., enterprise information system, etc. Figure 2 shows the meta-model of AALAADIN.

5 Conclusions

Organization and social metaphors are important in AOSE because they provide us with abstraction that are significant in software engineering to naturally model MAS and effectively control system complexity. By raising the level of abstraction in software engineering models, they can serve to facilitate understanding among developers, users and stakeholders, and can help to reduce the conceptual distance between the real world and the systems that we develop.

The research in this paper shows that different organizational and social concepts have different modeling purposes and are used in different modeling construct levels for various MAS with different social premises. Although some methodologies and models claim that they support the development of open and complex system, the existing methodologies are still weak in modeling the open, dynamic organization with self-interested agents. We believe that more modeling mechanisms such as concepts and models should be introduced and developed in order to specify and analyze the self-interested agent and the open and dynamic properties of systems. While different organizational and social concepts may be needed to serve a range of purposes in different methodologies, it would be desirable to have some consolidation and standardization of terminology and semantics as the field matures.

Acknowledgements. The first author gratefully acknowledges financial support from Chinese government and Natural Science Foundation of China for his one-year visiting in University of Toronto. The second author gratefully acknowledges financial support from the Natural Sciences and Engineering Research Council of Canada.

References

1. Y Shoham and M Tennenholtz, On the synthesis of the useful social laws for the artificial agents societies, in Proc. AAAI-92: 276-281, AAAI press, 1992.
2. Y Shoham and M Tennenholtz, On Social Laws for Artificial Agent Societies: Off-Line Design, Artificial Intelligence, Artificial Intelligence 73(1-2): 231-252, 1995.
3. E Alonso, Rights for Multi-agent Systems, UKMAS 2002, Springer, LNAI 2403, 59-72, 2002.
4. F. Zambonelli, N. Jennings, M. Wooldridge, Organizational Rules as an Abstraction for the Analysis and Design of Multi-agent Systems, Journal of Knowledge and Software Engineering, 11(3), 303-328, 2001.

5. F. Zambonelli, N R.Jennings, M Wooldridge, Organizational Abstractions for the Analysis and Design of Multi-agent System, AOSE'2001, LNCS2222, 127-141, Springer, 2002.

6. F. Zambonelli, N. R. Jennings, and M. Wooldridge, Developing Multiagent Systems: The Gaia Methodology, ACM Transactions on Software Engineering Methodology, 12(3): 317- 370, 2003.

7. F. Zambonelli, A.Omicini, and M. Wooldridge, Agent-Oriented Software Engineering for Internet Applications, in Coordination of Internet Agents: Models, Technologies and Applications, 326-346, Springer, 2000.

8. Wooldridge, N R.Jennings, and D.Kinny, The Gaia Methodology for Agent-Oriented Analysis and Design, International Journal of Autonomous Agents and Multi-agent System, 3(3):285-312, 2000.

9. N.R.Jennings, An agent-based approach for building complex software systems, Communication of ACM, 44(4): 35-41, 2001.

10. N.R.Jennings, On Agent-based Software Engineering, Artificial Intelligence, 117(2): 277-296, 2000.

11. S A. DeLoach, Modeling Organizational Rules in the Multiagent Systems Engineering Methodology, Proc. of the 15th Canadian Conference on Artificial Intelligence Calgary, Alberta, Canada. May 27-29, 2002.

12. S A. Deloach, M F.Wood, and C H.Sparkman, Multiagents Systems Engineering, International Journal of Software Engineering and Knowledge Engineering, 11(3):231-258, 2001.

13. E. Yu, Agent-Oriented Modelling: Software Versus the World, Proc. Of Agent-Oriented Software Engineering, Springer, LNCS 2222: 206-225, Springer-Verlag, 2001.

14. E. Yu, et.al., From Organization Models to System Requirements: A Cooperative Agents Approach, in Cooperative Information Systems: Trends and Directions, 194-204, 1997.

15. E Yu, Towards Modeling and Reasoning Support for Early-Phase Requirements Engineering, Proceedings of the 3rd IEEE Int. Symp. on Requirements Engineering, 226-235, 1997.

16. F Giunchiglia, John Mylopoulos and A Perini, The Tropos Development Methodology: Processes, Models and Diagrams, Proc. Of AAMAS: 35 - 36, 2002.

17. P Massonet, Yves Deville and C Neve, From AOSE Methodology to Agent Implementation, Proc of AAMAS'02, 2002.

18. Massimo Cossentino, Different Perspective in Designing Multi-Agent Systems, Proc. of AGES '02 workshop, Germany, 2002.

19. G Caire, et.al., Agent Oriented Analysis Using MESSAGE/UML, Proc. of Second International Workshop on Agent-Oriented Software Engineering, 101-108, 2002.

20. Thomas Juan, Adrian Pearce and Leon Sterling, ROADMAP: Extending the Gaia Methodology for Complex Open System, Proc. of AAMAS'02, 3-10, 2002.

21. Thomas Juan, Leon Sterling and Michael Winikoff, Assembling Agent Oriented Engineering Methodologies from Feature, In Proc. of AOSE, 2002.

22. J Pavon and J Gomez-Sanz, Agent Oriented Software Engineering with INGENIAS, Proc of CEEMAS 2003, LNAI 2691, 394-403, 2003.

23. Gerhard Weib, Agent Orientation in Software Engineering, The Knowledge Engineering Review, 16(4): 349-373, 2001.

24. Ofer Arazy and Carson C.Woo, Analysis and design of agent-oriented information systems, The knowledge engineering review, 17(3): 215-260, 2002.

25. M Kim, et.al., Agent-Oriented Software Modeling, Proc. of Sixth Asia Pacific Software Engineering Conference, 318-325, 1999.

26. K H Dam and M Winikoff, Comparing Agent-Oriented Methodologies, in the proceedings of the Fifth International Bi-Conference Workshop on Agent-Oriented Information System, 78-93, 2003.

27. Luca Cernuzzi and Gustavo Rossi, On the Evaluation of Agent Oriented Modeling Methods, Proceedings of the 3rd International Conference on Enterprise Information Systems, 2001.
28. Amon Sturm and Onn Shehory, A Framework for Evaluating Agent-Oriented Methodologies, Proc. Of AOIS, 94-109, 2003.
29. Andres Omicini, SODA; Societies and Infraestructures in the analysis and Design of agent-based System. Proc. of AOSE, 2001.
30. Andrea Omicini, From Object to Agent Societies: Abstractions and Methodologies for the Engineering of Open Distributed Systems, AI*IA/TABOO Joint Workshop, 2000.
31. H.V D Parunak and J J.Odell, Representing Social Structure in UML, AOSE 2001, LNCS 2222, 2002.
32. M. Dastani, V. Dignum, F. Dignum, Organizations and Normative Agents. In Proceedings of the First Eurasian Conference on Advances in Information and Communication Technology, 2002.
33. Christian Lemaître and Cora B. Excelente, Multi-Agent Organization Approach, 2nd Iberoamerican Workshop on Distributed Artificial Intelligence and Multi-Agent Systems, 1998
34. Jan Sudeikat, Lars Braubach, Alexander Pokahr, and Winfried Lamersdorf, Evaluation of Agent-Oriented Software Methodologies – Examination of the Gap Between the Modeling and Platform, Proceedings of AOSE 2004, Springer Verlag, 2005.
35. J. Ferber and O. Gutknecht. A meta-model for the analysis and design of organizations in multi-agent systems. In Proceedings of Third International Conference on MultiAgent Systems, IEEE Computer Society, 128-135, 1998.
36. J Ferber, Olivier Gutknecht, Fabien Michel: From Agents to Organizations: An Organizational View of Multi-agent Systems. Proc of AOSE 2003, 214-230, 2003.
37. J Ferber, et.al., Organization Models and Behavioural Requirements Specification for Multi-Agent Systems, Proc. of the ECAI 2000 Workshop on Modelling Artificial Societies and Hybrid Organizations, 2000.

Representing Agent Interaction Protocols with Agent UML

Marc-Philippe Huget[1] and James Odell[2]

[1] Leibniz-IMAG/MAGMA, 46, Avenue Félix Viallet,
F-38031 Grenoble Cedex, France
Marc-Philippe.Huget@imag.fr
[2] Agentis Software, Inc.,
3646 W. Huron River Dr. Ann Arbor, MI 48103, USA
jamesodell.com

Abstract. Several modeling techniques exist to represent agent interaction protocols mostly based on work done in distributed systems. These modeling techniques do not take the agent features such as the autonomy into account. Agent Interaction Protocol designers are now considering specific modeling techniques that contain these features. In this paper, we present the second version of the Agent UML interaction diagrams dedicated to interaction protocols, and based on UML 2.0.

1 Introduction

Designing an agent interaction protocol is realized via several steps (mostly based on the ones found in communication protocol engineering [3]). The main step is certainly the formal description phase in which the informal description of the protocol is formalized into a formal description. This step is crucial since it conditions the protocol design success: an incomplete formal description will lead to an implemented protocol that does not answer to user needs. Currently, there exist several (formal and semi-formal) description techniques to describe protocols mostly based on work performed in communication protocol engineering (such as automata [1] or Petri nets [4]) or specifically designed to agent interaction protocols (such as Agent UML or ANML [8]). Agent Interaction Protocol designers create from scratch new formal description techniques in order to cope with agent requirements such as autonomy. Agent UML was designed with this requirement in mind. Actually, Odell and Bauer—the fathers of Agent UML—designed a modeling language which is an extension of an acknowledged modeling language, UML [7]. As Odell et al. explain it in [6], it is worthwhile to define a modeling language that is a refinement of a well-known modeling language since in this case, learning this one will be simplified. Moreover, UML is widespread in industry, thus it will help software engineers moving from software systems to multiagent systems. Finally, several strong industrial tools already exist for UML. All these concerns give birth to Agent UML in 1999.

J. Odell et al. (Eds.): AOSE 2004, LNCS 3382, pp. 16–30, 2005.

Recently, UML knew a major improvement via the UML 2.0 specification [7] and past UML 1.x sequence diagrams were greatly modified. Thus, it seems reasonable to update Agent UML in order to now consider the UML 2.0 interaction diagrams as background of Agent UML. In this paper, we present the new specification of Agent UML Interaction diagrams based on UML 2.0 Interaction diagrams.

The remaining of this paper is structured as follows. Section 2 describes the UML 2.0 Interaction diagram specification. For sake of simplicity and brevity, we omit some parts in the description. This is due to the relationships of elements in the Interaction diagram with elements outside this diagram. For instance, an Interaction is a specialization of InteractionFragment and Behavior, an InteractionFragment is a specialization of NamedElement and so on. As much as possible, we try to let the section readable by readers that are not expert in UML 2.0. The Agent UML Interaction diagrams are defined as a profile. It means that an Agent UML Interaction diagram is defined from UML Interaction diagrams to which some elements are modified, and some new elements are added. We do not present here in details how this profile is created due to space restriction. This is the subject of another paper. Section 3 depicts the Agent UML Interaction diagram profile. Section 4 describes an example of Agent UML Interaction diagram. Finally, Section 5 concludes the paper and discusses future directions of this work.

2   UML 2.0 Interaction Diagrams

The inter-process communication is captured by the set of Interaction diagrams in UML 2.0 [7]. Actually, the Interaction diagrams represent a family of diagrams:

Sequence Diagrams. A diagram that depicts an interaction by focusing on the sequence of messages that are exchanged, along with their corresponding event occurrences on the lifelines. Unlike a communication diagram, a sequence diagram includes time sequences but does not include object relationships. A sequence diagram can exist in a generic form (describes all possible scenarios), and in an instance form (describes one actual scenario). Sequence diagrams are the most common form to represent protocols.

Interaction Overview Diagrams. A diagram that depicts interactions through a variant of activity diagrams in a way that promotes overview of the control flow. It focuses on the overview of the flow of control where each node can be an interaction diagram.

Communication Diagram. A diagram that focuses on object relationships where the message passing is central. The sequencing of messages is given through a sequence numbering scheme. Sequence diagrams and communication diagrams express similar information but show it in different ways.

Timing Diagram. An interaction diagram that shows the change in state or condition of a lifeline over linear time. The most common usage is to show the change in state of an object over time in response to accepted events or stimuli.

In this paper, we focus on the sequence diagrams since it is the main one. We briefly consider the other diagrams in Section 5 and particularly, their possible use for agent interaction protocols. The remaining of this section describes the different classes in the UML 2.0 Interaction diagram specification. For sake of simplicity, we direct the explanations to be more readable. As a consequence, some classes are omitted or explanations are reduced. For a detailed description of the specification, readers can consult [7].

Even if it is not written in the UML 2.0 Interaction diagram specification, sequence diagrams are timely ordered from the top of the diagram to the bottom. It means that, except if we are using Continuations[1], it is possible to easily order message sequences by reading the diagram from top to bottom. The X axis represents the different participants in the communication. Three notions are integrated within UML 2.0 Interaction diagrams: *traces*, *event occurrences* and *fragments*. If we do a parallel with protocols, a trace is a legal sequence of messages. An event occurrence is any event that can intervene during the communication such as message sending or receiving. A fragment is a piece of an interaction. It means a fragment is the lifelines involved in the fragment and the set of traces (eventually modified by some operators defined below).

2.1   Interaction

A sequence diagram in UML 2.0 is organized around a frame called *Interaction*. This frame is defined as a unit of behavior and contains, among others, the protocol name (prefixed by the keyword *sd* for sequence diagram), the set of objects that are in relation and the sequences of messages between these objects. This Interaction is not a closed unit since it can send (receive) messages from (to) other sequence diagrams via *Gates*. An Interaction is depicted by a solid-outline rectangle with a pentagon in the upper left corner of the rectangle as shown on Figure 1. The content of the pentagon is the keyword *sd* followed by the protocol name and eventually parameters. The notation within the frame comes in several forms Sequence diagrams, Interaction Overview diagrams, Communication diagrams or Timing diagrams.

2.2   Lifeline

A Lifeline in UML 2.0 represents an individual participant in the interaction. A Lifeline describes as well the presence of the participant in the interaction. A participant entering later in the interaction has a Lifeline lower than others. A participant ending prematurely the interaction has a Lifeline finishing before the others. The Lifeline notation is a symbol consisting of a rectangle forming its head followed by a vertical line that represents the lifeline of the participant as shown on Figure 1. Information identifying the lifeline is displayed inside the rectangle in the following format: *name : class name* where *name* is the instance of the class called *class name*. On Figure 1, : *xx* is a class name and *w* is a class instance.

---

[1] Classes from UML 2.0 or from Agent UML have their first letter capitalized.

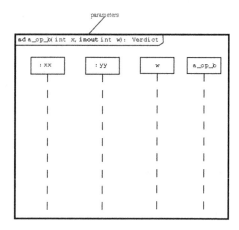

Fig. 1. The UML 2.0 Interaction Notation

2.3   Message

A Message defines a particular communication between Lifelines of an interaction. A Message is defined between a sender and a receiver. There are several kinds of Message in UML 2.0:

- a message is *complete* if there is a sending event occurrence and a receiving event occurrence.
- a message is *lost* if it is known that there is a sending event occurrence but there is no receiving event occurrence. This is particularly the case in unreliable communication.
- a message is *found* if a receiving event occurrence is known but there is no (known) sending event occurrence. This is the case where the sender is outside the scope of the description. It could be an activity that this communication does not take into account.

The Message notation is a directed line from the sender lifeline to the receiver lifeline. The form of the line or the arrow head reflects the properties of the message:

- an asynchronous message has an open arrow head.
- a synchronous message typically represents method calls and is shown with a filled arrow head. The reply message from a method has a dashed line.
- an object creation message has a dashed line with an open arrow head.
- a lost message is described as a small black circle at the arrow end of the message.
- a found message is described as a small black circle at the beginning of the message.

2.4   Constraint

A constraint in UML 2.0 is called a *StateInvariant*. It describes a constraint on the state of a Lifeline. If the constraint is evaluated to false, next event

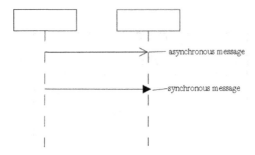

Fig. 2. The UML 2.0 Message Notation

occurrences are considered as invalid and are not executed. The StateInvariant notation is shown as a text in curly brackets on the lifeline on which the constraint is applied. A second kind of constraints exists in the specification: the InteractionConstraint. This constraint is used in conjunction with Combined-Fragments. The notation is a text within square brackets.

2.5   CombinedFragment

The CombinedFragment class in UML 2.0 represents a concise manner to represent several traces. The semantics of the CombinedFragment depends of the InteractionOperator used. There are several InteractionOperators:

Alternative. This InteractionOperator describes that several traces in the interaction are possible but at most one will be executed. The selection is based on guards. At most one guard is satisfied. The associated trace is executed. A default trace *else* can be added if no other trace can be executed.

Option. This InteractionOperator contains a single trace. Two situations are possible: if the guard associated to the trace is satisfied, then the trace is executed else nothing happens. This InteractionOperator is a particular case of the InteractionOperator Alternative.

Break. The InteractionOperator Break represents a breaking scenario that stops the current trace execution and executes the trace present in the Combined-Fragment. The broken current execution will not be resumed.

Parallel. The InteractionOperator Parallel describes that several traces can be executed concurrently. The set of traces can be interleaved in any order.

Weak Sequencing. This InteractionOperator represents a weak sequencing between the different event occurrences in the CombinedFragment. It implies that it is possible to order the Message on a same Lifeline but it is not possible to make any assumption for Message ordering of other Lifelines in the same CombinedFragment.

Strict Sequencing. This InteractionOperator refines the InteractionOperator Weak Sequencing by requiring that all Messages in the CombinedFragment are timely ordered.

Negative. This InteractionOperator describes the set of traces that are invalid.

Critical Region. The InteractionOperator Critical Region describes a region on which it is not possible to interleave the set of traces within the Critical region with other messages outside the Critical Region. It corresponds to the critical section in distributed systems.

Ignore/Consider. The InteractionOperator Ignore describes the set of traces that can occur during the communication but has to be considered as insignificant and has to be treated like that. The InteractionOperator Consider is the converse of the InteractionOperator Ignore. It represents the set of messages that has to be considered.

Assertion. The InteractionOperator Assertion describes the only set of traces that is valid. This InteractionOperator is often combined with the InteractionOperators Ignore and Consider.

Loop. The InteractionOperator Loop depicts that the CombinedFragment represents a loop. The guard associated with the iteration is either a range with a lower and an upper bounds, or a boolean expression. The loop is executed as long as the guard is satisfied.

The CombinedFragment notation is a solid-outline rectangle with a pentagon in which the InteractionOperator is written. InteractionOperators are written as follows: *alt* for alternatives, *opt* for options, *break* for break, *par* for parallel, *seq* for weak sequencing, *strict* for strict sequencing, *neg* for negative, *critical* for critical region, *ignore* for ignore, *consider* for consider, *assertion* for assertion and *loop* for loop.

Some InteractionOperators have a special notation: (ignore — consider) {<message name> {, message}*} and loop [<min int>, <max int>].

A CombinedFragment example can be found on Figure 11.

2.6   Continuation

A Continuation is a syntactic way to represent continuations of different branches of an Alternative CombinedFragment. Continuations is intuitively similar to labels representing intermediate points in a flow of control. The notation is a rounded-rectangle with a name within. The name corresponds to the label.

2.7   InteractionOccurrence

An InteractionOccurrence corresponds to a call to another interaction diagram. The current interaction diagram is resumed when the called interaction diagram ends. The notation of an InteractionOccurrence is a solid-outline rectangle with a pentagon. The keyword *ref* is written within the pentagon. The name of the called interaction diagram is written within the rectangle.

2.8   Gate

A Gate is a connection point to relate a Message outside the Interaction with a Message inside the Interaction. Gates are points on the frame corresponding to the end of Messages, the one outgoing the Interaction and the one incoming the Interaction.

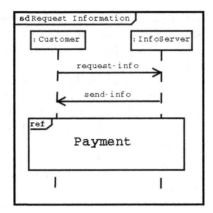

Fig. 3. The UML 2.0 InteractionOccurrence Notation

2.9   Termination

The Stop denotes the end of participation of a lifeline in the communication. The Stop is depicted by a cross in the form of an X at the bottom of a Lifeline. An example can be found on Figure 11.

3   Agent UML Interaction Protocol Profile

UML is an extensible language through stereotypes and tagged values. We have defined the Agent UML Interaction diagram specification as a UML profile. We define in this section the modification we have done on the UML Interaction diagram specification to give birth to Agent UML Interaction diagram specification. This description is high level and does not present in details which attributes and methods are added and removed in each class of the UML 2.O Interaction diagram package. This description profile will be the subject of another paper.

3.1   Interaction

There are two kinds of protocols in multiagent systems: protocol templates and instantiated protocols. Template protocols represent reusable patterns for useful protocol instances. The protocol as a whole is treated as an entity in its own right, which can be customized for other problem domains. A protocol template is not a directly usable protocol because it has unbound parameters. Its parameters must be bound to actual values to create a bound form that is an instantiated protocol. Protocol templates refer to abstract classes in object-oriented theory.

A protocol template is depicted by an Interaction where the pentagon contains the keyword <<*template*>> between the keyword *sd* and the protocol name. An instantiated protocol has parameters that are depicted as a Note linked to the Interaction via a dashed line. The first element in the Note is the keyword <<*parameters*>>. Frequent parameters are the ontology, the content language and the agent communication language as shown on Figure 4. These three parameters are introduced by the keywords *ontology, CL* and *ACL*. As a consequence, parameters in UML 2.0 Interaction are removed and replace by these ones. Parameters can be written without referring to an unbound parameter as long as there is no confusion.

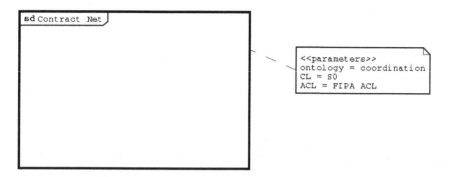

Fig. 4. The Agent UML Interaction Notation

3.2   Lifeline

Lifelines are the elements that were the most modified in the Agent UML Interaction diagram specification. First, Lifelines in Agent UML can represent a set of agents and not a unique agent as sketched in UML 2.0. Agent UML proposes to add roles in order to reduce the size of interaction diagrams and group agents that have the same behavior in this interaction. Actually, an agent can be described with its role or with its role and its group. There are five possible ways to represent the content of the head of the lifeline:

1. an agent identity denotes an agent instance, for instance Smith,
2. an agent identity with a role denotes an agent instance playing a specific role, for instance Smith:Employee,
3. an agent identity with a role and a group denotes an agent instance playing a specific role in a particular group, for instance Smith:Employee/ACME,
4. a role denotes a role regardless of the agents playing this role and,
5. a role and a group denotes a role in a group regardless of the agents playing this role.

A role is prefixed by a colon. A group is prefixed by a slash. A cardinality can be added to represent the number of agents playing a specific role. The cardinality can be an exact number, a range or a logic formula or a condition. Figure 5 summarizes the different notation.

The second important modification is the ability to write the role dynamics. An agent is able to add a new role or to change from one role to another one. We add two new stereotypes for this role dynamics: *<<add role>>* and *<<change role>>*. Changing or adding a role consists in drawing a directed line with an

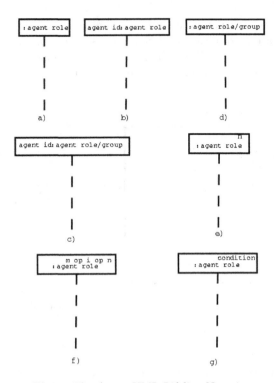

Fig. 5. The Agent UML Lifeline Notation

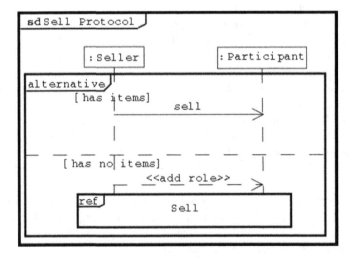

Fig. 6. The Agent UML Role Dynamics Notation

open arrow head from the current agent instance with the roles it plays to the new situation. The stereotype is written on the directed line as shown on Figure 6.

3.3   Message

We add new stereotypes in Agent UML Message in order to take account of roles, communication on the same lifeline and message delay.

Agent UML interaction diagrams can address a specific agent instance or a set of agents denoting by their role. As a consequence, it is required to write on message if it addresses a specific agent when the Lifeline only refers a role. The notation is to write the name of the agent instance on the Message close to the receiver Lifeline. A second point is issued from the use of roles. It is possible that a portion of the agent instances playing this role is concerned by this Message. A cardinality is adorned on the message to denote the number of agents that will receive this Message.

Since Agent UML considers roles, it is possible that a Message is sent from one agent instance in this role to another agents in this same role. It is important to address the case whether the sender wants to receive the Message as well. We add one new stereotype to cope the situation where the sender does not want to receive the Message in an asynchronous communication. It is not possible to have the sender in the list of receivers if the communication is synchronous since in this case, the sender will be deadlocked.

Figure 7 summarizes the Agent UML Message notation. The notation a corresponds to an asynchronous message sending. The notation b corresponds to a synchronous message. The notation c gives the cardinality for both sender and receiver. The notation d depicts the cardinality for the receiver in terms of a range. The notation e denotes the cardinality for the receiver in terms of a condition. The notation f denotes that this Message is sent to a specific agent instance when the Lifeline only refers to a role. The notation g corresponds to sending asynchronously the Message to the same Lifeline, the sender will receive a copy of the Message. The notation h depicts sending asynchronously the Message to the same Lifeline and the sender will not receive a copy of the Message. The notation i denotes to sending synchronously the Message to the same Lifeline, the sender will not receive a copy of the Message.

Finally, a Message can be delayed due to network congestion. It is then required to add that a specific message sent before another one can arrive after it. A new stereotype is added to denote this message switching. The delayed Message is represented as a multi-directed line and its point on the receiver Lifeline is after the Message sent after it. The Message that arrives before the Message sent before it is represented with a bridge on the directed line to avoid line crossing as shown on Figure 8.

3.4   Constraint

Two kinds of constraints are considered in Agent UML interaction diagrams: constraints and timing constraints. Timing constraints are conformed to the one defined in UML 2.0. Constraints are refined into two categories: blocking constraints and non-blocking constraints. Non-blocking constraints correspond to the constraints defined in UML 2.0. If the constraints are satisfied then the InteractionFragment is executed. In the case of blocking constraints, agents are

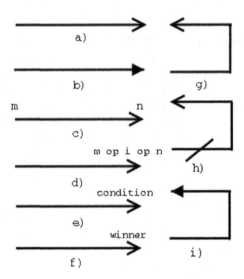

Fig. 7. The Agent UML Message Notation

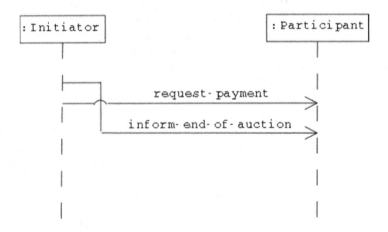

Fig. 8. The Agent UML Delayed Message Notation

blocked as long as the constraints are not satisfied. If a blocking constraint is applied to a Lifeline where a role is declared without agent instances, all the agent instances playing this role are blocked as long as the constraints are not satisfied. The stereotype <<*blocking*>> is added to represent blocking constraints as shown on Figure 9.

3.5   Protocol Template

The purpose of protocol templates is to create reusable patterns for useful protocol instances. The protocol as a whole is treated as an entity in its own right,

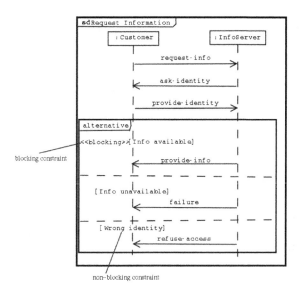

Fig. 9. The Agent UML Blocking Constraint Notation

which can be customized for other problem domains. A parameterized proto-col is not a directly usable protocol because it has unbound parameters. Un-bound parameters are distinguised from bound parameters by the stereotype <<*unbound*>>. Unbound parameters will be bound in instantiated protocols via the note linked to the interaction diagram as shown on Figure 4.

3.6 Action

Sending and receiving messages imply performing actions within agents. For instance, if we refer to FIPA ACL, sending a inform message implies verifying that the sender believes the content of the message; and receiving the inform message entails that the receiver believes the message content. An action is depicted as a round-cornered rectangle linked to the message that triggers it by an association. The action is written within the round-cornered rectangle. The action is written as a text independent of any programming language. The executable language from Mellor and Balcer is a possible language to represent actions in Agent UML [5].

4   Agent UML Sequence Diagram Example

We take the example of the FIPA Request When protocol to exemplify some classes, we described in Section 3. The FIPA Request When protocol allows an agent to request that the receiver performs some action at the time a given pre-condition becomes true. The Agent UML representation of this protocol is given on Figure 11. The protocol is composed of two roles: *Initiator* and *Participant*

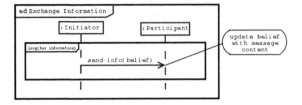

Fig. 10. The Agent UML Action Notation

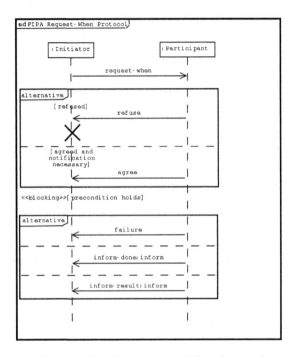

Fig. 11. The FIPA Request When Protocol

denoted by the two Lifelines. Since there are Lifelines with roles regardless of the agent instances, each Lifeline can represent several agents. However, a piece of information may be added on the first Lifeline that there is one and only one Initiator.

All the Messages are asynchronous. The first one is sent from the Initiator role to the Participant role. After this sending, the receiver role can answer either with a refuse Message or with an agree Message denoted by the CombinedFragment with the InteractionOperator Alternative. We do not add an *else* clause since the two conditions are opposite. The conditions are written as InteractionConstraint within square brackets. Here, the conditions are written as text but it is also possible to use some logic formulae. In case, the Participant refuses to answer to the request of the Initiator, it replies by the refuse Message. Just after, the Interaction stops since there has a Stop. If the Participant accepts, it replies by the accept Message and the Interaction continues. We add a blocking constraint. As long as the precondition holds, the Interaction is blocked and the agent instances as well. When the preconditions are no longer satisfied, the Participant has three different answers, either a failure Message if it fails performing the action, an inform-done Message to inform that the action is performed or an inform-result Message to give the result of the action. Since there is no more Messages in the Interaction, the Interaction stops.

5   Conclusion

Describing agent interaction protocols is an important task in multiagent system design since a faulty protocol can affect the way agents behave and cooperate. There exist several different formal description techniques available to agent interaction protocol designers: automata, Petri nets and logic to name a few. Some description techniques fit more or less the agent desiderata and particularly the decision autonomy. To tackle this point, agent interaction protocol designers considered new description techniques and among others, the Agent UML [6]. The Agent UML idea presents several interesting ideas:

1. It is rooted on the well-known and acknowledged modeling language UML
2. Thanks to UML, it eases the gap between industrial concerns and research concerns. It is easier to learn it than a complex or a logic formal description technique
3. Several industrial tools are available for UML
4. It covers the agent needs in terms of interaction

Even if this picture is quite idyllic, the first version of the Agent UML was of limited scope and does not take account of several operators such as the InteractionOperator break or loop. Moreover, the timing constraints were written as a note reducing its use when automatically implementing this protocol. Thanks to a growning effort from the community and particularly via the FIPA Modeling technical committee, the Agent UML takes a second birth. The new Agent UML is now rooted on the UML 2.0 Interaction diagram specification, which offers more possibilities for agent interaction protocols.

As stated in the introduction, the interaction diagram family contains four different diagrams. We only address here the sequence diagram but there are as well the interaction overview diagram, the communication diagram and the timing diagram. Even if we do not speak about them, they can be of interest for agent interaction protocols. The interaction overview diagram can be used to interleave agent interactions and control flow, and particularly the relationships between different protocols. The communication diagram can help designers during validation to test if agents correctly receive the message and the message ordering. Finally, timing diagrams can be used to check agent design and agent interaction protocol. It is then possible to verify that an agent takes a specific state when sending or receiving a message.

Several directions are already written in the agenda of Agent UML:

1. A comparative study between existing formal description techniques and Agent UML has to be performed in order to check what is missing and what is the expressive power of Agent UML. We particularly think about Petri nets and the study done on the previous version of Agent UML [4],
2. UML presents a main issue, this is a semi-formal language since there is no formal semantics of the Interaction diagrams. As a consequence, ambiguities and misunderstandings are possible. Moreover, such semantics is required when designers want to realize tools and implementation of Agent UML Interaction diagrams. In order to tackle this point, we envisage to describe the Agent UML sequence diagrams via communicating extended finite state machines. Petri nets are also used for describing the semantics of the Agent UML Interaction diagram specification [2],
3. Agent UML is a new modeling language and, as a consequence, there is actually no tools for the diagram design, validation or implementation. One idea is to reuse a tool that considers UML 2.0 as soon as one will be available,
4. Agent UML Interaction diagrams are actually only applied to the FIPA Interaction protocol library. We envisage to search for other protocols in order to check if this specification is consistent and answers user needs.

Acknowledgements

Authors would like to thank people who contribute directly or indirectly to this specification via the FIPA Modeling technical committee or via mails.

References

1. M. Barbuceanu and M. S. Fox. COOL : A language for describing coordination in multiagent system. In *First International Conference on Multi-Agent Systems (ICMAS-95)*, pages 17–24, San Francisco, USA, June 1995. AAAI Press.
2. L. Cabac and D. Moldt. Formal Semantics for Agent UML Agent Interaction Protocols Diagrams. In this volume.
3. G. J. Holzmann. *Design and Validation of Computer Protocols*. Prentice-Hall, 1991.
4. H. Mazouzi, A. El Fallah Seghrouchni, and S. Haddad. Open protocol design for complex interactions in multi-agent systems. In *Proceedings of the First International Joint Conference on Autonomous Agents and Multi-Agent Systems (AAMAS 2002)*, Bologna, Italy, July 2002.
5. S. J. Mellor and M. Balcer. *Executable UML*. Addison-Wesley, 2002.
6. J. Odell, H. V. D. Parunak, and B. Bauer. Extending UML for agents. In G. Wagner, Y. Lesperance, and E. Yu, editors, *Proceedings of the Agent-Oriented Information Systems Workshop at the 17th National conference on Artificial Intelligence*, Austin, Texas, july, 30 2000. ICue Publishing.
7. O. M. G. (OMG). *Unified Modeling Language: Superstructure version 2.0*, 03-04-01 edition, 2003.
8. S. Paurobally. *Rational Agents and the Processes and States of Negotiation*. PhD thesis, Imperial College, University of London, 2003.

AML: Agent Modeling Language
Toward Industry-Grade Agent-Based Modeling

Radovan Červenka, Ivan Trenčanský, Monique Calisti, and Dominic Greenwood

Whitestein Technologies, Panenská 28, 811 03 Bratislava, Slovakia
Tel +421 (2) 5443-5502, Fax +421 (2) 5443-5512
{rce, itr, mca, dgr}@whitestein.com
http://www.whitestein.com

Abstract. The *Agent Modeling Language (AML)* is a semi-formal visual modeling language, specified as an extension to UML 2.0. It is a consistent set of modeling constructs designed to capture the aspects of multi-agent systems. The ultimate objective for AML is to provide a means for software engineers to incorporate aspects of multi-agent system engineering into their analysis and design processes. This paper presents an introductory overview of AML, discussing the motivations driving the development of the language, the scope and approach taken, the specific language structure and optional extensibility. The core AML modeling constructs are explained and demonstrated by example where possible. Extensions to OCL and CASE tool support are also discussed.

1 Introduction

The Agent Modeling Language (AML) is a semi-formal[1] visual modeling language for specifying, modeling and documenting systems that incorporate concepts drawn from Multi-Agent Systems (MAS) theory.

The primary application context of AML is to systems explicitly designed using software multi-agent system concepts. AML can however also be applied to other domains such as business systems, social systems, robotics, etc. In general, AML can be used whenever it is suitable or useful to build models that (1) consist of a number of autonomous, concurrent and/or asynchronous (possibly proactive) entities, (2) comprise entities that are able to observe and/or interact with their environment, (3) make use of complex interactions and aggregated services, (4) employ social structures, and (5) capture mental characteristics of systems and/or their parts.

Why Another Modeling Language? The most significant motivation driving the development of AML stems from the extant need for a ready-to-use, complete

---

[1] The term "semi-formal" implies that the language offers the means to specify systems using a combination of natural language, graphical notation, and formal language specification. It is not based on a strict formal (e.g. mathematical) theory.

J. Odell et al. (Eds.): AOSE 2004, LNCS 3382, pp. 31–46, 2005.

and highly expressive modeling language suitable for the development of commercial software solutions based on multi-agent technologies. To qualify this more precisely, AML was intended to be a language that:

- is built on proven technical foundations,
- integrates best practices from agent-oriented software engineering (AOSE) and object-oriented software engineering (OOSE) domains,
- is well specified and documented,
- is internally consistent from the conceptual, semantic and syntactic perspectives,
- is versatile and easy to extend,
- is independent of any particular theory, software development process or implementation environment, and
- is supported by Computer-Aided Software Engineering (CASE) tools.

Given these requirements, AML is designed to address and satisfy the most significant deficiencies with current state-of-the-art and practice in the area of MAS oriented modeling languages, which are often:

- insufficiently documented and/or specified, or
- using proprietary and/or non-intuitive modeling constructs, or
- aimed at modeling only a limited set of MAS aspects, or
- applicable only to a specific theory, application domain, MAS architecture, or technology, or
- mutually incompatible, or
- insufficiently supported by CASE tools.

Paper Layout. The purpose of this paper is to present an overview of AML. However, due to limitations in paper length it is not possible to provide a comprehensive description of AML including its abstract syntax, semantics, notation, and UML profiles. Therefore we have chosen to discuss the principles that guided the specification of AML, our specific approach and a brief overview of the various AML modeling constructs. Using concrete examples, we also illustrate some of the more essential AML concepts. The paper is structured as follows:

Section 2 presents our approach in terms of language definition and specification, scope of the language, foundations, and structure and extensibility. Sections 3, 4, 5, and 6 then present the overview of AML organized according to the packages defined in the AML metamodel: Architecture, Behavior, Mental Aspects, and Contexts. Section 7 describes an extension of the OCL Standard Library required for modeling modal, deontic, and temporal logic, and cognitive primitives. Section 8 provides an overview of the CASE tool support for AML and Section 9 draws conclusions and recommendations for further work.

2   The AML Approach

Toward achieving the stated goals and overcoming the deficiencies associated with many existing approaches, AML has been designed as a language, which:

- incorporates and unifies the most significant concepts from the broadest set of existing multi-agent theories and abstract models (e.g. DAI [1], BDI [2], SMART [3]), modeling and specification languages (e.g. AUML [4, 5, 6], GRL [7], TAO [8], OPM/MAS [9], AOR [10], UML [11], OCL [12], OWL [13], UML-based ontology modeling [14], OWL-S [15]), methodologies (e.g. MES-SAGE [16], Gaia [17], TROPOS [18], PASSI [19], Prometheus [20], MAS CommonKADS [21], MaSE [22]), agent platforms (e.g. Jade, FIPA-OS, Jack, Cougaar) and multi-agent driven applications,
- extends the above with new modeling concepts to account for aspects of multi-agent systems thus far covered insufficiently, inappropriately or not at all,
- assembles them into a consistent framework specified by the AML meta-model (covering abstract syntax and semantics of the language) and notation (covering the concrete syntax), and
- is specified as a *conservative extension of UML*^{2} to the maximum possible extent.

2.1   Scope

AML is designed to support business modeling, requirements specification, analysis, and design of software systems that use software agent concepts and principles.

The current version of AML offers:

- Support for the human mental process of requirements specification and analysis of complex problems/systems, particularly (1) mental aspects, which can be used for modeling intentionality in use case models, goal-based requirements, problem decomposition, etc. (Sect. 5), and (2) contexts, which can be used for situation-based modeling (Sect. 6).
- Support for the abstraction of architectural and behavioral concepts associated with multi-agent systems, i.e. ontologies (Sect. 3.1), MAS entities (Sect. 3.2), social aspects (Sect. 3.3), behavior abstraction and decomposition (Sect. 4.1), communicative interactions (Sect. 4.2), services (Sect. 4.3), observations and effecting interactions (Sect. 4.4), mental aspects used for modeling mental attitudes of entities (Sect. 5), MAS deployment and agent mobility (Sect. 3.4).

2.2   Outside the Scope of AML

AML does not cover most of operational semantics, which might be dependent on a specific execution model given by an applied theory or deployment environment (e.g. agent platforms, reasoning engines, other technologies used).

2.3   UML 2.0 as a Base

AML is based on the Unified Modeling Language (UML) 2.0 Superstructure [11], augmenting it with several new modeling concepts appropriate for capturing the typical features of multi-agent systems.

The main advantages of this approach are:

---

^{2} A conservative extension of UML is a strict extension of UML which retains the standard UML semantics in unaltered form[23].

- Reuse of well-defined, well-founded, and commonly used concepts of UML.
- Use of existing mechanisms for specifying and extending UML-based languages (metamodel extensions and UML profiles).
- Ease of incorporation into existing UML-based CASE tools.

2.4   Structure of AML

AML is defined at two distinct levels – *AML Metamodel and Notation* and *AML Profiles*. Fig. 1 depicts these two levels, their derivation from UML 2.0 and optional extensions based on UML 1.* and 2.0.

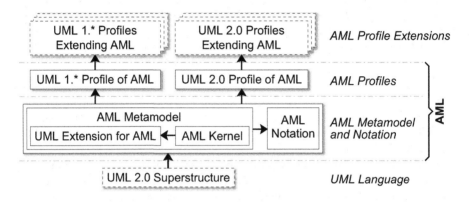

Fig. 1. Levels of AML definition

With reference to Fig. 1, the *UML Language* level contains the UML 2.0 Superstructure defining the abstract syntax, semantics and notation of UML. AML uses this level as the foundation upon which to define MAS-specific modeling constructs.

The *AML Metamodel and Notation* level defines the AML abstract syntax, semantics and notation, structured into two packages: *AML Kernel* and *UML Extension for AML*.

The *AML Kernel* package is the core of AML where the AML specific modeling elements are defined. It is logically structured into several packages, each of which covers a specific aspect of MAS. The most significant of these packages are described in sections 3, 4, 5, and 6. The AML Kernel is a conservative extension of UML 2.0.

The *UML Extension for AML* package adds meta-properties and structural constraints to the standard UML elements. It is a non-conservative extension of UML, and thus is an optional part of the language. However, the extensions contained within are simple and can be easily implemented in most existing UML-based CASE tools.

At the level of *AML Profiles*, two UML profiles built upon the AML Metamodel and Notation are provided: *UML 1.* Profile for AML* (based on UML 1.*) and *UML 2.0 Profile for AML* (based on UML 2.0). These profiles, inter alia, enable implementation of AML within UML 1.* and UML 2.0 based CASE tools, respectively.

Based on AML Profiles, users are free to define their own language extensions to customize AML for specific modeling techniques, implementation environments, technologies, development processes, etc. The extensions can be defined as standard UML 1.* or 2.0 profiles. They are commonly referred to as *AML Profile Extensions*.

2.5   Extensibility of AML

AML is designed to encompass a broad set of relevant theories and modeling approaches, it being essentially impossible to cover all inclusively. In those cases where AML is insufficient, several mechanisms can be used to extend or customize AML as required.

Each of the following extension methods (and combinations thereof) can be used:

- *Metamodel extension.* This offers first-class extensibility (as defined by MOF [24]) of the AML metamodel and notation.
- *AML profile extension.* This offers the possibility to adapt AML Profiles using constructs specific to a given domain, platform, or development method, without the need to modify the underlying AML metamodel.
- *Concrete model extension.* This offers the means to employ alternative MAS modeling approaches as complementary specifications to the AML model.

3   Architecture

This section provides an overview of the AML constructs used to model architectural aspects of multi-agent systems.

3.1   Ontology

AML supports ontology modeling in terms of ontology classes and instances, their relationships, constraints, ontology utilities, and ontology packages.

Ontology package is a specialized UML package used to specify a single ontology. By utilizing the features inherited from UML package (package nesting, element import, package merge, etc.), ontologies can be logically structured.

Ontology class is a specialized UML class used to represent an ontology concept. Attributes and operations of the ontology class represent its slots. Ontology functions, actions, and predicates belonging to a concept modeled by the ontology class are modeled by its operations. Ontology class can use all types of relationships allowed for UML class (association, generalization, dependency, etc.) with their standard UML semantics.

Ontology utility is a specialized UML Class used to cluster global ontology constants, variables, functions, actions, and predicates, which are modeled as its features. These features can be used by (referred to) other elements within the owning ontology. One ontology package can contain several ontology utilities allowing logical clustering of the features.

The diagram in Fig. 2 depicts a simplified version of a `SoccerMatch` ontology. Rectangles with the special icon ("C" placed in a rounded square) represent ontology classes that model concepts from the domain. Their relationships are modeled by standard UML relationships with standard semantics.

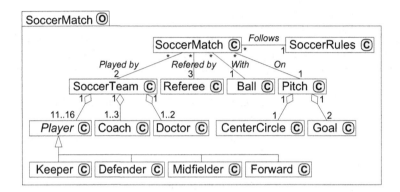

Fig. 2. Example of an ontology

3.2 Fundamental Entity Types

In general, *entities* represent objects that can exist in the system independently of other objects. AML defines three modeling constructs used to model types of MAS entities, namely: Agents, environments, and resources. Entities can also be modeled at the instance level by UML instance specifications categorized according to the corresponding types:

Agent type is a specialized UML class used to model the type of an *agent*, i.e. self contained entities that are capable of interactions, observations and autonomous behavior within their environment.

Resource type is a specialized UML class used to model the type of a resource within the system[3]. A *resource* is a physical or informational entity with which the main concern is availability (in terms of its quantity, access rights, conditions of usage/consumption, etc.).

Environment type is a specialized UML class used to model the type of a system's inner environment[4], i.e. the logical or physical surroundings of entities which provide conditions under which the entities exist and function. As environments are usually complex entities, different environment types are usually used to model different aspects of the environment.

---

[3] A resource positioned outside a system is modeled as a UML actor.

[4] *Inner environment* is that part of an entity's environment that is contained within the boundaries of the system.

In AML, all the aforementioned entity types are collectively called *behavioral entities*. They can own capabilities, be decomposed into behavior fragments (see Sect. 4.1), provide and use services (see Sect. 4.3), and own perceptors and effectors (see Sect. 4.4). Additionally, agent and environment types are *autonomous entities* that can be characterized in terms of their mental attitudes (see Sect. 5). All entities can make use of modeling mechanisms inherited from UML class, i.e. they can own features, participate in varied relationship types, be internally structured into parts, own behaviors, etc.

Fig. 3 shows a definition of an abstract class 3DObject that represents spatial objects, characterized by shape and position, existing inside a containing space. An abstract environment type 3DSpace represents a three dimensional space. This is a special 3DObject and as such can contain other spatial objects. 3DSpace provides a service Motion to the objects contained within (for details about services see Sect. 4.3).

Three concrete 3DObjects are defined: an agent type Person, a resource type Ball and a class Goal. 3DSpace is furthermore specialized into a concrete environment type Pitch representing a soccer pitch containing two goals and a ball.

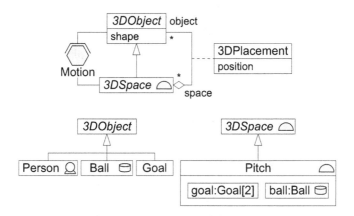

Fig. 3. Example of entities, their relationships, service provision and usage

3.3   Social Aspects

AML defines several elements for modeling the social aspects of MAS, including structural characteristics of socialized entities and certain aspects of their social behavior.

Organization unit type is a specialized environment type used to model the type of an *organization unit*. From an external perspective, organization units represent coherent autonomous entities, the properties and behavior of which are both (1) emergent properties and behavior of all their constituents, their mutual relationships, observations and interactions, and (2) the features and behavior of organization units themselves. From an internal perspective, organization units are types of environment that specify the social arrangements of entities in terms of structures, interactions, roles, constraints, norms, etc.

Social Relationships are modeled by *social properties* and *social associations*. The current version of AML supports the modeling of superordinate-subordinate and peer-to-peer relationships, but this set can be extended as required (e.g. to model producer-consumer, competitive, or cooperative relationships).

Entity role type is a specialized UML class used to represent a coherent set of features, behaviors, participation in interactions, and services offered or required by behavioral entities participating in a particular context. Each entity role type, being an abstraction of a set of capabilities, should be realized by a specific implementation possessed by a behavioral entity that can play that entity role type.

An instance of the entity role type is called an *entity role*[5]. It represents the execution of behaviors, usage of features and/or participation in interactions as defined by the particular entity role type. A given entity role exists only while a behavioral entity instance plays it.

To allow explicit manipulation of entity roles in UML activities and state machines, AML defines a set of actions for entity role creation and disposal, and related triggers.

The possibility of playing an entity role by a behavioral entity is modeled by *role property* and *play association*. Mechanisms are also offered for modeling dynamic changes of roles, reasoning about played roles, expressing multiplicities and constraints on played entity roles and navigation through the structural features and capabilities of entity roles types from their playing entities (used for example in model navigation expressions).

Fig. 4 part (a) contains a diagram which express that an agent of type `Person` can play entity roles of type `Player`, `Doctor`, `Coach`, and `Referee`. The possibility of playing entity roles of a particular type is modeled by play associations. Fig. 4 part (b) depicts an organization structure containing the entities participating in a soccer match. An environment type `Pitch` contains one `referee` (of the `Referee` entity role type) and two `teams` (of the `SoccerTeam` organization unit type). `SoccerTeam` itself consists of one to three `coaches`, one or two `doctors`, and seven to eleven `players`. The `players` are subordinate to the `coaches` (by the `lead` connector), and to `referees` (by the `refer` connector), but peers to `doctors` (by the `treat` connector).

3.4   MAS Deployment and Mobility

To model deployment of an MAS to a physical environment, AML extends the UML deployment model with *agent platform* as a specialized execution environment, and specialized types of artifacts representing deployed entities. Particularly, *agent artifact*, *environment artifact*, and *resource artifact*.

Modeling of structural and behavioral aspects of agent mobility is also provided. The structural aspects allow the specification of which agent artifacts are

---

[5] AML uses the term "entity role" to differentiate agent-related roles from the roles defined by the UML 2.0, i.e. roles used for collaborations, parts, and associations.

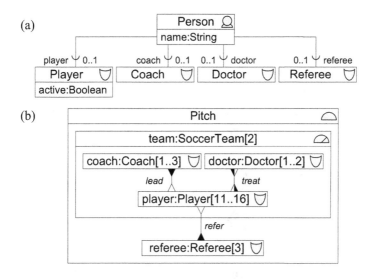

Fig. 4. Example of social structure modeling

mobile, on what deployment targets they can appear, their relationships to deployment targets, and what actions (move or clone) can make them appear on a particular deployment target. The behavioral aspects allow the specification of the move and clone actions and the corresponding triggers used in activities and state machines to incorporate mobility into behavior specifications.

4   Behavior

This section contains an overview of the AML constructs used to model behavioral aspects of multi-agent systems.

4.1   Behavior Abstraction and Decomposition

AML extends the capacity of UML to abstract and decompose behavior by the addition of two modeling elements: capability and behavior fragment.

Capability is used to model an abstract specification of a behavior that allows reasoning about and operations on that specification. Technically, a capability represents a unification of the common specification properties of UML's behavioral features and behaviors expressed in terms of inputs outputs, pre- and post-conditions.

Behavior fragment is a specialized class used to model a coherent re-usable fragment of behavior. It enables the decomposition of a complex behavior into simpler and (possibly) concurrently executable fragments. A behavior fragment can be shared by several entities and the behavior of an entity can, possibly recursively, be decomposed into several behavior fragments.

Fig. 5 part (a) shows the decomposition of the Player entity role type's behavior into a structure of behavior fragments. In part (b) two fragments, Mobility and BallHandling are described in terms of their owned capabilities (turn, walk, catch, etc.).

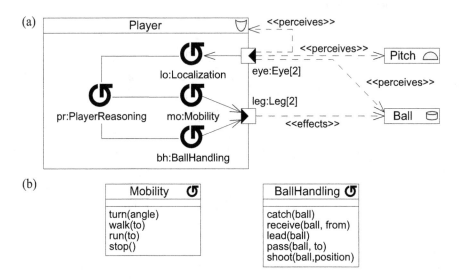

Fig. 5. Example of behavior fragments, observations and effecting interactions

4.2   Communicative Interactions

AML provides generic extensions to UML interactions in order to model interactions between groups of objects (using *multi-message* and *multi-lifeline*), dynamic change of an object's attributes induced by interactions (using *role change*), modeling of messages and signals not explicitly associated with an invocation of corresponding methods and receptions (using *agentified message* and *agentified signal*).

In addition to these generic concepts, AML also models communicative act based interactions commonly used in multi-agent systems, particularly: *communicative acts* (specialized agentified messages), *communicative interactions* (specialized UML interactions used to model communicative act based interactions), and *interaction protocols* (parametrized communicative interactions used to model patterns of interactions).

A simplified interaction between entities taking part in a player substitution is depicted in Fig. 6. Once the main coach decides which players are to be substituted (p1 to be substituted and p2 the substitute), he first notifies player p2 to get ready and then asks the main referee for permission to make the substitution. The main referee in turn replies by an answer. If the answer is "yes", the substitution process waits until the game is interrupted. If so, the coach instructs player p1 to exit and p2 to enter. Player p1 then leaves the pitch

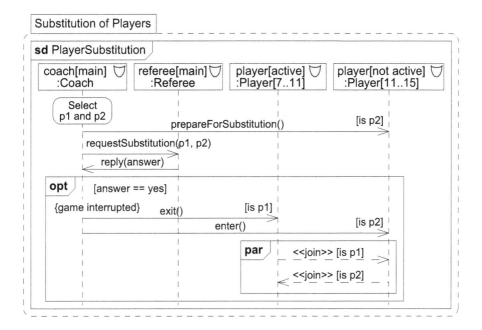

Fig. 6. Example of a communicative interaction

and joins the group of inactive players and p2 joins the pitch and thereby the group of active players.

4.3   Services

Services are encapsulated blocks of functionality that entities can offer to perform upon request. They are modeled in AML in terms of service specifications, service provisionings and service usages.

Service specification is a modeling element for specifying the functionality and accessibility of a service. Technically it specifies a set of specialized interaction protocols (called *service protocols*) each of which determines two sets of template parameters that must be bound by the service's providers and clients.

Service provision is a specialized dependency used to model provision of a service by particular entities, together with the binding of template parameters that are declared to be bound by service providers.

Service usage is a specialized dependency used to model usage of a service by particular entities, together with the binding of template parameters that are declared to be bound by service clients.

Fig. 7 shows a specification of the Motion service defined as a collection of three service protocols. The CanMove service protocol is based on the standard FIPA protocol FIPA-Query-Protocol [25] and binds the proposition parameter (the content of a query-if message) to the capability canMove(what, to) of a service provider. The participant parameter of the FIPA-Query-Protocol

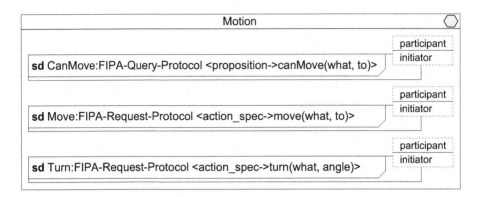

Fig. 7. Example of service specification

is mapped to a service provider and the `initiator` parameter to a service client. The `CanMove` service protocol is used by the service client to ask if an object referred by the `what` parameter can be moved to the position referred by the `to` parameter. The remaining service protocols `Move` and `Turn` are based on the `FIPA-Request-Protocol` [25] and are used to change the position or direction of a spatial object.

Binding of the `Motion` service specification to the provider `3DSpace` and the client `3DObject` is depicted in Fig. 3.

4.4   Observations and Effecting Interactions

AML defines several constructs for modeling observations (i.e. the ability of entities to observe features of other entities) and effecting interactions (i.e. the ability of entities to manipulate, or modify the state of, other entities).

Observations are modeled as the ability of an entity to perceive the state of (or to receive a signal from) an observed entity by means of *perceptors*. *Perceptor types* are used to specify (by means of *perceiving acts*) the observations an owner of a perceptor of that type can make.

The specification of which entities can observe others, is modeled by a *perceives* dependency. For modeling behavioral aspects of observations, AML provides a specialized *percept action*.

Different aspects of effecting interactions are modeled analogously, by means of *effectors*, *effector types*, *effecting acts*, *effects* dependencies, and *effect actions*.

An example is depicted in Fig. 5 (a) which shows an entity role type `Player` with two eyes - perceptors called `eye` of type `Eye`, and two legs - effectors called `leg` of type `Leg`. Eyes are used to see other players, the pitch and the ball, and to provide localization information to the internal parts of a player. Legs are used to change the player's position within the pitch (modeled by changing of internal state implying that no effects dependency need be placed in the diagram), and to manipulate the ball.

5   Mental Aspects

This section provides an overview of the AML constructs used to model beliefs, goals, plans, and mental relationships. These can be used for:
1. Enriching use case modeling through the expression of intentionality, goal-based requirements modeling, problem decomposition, etc.
2. Modeling mental attitudes of autonomous entities, which represent their informational, motivational and deliberative states.

Belief is a specialized UML class used to model information which autonomous entities have about themselves or their environment with a certain degree of subjective confidence.

Goal is a specialized UML class used to model goals, i.e. conditions of states of affairs, the achievement or maintenance of which is controlled by an autonomous entity or to which a modeling element may contribute.

Plan is a specialized UML activity used to model either predefined plans or fragments of behavior from which plans can be composed.

Mental relationships are specialized UML relationships used to model different types of relationships between mental states, e.g. means-ends, (de)composition, dependency, correlation, commitment, contribution, etc.

6   Contexts

AML offers the means to logically structure models according to situations that can occur during a system's lifetime and to model elements involved in handling those situations. For this reason AML provides a modeling element called *context*, which is a specialized UML package used to contain a part of the model relevant for a particular situation. The situation is specified either as a constraint or an explicitly modeled state associated with the context.

Fig. 6 shows the interaction `PlayerSubstitution` placed within a context `Substitution of Players`. This context could also contain an activity diagram modeling the substitution algorithm, specification of necessary structural features, relationships, and capabilities of affected entity roles, etc.

7   Extension of OCL

AML defines a set of operators used to extend the OCL Standard Library [12] to include expressions belonging to modal logic (operators `possible` and `necessary`), deontic logic (operators `obliged` and `permitted`), temporal logic (operators `until`, `past`, `future`, `next`, etc.), and cognitive primitives (operators `believe`, `know`, `desire`, `intend`, `feasible`, etc.), see [1].

8   CASE Tools Support

A necessary condition of successful dissemination of a modeling language into the software engineering community is the provision of tools supporting that language. Therefore we provide an implementation of AML in two CASE tools: Rational Rose 2003 (modeling CASE tool supporting UML 1.4) and Enterprise Architect 4.0 (modeling CASE tool supporting UML 2.0). The AML implementation consists of support for UML 1.* and 2.0 profiles for AML, a set of modeling utilities (specialized element specification dialogs, model consistency checker, etc.), and forward-engineering tools for the agent platform TAP1[6].

9   Conclusions and Further Work

AML represents a consistent framework for modeling applications that embody and/or exhibit characteristics of multi-agent systems. It integrates best modeling practices and concepts from existing agent oriented modeling and specification languages into a unique framework built on foundations of UML 2.0 and OCL 2.0. AML is also specified in accordance with OMG modeling frameworks (MDA, MOF, and UML), see Sect. 2.3. The structure of the language specification (see Sect. 2.4) together with the MDA/MOF/UML "metamodeling technology" (UML profiles, first-class metamodel extension, etc., see Sect. 2.5) gives AML the advantage of natural extensibility and customization. In addition, AML is supported by CASE tools (see Sect. 8).

We feel confident that AML is sufficiently detailed, comprehensive and tangible to be a useful tool for software architects building systems based on, or exhibiting characteristics of, multi-agent technology. In this respect we anticipate that AML may form a significant contribution to the effort of bringing about widespread adoption of intelligent agents across varied commercial marketplaces.

Current status: AML is ready for use today. The AML Specification version 1.0 is available for public review and its suitability for large-scale software development projects is being validated in real customer software projects. Further evaluation and feedback is needed to identify the perceived and actual value of the work and establish contexts for future work.

Further work: In the immediate future we anticipate revising the AML specification according to feedback from the public review and ongoing commercial projects. Beyond this we intend to extend the scope of AML to incorporate additional aspects of MAS (e.g. security), and extend CASE tools support for other agent platforms (e.g. JADE).

References

1. Weiss, G.: Multiagent Systems - A Modern Approach to Distributed Artificial Intelligence. 3rd edn. The MIT Press (2001)
2. Rao, A., Georgeff, M.: Modeling rational agents within a BDI-architecture. In Allen, J., Fikes, R., Sandewall, E., eds.: KR'91: Principles of Knowledge Representation and Reasoning. Morgan Kaufmann, San Mateo, California (1991) 473–484

---

[6] TAP1 is the commercial agent platform of Whitestein Technologies AG.

3. d'Inverno, M., Luck, M.: Understanding Agent Systems. Springer-Verlag (2001)
4. Bauer, B., Muller, J., Odell, J.: Agent UML: A formalism for specifying multiagent interaction. In Ciancarini, P., Wooldridge, M., eds.: Agent-Oriented Software Engineering. Springer-Verlag (2001) 91–103
5. Odell, J., Parunak, H., Bauer, B.: Extending UML for agents. In Wagner, G., Lesperance, Y., Yu, E., eds.: Proceedings of the Agent-Oriented Information Systems Workshop at the 17th National conference on Artificial Intelligence, Austin, Texas, ICue Publishing (2000) 3–17
6. Odell, J., Parunak, H., Fleischer, M., Brueckner, S.: Modeling agents and their environment. In: Proceedings of AOSE 2002, Bologna, Italy, Springer (2002) 16–31
7. Liu, L., Yu, E.: From requirements to architectural design using goals and scenarios. In: Software Requirements to Architectures Workshop (STRAW 2001), Toronto, Canada (2001)
8. Silva, V., Garcia, A., Brandao, A., Chavez, C., Lucena, C., Alencar, P.: Taming agents and objects in software engineering. In Garcia, A., Lucena, C., Castro, J., Omicini, A., Zambonelli, F., eds.: Software Engineering for Large-Scale Multi-Agent Systems: Research Issues and Practical Applications. Volume LNCS 2603. Springer-Verlag (2003) 1–25
9. Sturm, A., Dori, D., Shehory, O.: Single-model method for specifying multi-agent systems. In: 2nd International Joint Conference on Autonomous Agents and Multiagent Systems (AAMAS 2003), Melbourne, Australia (2003)
10. Wagner, G.: The agent-object-relationship meta-model: Towards a unified conceptual view of state and behavior. Information Systems **28** (2003)
11. OMG: Unified modeling language: Superstructure version 2.0. ptc/03-08-02 (2003)
12. OMG: UML 2.0 OCL specification. ptc/03-10-14 (2003)
13. Smith, M., McGuinness, D., Volz, R., Welty, C.: Web ontology language (OWL), guide version 1.0, W3C working draft. URL: http://www.w3.org/TR/2002/WD-owl-guide-20021104 (2002)
14. Cranefield, S., Haustein, S., Purvis, M.: UML-based ontology modelling for software agents. In: Proceedings of the Workshop on Ontologies in Agent, 2001. (2001)
15. Martin, D.e.: OWL-S 1.0 release. URL: http://www.daml.org/services/ (2003)
16. Evans, R., Kearny, P., Stark, J., Caire, G., Garijo, F., Sanz, G., Leal, F., Chainho, P., Massonet, P.: MESSAGE: Methodology for engineering systems of software agents. Technical Report P907, EURESCOM (2001)
17. Zambonelli, F., Jennings, N., Wooldridge, M.: Developing multiagent systems: the Gaia methodology. ACM Trans on Software Engineering and Methodology **12** (2003) 317–370
18. Bresciani, P., Giorgini, P., Giunchiglia, F., Mylopoulos, J., Perini, A.: TROPOS: An agent-oriented software development methodology. Autonomous Agents and Multi-Agent Systems **2** (2004) 203–236
19. Cossentino, M., Sabatucci, L., Chella, A.: A possible approach to the development of robotic multi-agent systems. In: IEEE/WIC Conference on Intelligent Agent Technology (IAT'03), Halifax, Canada (2003)
20. Padgham, L., Winikoff, M.: Prometheus: A methodology for developing intelligent agents. In: Proceedings of the First International Joint Conference on Autonomous Agents and Multi-Agent Systems (AAMAS 2002), Bologna, Italy (2002)
21. Iglesias, C., Garijo, M., Gonzalez, J., Velasco, J.: Analysis and design of multiagent systems using MAS-CommonKADS. In Singh, M., Rao, A., Wooldridge, M., eds.: Intelligent Agents IV (LNAI Vol. 1365). Volume 1365. Springer-Verlag (1998) 313–326

22. DeLoach, S.: Multiagent systems engineering: A methodology and language for designing agent systems. In: Agent-Oriented Information Systems '99 (AOIS'99), Seattle, WA (1999)
23. Turski, W., Maibaum, T.: The Specification of Computer Programs. Addison-Wesley (1987)
24. OMG: Meta object facility (MOF) specification. Version 1.4, formal/2002-04-03 (2002)
25. The Foundation for Intelligent Physical Agents: FIPA specifications repository. URL: http://www.fipa.org/repository/index.html (2004)
26. Jennings, N.R.: On agent-based software engineering. Artificial Intelligence **117** (2000) 277–296
27. Jennings, N., Wooldridge, M.: Software agents. IEEE Review **42** (1996) 17–21
28. Wooldridge, M., Ciancarini, P.: Agent-oriented software engineering: The state of the art. In: Handbook of Software Engineering and Knowledge Engineering. World Scientific Publishing Co. (2001)

Formal Semantics for AUML Agent Interaction Protocol Diagrams

Lawrence Cabac and Daniel Moldt

Department of Computer Science, TGI, University of Hamburg
{cabac, moldt}@informatik.uni-hamburg.de

Abstract. In this paper we introduce an approach for defining semantics for AUML agent interaction protocol diagrams using Petri net code structures. This approach is based on the usage of net components which provide basic tasks and the structure for Petri nets. Agent interaction protocol diagrams are used to model agent conversations on an abstract level. By mapping elements of the diagrams to net components we are able to translate the diagrams into Petri nets, i.e to generate code structures from the drawings. We provide tool support for this approach by combining a tool for net components with a tool for drawing agent interaction protocol diagrams. This combined tool is available as a plug-in for RENEW (**R**eference **N**et **W**orkshop).

Keywords: agents, agent interaction protocols, AUML, CAPA, high-level Petri nets, MULAN, net components, operational semantics, reference nets, RENEW.

1 Introduction

Computer aided software engineering (CASE) tools are programs that support the development of large software systems. They provide tools for modeling and constructing applications. Furthermore, they provide the possibility to generate code from models, to facilitate the development and to strip the development process of unnecessary recurrent and error-prone manual tasks. Successful tools for various programming languages exist and are in extensive use.

Especially for the usage of the Agent Unified Modeling Language (AUML) within CASE tools, a well defined semantics is required. However, the semantics of agent interaction protocols (AIP) is usually defined by the semantics of sequence diagrams and descriptions in natural languages. These semantics are usually ambiguous and vague. To address the challenge of defining a formal semantics for agent interaction protocols, we use high-level Petri nets. Since Petri nets do not only offer a well defined formal, but also operational semantics, we can by this means, not only provide formal semantics, but also operational semantics to agent interaction protocol diagrams.

While modeling with Petri nets is common, the idea of programming with Petri nets has not been widely accepted yet. But especially when it comes to concurrent and distributed processes, e.g. multi-agent systems, the advantages

J. Odell et al. (Eds.): AOSE 2004, LNCS 3382, pp. 47–61, 2005.

of Petri nets are obvious. For this reason, we build concurrent and distributed software systems as multi-agent systems on the basis of reference nets [11] – a high-level Petri net formalism, which is enriched with Java as inscription language. The framework's reference architecture for the multi-agent system is MULAN[1]/CAPA[2]. It is implemented in reference nets and can be executed efficiently in Renew[3].

The process of implementing application software in MULAN requires the construction of Mulan protocols which define the behavior of the agents. A Mulan protocol is a reference net that describes the communication and the internal behavior of an agent. Since the construction of a large system requires building many Mulan protocols, which frequently require similar parts of functionality, the need for software engineering methods and techniques becomes evident. This includes standardizations, conventions and tool support.

We have established two methods to handle the complexity of Mulan protocols and support their construction. First, we use net components [2] to construct the Mulan protocols and to achieve a unified and structured form of the protocols. Second, we model the agents' interactions on an abstract level using agent interaction protocol diagrams [4]. Agent interaction protocol diagrams are defined by the FIPA (Foundation for Intelligent Physical Agents [6]) in AUML [7]. The advantage of modeling in AUML is its intuitive graphical representation of the architecture and processes.

By offering tool support for the construction and modeling of Mulan protocols, we have succeeded in speeding up their development. Also, the form and the structure of Mulan protocols have become unified and easily readable. Another advantage is that the agents' communications are documented in the agent interaction protocol diagrams. Therefore, the overview of the system has been simplified and enhanced.

In this paper we want to describe one further step towards an integrated development environment for MULAN applications. By combining the two described approaches we are able to generate code (here: Petri net) structures from the agent interaction protocol diagrams.

The following pages briefly introduce the MULAN net components and the modeling of agent conversations with agent interaction protocol diagrams. Finally, a prototype tool for code generation will be presented together with a simple example.

2   AUML and Petri Nets

This section describes how agent interaction protocol diagrams semantics can be defined with the help of Petri nets. Examples for some expressions of the diagrams are given to show the general notion.

---

[1] **Multi-Agent Nets**, [9]
[2] **Concurrent Agent Platform Architecture**, [5]
[3] **Reference Net Workshop**, [12], [11], [13]

Different versions or flavors of AUML have been presented and discussed. See [16], [15] and [10] for the old version (version 1) and their extensions. These are also used by the FIPA to describe the Interaction Protocols [7]. The new version (version 2) is still under development (see [8], [14]). However, we are not concerned with the different flavors of the AUML agent interaction protocol diagrams. Since the meaning behind these flavors is basically the same, which makes the graphical representation interchangeable, it is superfluous to discuss this matter here. The shown examples are given in agent interaction protocol diagrams of the old version (version 1). If semantics is defined for one of the flavors, it can easily be translated to the other flavors.

2.1   AUML Flavors

Each of the different flavors of AUML agent interaction protocol diagrams have advantages and disadvantages. We favor the old version of the AUML agent interaction protocol diagrams for several reasons. First, we think that the old representation of agent interactions is more intuitive and clearer in appearance than the new style that is oriented towards the UML 2.0 standard. Second, through dropping the threads, the new version of AUML (version 2) does not reflect concurrency in a sufficient way. Third, we have been working with the old version successfully over the last two years in several teaching projects with over one hundred students. The modeling technique - although new to the students - was well accepted and successfully used in the development of multi-agent applications.

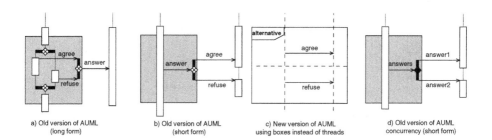

a) Old version of AUML (long form) b) Old version of AUML (short form) c) New version of AUML using boxes instead of threads d) Old version of AUML concurrency (short form)

Fig. 1. Flavors of AUML, representing the alternative of sending one of two possible (a,b,c) / concurrently sent (d) messages

Figure 1 shows the representation of the alternative to send one message out of two possible messages as an example for the different flavors of AUML agent interaction protocol diagrams.[4] This example shows another advantage of the old long (or explicit) version (Figure 1 a) of agent interaction protocol diagrams. With the usage of message join figures we are able to represent the fact that only one message is actually received by the receiver of the message. Instead, in the

---

[4] Only parts of the diagrams are shown in the image.

short version (b) and also in the new version (c) of AUML there is no *structural* difference in the representation of receiving one message (of for example two possible messages) and the representation of two concurrently sent / received messages (d), although the syntax itself is unambiguous.

2.2   Semantics for AUML

By using Petri nets, which offer a well defined operational semantics, it is possible to describe the operational semantics of agent interaction protocol diagrams. To demonstrate how this is done, the example of Figure 1 (see also Figure 2 a) is used and modeled as Petri net in an abstract (or simplified) fashion. Figure 2 shows the representation of two alternatively sent messages modeled with a Petri net[5] (b). In addition, Petri nets also offer the possibility of coarsening (respectively refining) nets. The coarsened Petri net is shown in (c) which can be interpreted in the coarsened agent interaction protocol diagrams as shown in (d). This way of modeling offers the possibility to use abstractions that can clarify the models. It also offers the possibility to exchange one agent's behavior with another possible behavior without the need to alter the behavior of the communicating agent. For instance, the sending agent can always reply with an *agree* and the receiving agent's behavior would not have to be altered.

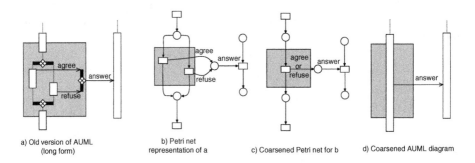

a) Old version of AUML (long form)   b) Petri net representation of a   c) Coarsened Petri net for b   d) Coarsened AUML diagram

Fig. 2. Semantics for the alternative message provided by Petri net and coarsened descriptions

By translating AUML agent interaction protocol diagrams into Petri nets we manage to define the operational semantics of the agent interaction protocol diagrams, i.e. the semantics of the diagrams is defined through the semantics of Petri nets. However, the translation is not done on the abstract level as shown in Figure 2. For a translation into a form of Petri nets that is also executable we need to use more elaborate and concrete methods. These methods are a framework architecture for the execution of the resulting protocols and a mapping from agent interaction protocol diagram expressions onto (unified) expressions of Petri net code that can be executed in the framework's architecture. The

---

[5] For the exact semantics including inscriptions and pattern variations see [3].

first is given through MULAN/CAPA ([9], [5]), which offers a Petri net-based infrastructure as a reference model for a FIPA-compliant multi-agent system. In
addition, the multi-agent applications built on MULAN/CAPA are also executable
within the framework. The second is achieved through mapping the agent interaction protocol diagram expressions onto net components. Net components [4]
and the way they can be used to compose Mulan protocols are presented in the
next section.

3   Net Structures

In this section we introduce net components, show how they provide a structure for Mulan protocols, describe the way we model agent communication
with AUML diagrams and present how agent interaction protocol diagrams are
mapped to Petri net structures using the net components for Mulan protocols.
While agent interaction protocol diagrams describe the conversations of agents,
Mulan protocols define the behavior of the MULAN agents and net components
are descriptions of basic tasks in the Mulan protocols.

3.1   Net Components

A net component is a subnet. It consists of net elements and additional elements
such as default inscriptions or comments. It fulfills one basic task that is so
general that the net component can be applied to a broad variety of nets.

A net component is defined by its net elements, but it also has a fixed geometrical structure and orientation. This structure contributes to the net structure
of the net in which the net component is used. In addition, the geometrical
form makes the net component easily identifiable to the developer. A set of
net components for the Mulan protocols exists that facilitates the construction
(modeling) of these Petri nets. Figure 3 shows a selection of the most frequently
used MULAN net components. The readability of Mulan protocols that are built

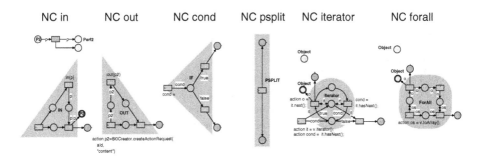

Fig. 3. A selection of the MULAN net components responsible for message passing,
splits and loops

with net components increases significantly. Furthermore, the structure of the net is unified since it depends on the structure of the net components.

3.2   Structured Petri Nets

Petri nets are graphs, i.e. they have a graphical representation. A graphical representation is useful for the understanding of the behavior of a model. A graphic/diagrammatic representation can be more comprehensive than a textual one. However, a diagram can also be very confusing if it does not provide a clear structure or if substructures of similar behavior are displayed in many different ways. One of the greatest advantages of a diagrammatic representation is the fact that reappearing structures can be perceived by the human cognitive system without effort.

The usage of net components enables developers to recognize reappearing net structures in Mulan protocols effortlessly. Furthermore, a conventionalized style of the developed Petri nets is achieved.

3.3   Modeling Agent Interaction

Modeling agent interaction can be done by using several means. The FIPA [6] uses the AUML agent interaction protocol diagrams [7] for modeling interactions between agents. These diagrams are an extension of the Unified Modeling Language (UML) sequence diagrams [1] but they are more powerful in their expressiveness. They can fold several sequences into one diagram by adding additional elements (AND, XOR and OR) to the usual sequence diagram. Thus, they are able to describe a set of scenarios. Figure 4 shows the FIPA Request Protocol and a compliant Producer-Consumer example.

There are several advantages in the method of modeling agent interactions with agent interaction protocol diagrams. Three of them are:

- The models are easily readable by all participants, because of the similarity to UML.
- Abstract modeling increases the overview over the system.
- A means of communication, specification and documentation is established.

3.4   Mapping Agent Interaction Protocol Diagrams to Mulan Protocols

The combination of the two tools – the tool for applying net components and the tool for drawing diagrams – is done as follows. By using agent interaction protocol diagrams for modeling agent communication the structure of the Mulan protocols can be derived directly from the diagram. This is done by mapping the relating elements in the agent interaction protocol diagrams to the net components. In detail this means (compare with Figures 3 and 6 to 11):

- A message arc is the abstract representation of the basic messaging net components (*NC out* and *NC in*).
- A split figure is the abstract representation of the conditional (*NC cond*) or a parallel split (*NC psplit*).

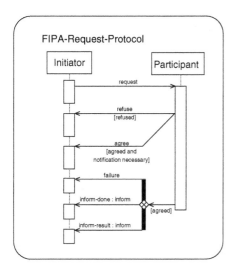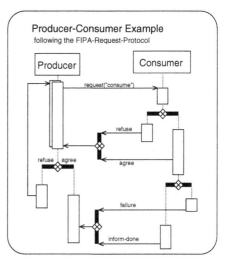

Fig. 4. Agent interaction protocol diagrams of the FIPA Request Protocol and a compliant Producer-Consumer example

- A life line between a role descriptor and an activation marks the start of a protocol (*NC start*)

Several other net components (loops, subcalls) and also possibilities to handle instances of protocols (indicated by the shadow activation figure in Figure 4 in the Producer thread) are not yet represented in our tool for agent interaction protocol diagrams, since the elements to represent that kind of functionality do not exist in the abstract model. It seems that for some of these basic tasks/features the notation of the agent interaction protocol diagrams has to be extended. However, the possibility to model that kind of functionality exists in Petri net protocols and are applied using net components. For that functionality agent interaction protocol representation offers no equivalent.

- Loops are not well represented yet. Proposals exist for their representation, but so far there has been no way to determine whether a sequential or a concurrent process is desired.
- Sub-calls: It is possible to nest agent interaction protocol diagrams, but semantics is ambiguous.

These and some other challenges are for instance addressed in the development of the AUML version 2.0 [8].

In general, the main problem is the vague semantics of the agent interaction protocol diagrams. Although the lack of specification of detail within a model that results from abstraction can be of advantage while modeling, the semantics of notation should be clear and well defined. The process of modeling can be accelerated by postponing the description of details to the implementation or by relying on implicit knowledge that defines the missing semantics.

In contrast, if there is the need to define a specific mapping, clear semantics is desired/necessary. This can be described as implementing through model refinement ("Implementing by Modeling"), i.e. the model's details are progressively worked out.

4   From Model to Net

This section describes the tool support for mapping agent interaction protocol diagrams to Mulan protocol structures. The tool generates Petri net structures that can be compared to program source code skeletons. To achieve a functional Mulan protocol, the inscriptions have to be adjusted and - if needed - the classes for the messages have to be implemented. Furthermore, the net has to be adjusted (refactored) if an element has to be used that is not yet provided, e.g. loops.

4.1   Code Generation

In the last developer version of RENEW[6], a tool – a RENEW plug-in– for applying net components to nets and a tool to draw agent interaction protocol diagrams were included. Therefore, developers of Mulan protocols were able to draw diagrams to model the behavior of agents with that version of the diagram tool. Diagrams were used as means of specification, documentation and communication among the developers of MULAN applications. The basic communication protocols were established and defined using these diagrams. So agent interaction protocol diagrams only defined the way of communication between the agents, but not the internal behavior.

Usually, but not necessarily, different developers implement the Mulan protocols for each agent defining the external and the internal behavior of an agent. As long as the different developers constructed the Mulan protocol according to the given agent interaction protocol diagrams, the agents could communicate in a correct way.

Figure 5 displays the RENEW GUI including the control elements of the diagram plug-in. The last palette contains buttons for the drawing of role figures, activations, messages, life lines, split and join figures, note figures, frames and inscriptions.

The process of constructing a Mulan protocol requires the manual task of mapping the diagram structures to each Mulan protocol. This was done by connecting net components with each other using the net component tool. Many elements in the agent interaction protocol diagrams could be mapped onto net components in a straight forward fashion as described in section 3.4.

It seems obvious that this task can be performed automatically by the introduced tool. Since agent interaction protocol diagrams describe the interactions and the splitting of activities, we decided to implement a prototype that is capable of generating Petri net skeletons from the diagrams that reflect these

---

[6] See also RENEW 2.0, [13].

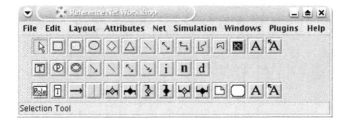

Fig. 5. The GUI of RENEW with the tool support for drawing diagrams

structures. To be able to execute the generated code, it has to be refactored
and adjusted with additional functionality. This is a common approach for code
generation: The parts that can be derived from the model are generated and the
rest is added manually.

4.2   Geometrical Arrangement of Mulan Protocols

In addition to textual code generation, the construction of Petri nets also has
to deal with the layout of the generated nets. The structure of nets is crucial to
readability. If the code is used as it is generated, there is no need to design the
layout of the code. But if the code has to be adjusted, the programmer has to
understand the code. Thus, the layout of the nets is an important issue.

Net components provide a structure for Petri nets. This is not only true for
the manually made nets but also for generated code. For each net component only
some additional information is needed that provides the knowledge of how it can
be connected to other net components and how this is reflected in the layout. The
net structure results from the smaller structure of the net components similar
to the structure of a snowflake, which results from the structures of molecules of
water. So net components provide the structure by imposing their own structure
onto the net structure. However, the generated Petri net code structures have
always the same form due to the automated generation.

Figure 7 shows the source of the model augmented with the geometrical
representation of the corresponding net components and Figures 8 and 10 show
the two parts of the model that match the two Mulan protocols, rotated by
ninety degrees. The resulting skeletons are shown in Figures 9 and 11.

All augmented models are just presented here to illustrate the matching of
diagram elements to net components. They are not necessary for the generation
of the Mulan protocols. The generated Mulan protocol skeletons are shown (Figures 9 and 11) as they have been generated, without any modification of nets or
inscriptions.

4.3   Example: Producer-Consumer

Generating code skeletons from the Producer-Consumer example agent interaction protocol diagram is possible and results in two Mulan protocol skeletons.
Figure 6 shows the diagram from which the code is generated.

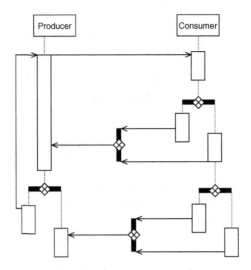

Fig. 6. Source for generation of the Producer-Consumer example

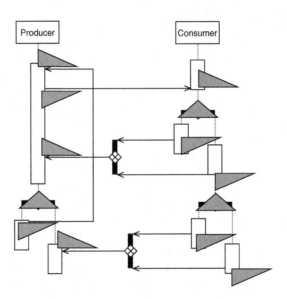

Fig. 7. The source from Figure 6, with the geometrical representation of the corresponding net components

The results of this simple example are satisfying. The Mulan protocols do not need to be refactored because the conversation deals only with communication and decisions. However, in order to convert these skeletons into executable Mulan

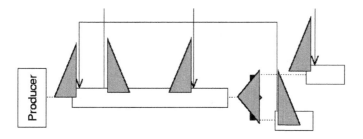

Fig. 8. The Producer part of the source from Figure 6, with the geometrical representation of the corresponding net components. Rotated by ninety degrees to fit the orientation of the resulting Mulan protocol

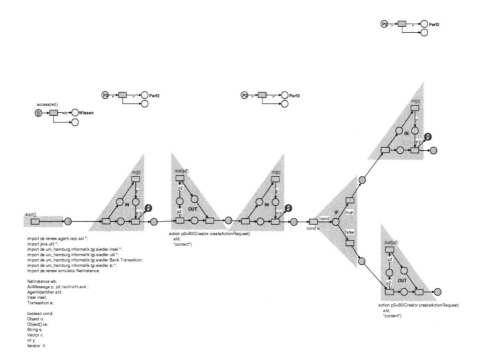

Fig. 9. Generated Producer Mulan protocol skeleton

protocols, we still have to work on them. The relevant data has to be extracted from the messages and from the agents' knowledge bases. Furthermore, we have to define the decisions and the outgoing messages.

It seems that for more complex communication protocols, dealing with internal behavior, loops or sub-calls, this simple approach is not powerful enough. But since most of the used net components deal with message passing, splits, starting and stopping, this approach will already generate more than ninety percent of the Petri net code structure. Only the parts that deal with broadcasting

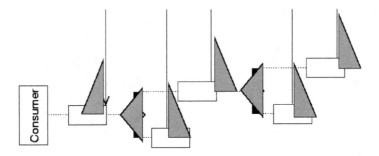

Fig. 10. The Consumer part of the source from Figure 6, with the geometrical representation of the corresponding net components. Rotated by ninety degrees to fit the orientation of the resulting Mulan protocol

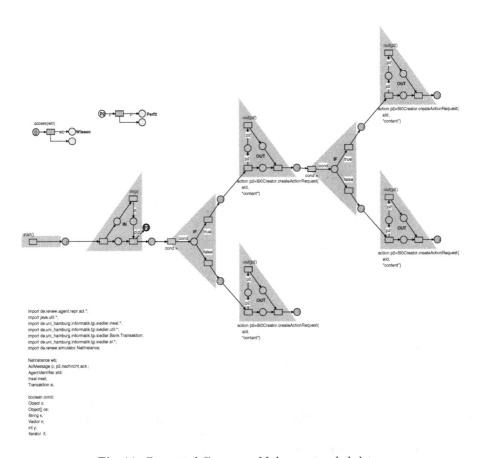

Fig. 11. Generated Consumer Mulan protocol skeleton

or multi-casting messages, or the parts that deal with internal behavior have to be adjusted manually.

5 Conclusion

Software engineering methods have been developed to enhance the construction of large software systems and are used and applied successfully. These methods can also be applied for software development based on high-level Petri nets. With more extensive use of these conventional techniques the process of Petri net-based software developing can be improved. The advantages of Petri nets lie in their inherent concurrency; UML is a powerful modeling language that is well accepted and widely spread. Both – UML and Petri nets – can contribute to the construction of large distributed and / or concurrent systems. Combining their advantages results in a powerful method to develop applications.

A crucial point is the semantics of the used AUML agent interaction protocol diagrams. It has to be well defined in developing / designing as well as for the generation of code (structures). We showed that the defining of agent interaction protocol diagram semantics can be achieved by mapping the diagrams onto Petri nets. For this a net component-based approach was used, which enables us to generate Petri net code structures from the diagrams. The net components provide the functionality of syntactic / semantic unities as well as the structure of the resulting Mulan protocols. However, the definition of semantics is realized in the tool and not explicitly given here.

In addition, by using net components, the Mulan protocols are structured and their structure is unified. This increases the readability of Mulan protocols and the software development is accelerated. The integration of UML-based modeling into the developing process has contributed to the clearness of the system and its overall structure. Apart from the development process, the focus of development was also altered by using AUML. The center of focus shifted from the agents' processes to the communication between the agents.

The introduction of UML-based modeling into the developing process and the unification of net structures turned out to be a successful approach. Nevertheless, the integration of conventional methods as UML and development of software with Petri nets can be driven further. In this paper we presented one step towards an integrated development environment for the construction of MULAN-based application software. By merging the two approaches – net components and agent interaction protocol diagrams – we are able to generate skeletons of Mulan protocols from interaction diagrams.

For the development of large applications on the basis of the Petri net-based multi-agent system MULAN / CAPA, tool support is needed on different levels of abstraction. This includes the construction of Mulan protocols, the modeling of agent interaction and the debugging of the system during development. The first two points are covered by the tool support for net components and agent interaction protocol diagrams. Additionally, we can now also ease the developing process by generating code in the form of Petri net structures from diagrams.

Even further integration of methods and techniques can be considered in the future. For a representation of all MULAN net components in the agent interaction protocol diagrams the notation for these diagrams has to be augmented by corresponding elements. Another useful approach is to integrate a round-trip engineering functionality into the diagram tool so that changes that are made in the Mulan protocols are reflected in the diagrams.

References

1. Grady Booch, James Rumbaugh, and Ivar Jacobson. *The Unified Modeling Language User Guide*. Addison-Wesley, Reading, Massachusetts, 1996.
2. Lawrence Cabac. *Entwicklung von geometrisch unterscheidbaren Komponenten zur Vereinheitlichung von Mulan-Protokollen*. Studienarbeit, University of Hamburg, Department of Computer Science, 2002.
3. Lawrence Cabac. *Modeling Agent Interaction with AUML Diagrams and Petri Nets*. diploma thesis, University of Hamburg, Department of Computer Science, Vogt-Kölln Str. 30, 22527 Hamburg, Germany, 2003.
4. Lawrence Cabac, Daniel Moldt, and Heiko Rölke. A proposal for structuring Petri net-based agent interaction protocols. In *24th International Conference on Application and Theory of Petri Nets, Eindhoven, Netherlands, June 2003*, volume 2679 of *"Lecture Notes in Computer Science"*, pages 102–120. Springer-Verlag, June 2003.
5. Michael Duvigneau, Daniel Moldt, and Heiko Rölke. Concurrent architecture for a multi-agent platform. In Fausto Giunchiglia, James Odell, and Gerhard Weiß, editors, *Agent-Oriented Software Engineering III. Third International Workshop, AOSE 2002, Bologna, Italy, July 2002. Revised Papers and Invited Contributions*, volume 1420 of *"Lecture Notes in Computer Science"*, pages 59–72. Springer-Verlag, 2003.
6. Foundation for Intelligent Physical Agents. http://www.fipa.org.
7. FIPA. FIPA Interaction Protocol Library Specification, August 2001. http://www.fipa.org/specs/fipa00025/XC00025E.pdf.
8. Marc-Philippe Huget and James Odell. Representing agent interaction protocols with agent UML. In James Odell, Paolo Ciorgini, and Jörg P. Müller, editors, *Proceedings of the Workshop on Agent-Oriented Software Engineering at the Conference on Autonomous Agents & Multi Agent Systems (AAMAS'04)*, New York, 2004. (also in this collection).
9. Michael Köhler, Daniel Moldt, and Heiko Rölke. Modeling the structure and behaviour of Petri net agents. In *Proceedings of the 22nd Conference on Application and Theory of Petri Nets*, volume 2075 of *"Lecture Notes in Computer Science"*, pages 224–241. Springer-Verlag, 2001.
10. Jean-Luc Koning, Marc-Philippe Huget, Jun Wei, and Xu Wang. Extended modeling languages for interaction protocol design. 2222:68–76, 2002.
11. Olaf Kummer. *Referenznetze*. Dissertation, University of Hamburg, Department of Computer Science, Logos-Verlag, Berlin, 2002.
12. Olaf Kummer, Frank Wienberg, and Michael Duvigneau. Renew - The Reference Net Workshop. In *Tool Demonstrations - 22nd International Conference on Application and Theory of Petri Nets*, 2001. See also http://www.renew.de.
13. Olaf Kummer, Frank Wienberg, Michael Duvigneau, Jörn Schumacher, Michael Köhler, Daniel Moldt, Heiko Rölke, and Rüdiger Valk. An extensible editor and simulation engine for Petri nets: Renew. In J. Cortadella and W. Reisig, editors, *25th International Conference on Application and Theory of Petri Nets 2004*, volume 3099 of *"Lecture Notes in Computer Science"*, pages 484–493. Springer-Verlag, 2004.

14. James Odell and Marc-Philippe Huget. FIPA Modeling: Interaction Diagrams. Working draft, Foundation for Intelligent Physical Agents, July 2003. http://www.auml.org/auml/documents/ID-03-07-02.pdf.
15. James Odell, H. Van Dyke Parunak, and Bernhard Bauer. Extending UML for agents. In Gerd Wagner, Yves Lesperance, and Eric Yu, editors, *Proc. of the Agent-Oriented Information Systems Workshop at the 17th National conference on Artificial Intelligence*, pages 3–17, 2000. http://www.jamesodell.com/ExtendingUML.pdf.
16. James Odell, H. Van Dyke Parunak, and Bernhard Bauer. Representing agent interaction protocols in UML. In Paolo Ciancarini and Michael Wooldridge, editors, *Agent-Oriented Software Engineering*, volume 1957 of *"Lecture Notes in Computer Science"*, pages 121–140. Springer-Verlag, 2001. http://www.auml.org/auml/supplements/Odell-AOSE2000.pdf.

A Study of Some Multi-agent Meta-models

Carole Bernon[1], Massimo Cossentino[2], Marie-Pierre Gleizes[1], Paola Turci[3], and Franco Zambonelli[4]

[1] IRIT - University Paul Sabatier - Toulouse, Cedex 4 (France)
{bernon, gleizes}@irit.fr
[2] Istituto di Calcolo e Reti ad Alte Prestazioni (ICAR) -
Consiglio Nazionale delle Ricerche (CNR)- Palermo, Italy
cossentino@pa.icar.cnr.it
[3] Dipartimento di Ingegneria dell'Informazione -
Universitá degli Studi di Parma - Parma, Italy
turci@ce.unipr.it
[4] Dipartimento di Scienze e Metodi dell'Ingegneria -
Universitá di Modena e Reggio Emilia - Reggio Emilia, Italy
franco.zambonelli@unimo.it

Abstract. Several agent-oriented methodologies have been proposed over the last few years. Unlike the object-oriented domain and unfortunately for designers, most of the time, each methodology has its own purposes and few standardization works have been done yet, limiting the impact of agent design on the industrial world. By studying three existing methodologies - ADELFE, Gaia and PASSI - and the concepts related to them, this paper tries to find a means to unify their meta-models. Comparing a certain number of features at the agent or system level (such as the agent structure, its society or organization, its interactions capacities or how agents may be implemented) has enabled us to draw up a first version of a unified meta-model proposed as a first step toward interoperability between agent-oriented methodologies.

1 Introduction

Over the years several methodologies and approaches have been proposed for the development of multi-agent systems. Nevertheless many users have still trouble finding a method and notation that would satisfy their needs completely. What seems to be widely accepted is that a unique specific methodology cannot be general enough to be useful to everyone without some level of personalization. As a matter of fact the need for systematic principles to develop situation-specific methods, perceived almost from the beginning by the object-oriented community, has led to the emergence of the proved successful in developing object-oriented information systems [1]. Its importance in the object-oriented context should be evaluated considering not only the direct influence (not so many companies and individuals work in this specific way) but mainly the indirect consequence. The most important and diffused development processes (e.g., the Rational Unified

J. Odell et al. (Eds.): AOSE 2004, LNCS 3382, pp. 62–77, 2005.

Process [2]) are in fact not rigid, instead they are a kind of framework within which the single designer can choose his/her own path.

We believe that the agent-oriented community should follow a similar path, trying to adapt the method engineering for using it in agent-oriented design. It is in this ambit that the FIPA Methodology TC[1] is situated. Its aim, and our aim as members of the committee, is to propose quite an open approach that allows the composition of a very large repository of human experiences (design process is first of all a human process) that could be expressed in terms of a standard notation.

Right from the beginning however it was clear that adopting the method engineering approach in the AOSE context is not a plain task. In the object-oriented context the construction of method fragments, the assembling of the methodology with them and the execution of the design rely on a common denominator, the universally accepted concept of object and related meta-model of the object-oriented system. The situation concerning the agent-oriented approach is quite different since there is not a commonly accepted definition of the concept of agent and related meta-model of the multi-agent system - a structural representation of the elements (agent, role, behavior, ontology, etc.) that will compose the actual system with their composing relationships. Since a meta-model is a means of unifying concepts, the lack of a unique MAS meta-model consequently leads to each methodology having its own concepts and system structure.

Analyzing the process of designing a system (object or agent-oriented) we have come to the conclusion that it consists in instantiating the system meta-model that the designers have in their mind in order to fulfill the specific problem requirements. In the agent world this means that the meta-model is the critical element when applying the method engineering paradigm, because of the variety of the methodology MAS meta-models. Indeed the first step of the composition process should consist in a selection of the elements that compose the meta-model of the MAS the designers will build. The MAS meta-model so derived will be useful in the method fragment selection phase at least in order to avoid the selection of methods referring to different elements. But without a unique MAS meta-model, the various concepts and system structures characterizing the different methodologies could make very laborious or even impossible to carry out the method fragment composition.

Bearing in mind the above described composition process centered on the MAS meta-model, the main scope of this work is two-fold: (i) to analyze the MAS meta-models of three existing design methodologies - ADELFE, Gaia and PASSI - in order to support what has been asserted above; (ii) to design a unifying MAS meta-model, obtained by merging the most interesting aspects of each meta-model, with the aim of making a significant step toward the definition of a unique omni-comprehensive MAS meta-model.

We would like to emphasize that despite the fact that the choice of the three methodologies was a logic consequence of the people involved in writing the

---

[1] http://www.fipa.org/activities/methodology.html

paper, we think that all in all the heterogeneousness of the three methodologies allows us to draw interesting remarks.

2   ADELFE Meta-model

ADELFE[2] is a methodology devoted to software engineering of adaptive multi-agent systems [3], [4]. Adaptive software is used in situations in which the environment is unpredictable or the system is open. To solve these problems ADELFE guarantees that the software is developed according to the AMAS (Adaptive Multi-Agent System) theory [5].

According to this theory, building a system which is functionally adequate (which realizes the right desired global function) is achieved by designing agents with a cooperation-driven social attitude. Agents composing an AMAS ignore the global function of the system, only pursue a local goal and try to always keep cooperative relations with one another. They are called "cooperative agents".

The MAS meta-model adopted for ADELFE (cf. Figure 1) is fundamentally explained by this specialization of ADELFE and by the features a cooperative agent possesses. Its life cycle is a classical one; it consists in having perceptions, taking decisions and then doing actions (perceive-decide-act).

Besides local cooperation rules are enabling it to detect and solve Non Cooperative Situations (NCS). These NCS are cooperation failures (e.g., cooperation protocol not obeyed, unpredictable situations) that are, from its point of view, inconsistent with its cooperative social attitude. Different kinds of such failures can be detected according to the context of the concerned application, such as Incomprehension (an agent does not understand a perceived signal), Ambiguity (it has several contradictory interpretations for a perceived signal), Incompetence (it cannot satisfy the request of another one), Unproductiveness (it receives an already known piece of information or some information that leads to no reasoning for it), Concurrency (several agents want to access an exclusive resource), Conflict (several agents want to realize the same activity) or Uselessness (an agent may make an action that is not beneficial, according to its beliefs, to other agents). When detecting a NCS, an agent does all it is able to do to solve it to stay cooperative for others. For example, faced up with an incomprehension situation, it does not ignore the message but will transmit it to agents that seem (from its point of view) relevant to deal with it.

An agent possesses world representations that are beliefs concerning other agents, the physical environment or the agent itself. These representations are used by the agent to determine its behavior. If an agent has representations that may evolve (e.g., a semantic network), these representations can be expressed using a multi-agent system. A representation can be shared by different agents.

---

[2] ADELFE is a French acronym meaning "toolkit to develop software with emergent functionalities". It was a French RNTL-funded project (2000-2003) which partners were: ARTAL Technologies and TNI-Valiosys from industry, and IRIT and L3I from academia. See http://www.irit.fr/ADELFE

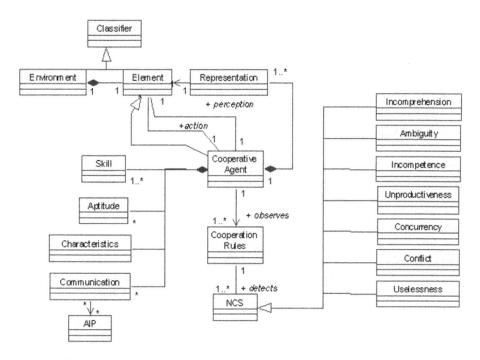

Fig. 1. The Multi-Agent System Meta-Model Adopted in ADELFE

An agent is able to communicate with other agents or its environment. This communication can be done in a direct manner (by exchanging messages) or an indirect one (through the environment). Tools that enable an agent to communicate are interaction languages. When an agent uses a direct communication through messages exchanges, AIPs may also be used to express the communication pattern between agents.

An agent can interact with its environment (physical or social) by means of perceptions and actions. For an agent, an action is a way to act on its environment during its action phase and a perception enables it to receive information from this environment.

Aptitudes show the ability of an agent to reason both about knowledge and beliefs it owns. For instance, an aptitude of a software agent can be expressed by an inference engine on a base of rules or any other processing on perceptions and world representations. Aptitudes can also be expressed using data, e.g. an integer value which represents the exploration depth of a planning tree.

An agent owns some skills that are specific knowledge that enable it to realize its own partial function. For instance, a skill may be a simple datum which is useful to act on the world (e.g., an integer distance which represents the minimal distance a robot has to respect to avoid obstacles) or may be more complex when expressing a reasoning that the agent makes during its decision phase (e.g., a reasoning to avoid obstacles). If they are complex and able to evolve, skills may also be implemented by MAS.

An agent may possess some characteristics which are its intrinsic or physical properties. It may be, for instance, the size of an agent or the number of legs of a robot-like or ant-like agent. A characteristic may also be something the agent can perform to modify or update one of its properties; for example, if the agent is an ant, enabling it to modify its number of legs.

3   Gaia Meta-model

The first version of the Gaia methodology was designed to handle small-scale, closed agent-based systems [6]. Consequently, it modeled agents, roles, interactions, but missed in modeling explicitly the social aspects of a multi-agent system. The official extension of Gaia extends Gaia based on the key consideration that an organization is more than simply a collection of roles and agents [7]. Therefore the main difference is that it has been designed in order to explicitly model and represent the social aspects of open agent systems, with particular attention to the social goals, social tasks or organizational rules. This is quite evident from the MAS meta-model (see Figure 2): the methodology is focused on the organizational structure of the system and all other concepts - agents, roles, services interactions - turn around the concept of organization and are modeled in order to better specify the relationship between the different entities in the context of a specific organization.

Having a deeper look at the MAS meta-model for the extended version of Gaia we notice that the basic building blocks of the former version of Gaia - namely agents, roles, activities, services, and protocols - are still present. In particular: an agent is an entity that plays one or more roles; a role is a specific behavior to be played by an agent, defined in terms of permission, responsibilities, and activities, and of its interactions with other roles; an agent plays a role by actualizing the behavior in terms of services to be activated and de-activated in dependence of specific pre- and post-conditions.

The extended version of Gaia starts from the above basic concepts and enriches them by putting them in the context of a specific environment and of a specific organization.

We emphasize Gaia does not deal with the requirements capture phase, and considers the requirements statement simply as an input for the methodology. However, the environment in which a multi-agent system is immersed is elected to a primary analysis and design abstraction in order to promote a clear understanding of the overall system. The environment abstraction explicitly specifies all the entities and resources a multi-agent system may interact with, restricting the interactions by means of the permitted actions. Thus, to some extent, the explicit representation of the environmental resources that can be manipulated by agents can be considered as a reference to the problem domain.

The explicit representation of an agent organization and the central role of organizational concepts come into play with the abstractions of organizational rules and organizational structures.

Organizational rules have the scope of specifying some constraints that the organization has to observe. They may be global, affecting the behavior of the

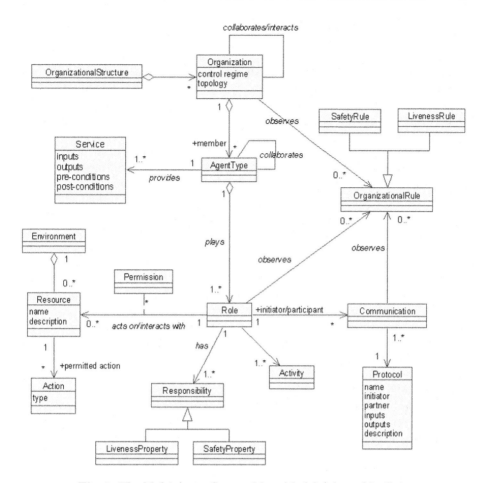

Fig. 2. The Multi-Agent System Meta-Model Adopted in Gaia

society as a whole, or concerning only specific roles or protocols. Organization structure on the other hand aims at making the overall architecture of the system, that is the position of each role in the organization and its relationship with other roles, explicit.

Organizational rules and organizational structures are strictly related, in that organizational rules may help designers in the identification of the organizational structures that more naturally suit these rules. Therefore, in the extended version of Gaia, the organizational structure is not implicitly defined via the role model, instead the identification of the roles is explicitly derived from an analysis of the chosen organizational structure. As a consequence the role model and the related interaction model will be completely defined in the design phase when an accurate identification of the organizational structure will take place.

4   PASSI Meta-model

System meta-models traditionally refer to two different domains: the problem domain (where the requirements are captured) and the solution domain (where the implemented system will be deployed). In conceiving the PASSI [8] MAS meta-model (see Figure 3) we found that this duality does not properly reflect the needs of an agent approach and therefore in our meta-model we introduce the agency domain. It represents the transition from problem-related concepts to the corresponding agent solution (that is not at an implementation level but it is still a logical abstraction). In this (agent) domain we will design all the agent-related elements like roles, communications, and the same agents, in order to define the solution to the requirements drawn in the problem domain. Since we decided to implement our solution with a FIPA-based infrastructure, we do not have any agent-oriented language that can be used to code the system but we map our choices to an object-oriented implementation level. In PASSI we do not think this is a limit because this presents several advantages, in fact the agent paradigm is used where it is more profitable: providing an abstraction level that could enable a simpler solution where classical software engineering concepts like decoupling, information hiding and responsibility division among components are naturally pursued. Moreover, final code-level implementation is devoted to affordable object-oriented languages that can be managed by several already skilled programmers and can be easily tested referring to a broad existing experience and a huge literature.

In the PASSI MAS meta-model (Figure 3), the Problem Domain deals with the user's problem in terms of scenarios, requirements, ontology and resources; scenarios describe a sequence of interactions among actors and the system. Requirements are represented with conventional use case diagrams. There is a strong point behind these choices: a lot of highly skilled designers are already present in different companies and can be more easily converted to the use of an agent-oriented approach if they are already confident with some of the key concepts used within it. Analysis related issues (like requirements and scenarios) being situated in the highest abstraction phase are strategic in enabling this skill reuse and allow a smooth entering in the new paradigm.

Ontological description of the domain is composed of concepts (categories of the domain), actions (performed in the domain and effecting the status of concepts) and predicates (asserting something about a portion of the domain). This represents the domain in a way that is substantially richer than the classic structural representations produced in the object-oriented analysis phase. As an instance, we can consider ontologies devoted to reasoning on strategies or problem solving methods whose essence is very difficultly captured in object-oriented structures [9].

Resources are the last element of the problem domain. They can be accessed/shared/manipulated by agents. A resource could be a repository of data (like a relational database), an image/video or also a good to be sold/bought. We prefer to expressly model them since goals of most systems are related to using and capitalizing available resources.

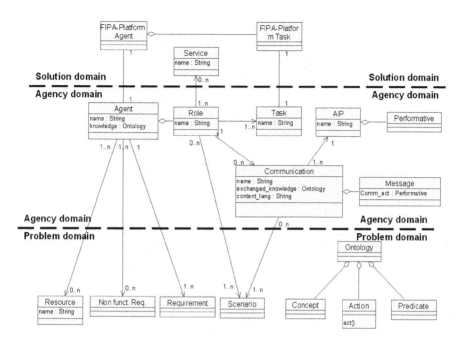

Fig. 3. The Multi-Agent System Meta-Model Adopted in PASSI

The Agency Domain contains the elements of the agent-based solution. None of these elements is directly implemented; they are converted to the correspondent object-oriented entity that constitutes the real code-level implementation. The concept of agent is the real center of this part of the model; each agent in PASSI is responsible for realizing some functionalities descending from one or more requirements. The direct link between a requirement and the responsible agent is one of the strategic decisions taken when conceiving PASSI. Sometimes an agent has also access to available resources. This could happen because it accesses the corresponding information (for example stored in a DB) or it can perceive it using its sensors (like in the case of embodied robotic agents sensing the environment). Each agent during its life plays some roles; that are portions of the agent social behavior characterized by some specificity such as a goal, or providing a functionality/service.

From this definition easily descends that roles could use communications in order to realize their relationships or portions of behavior (called tasks) to actuate the role proclivity. In PASSI, the term task is used with the significance of atomic part of the overall agent behavior and, therefore, an agent can accomplishing its duties by differently composing the set of its own tasks. Tasks cannot be shared among agents, but their possibilities could be offered by the agent to the society as services (often a service is obtained composing more than one task); obviously according to agent autonomy, each single agent has the possibility of accepting or refusing to provide a service if this does not match its personal attitudes and will.

A communication is composed of one or more messages expressed in an encoding language (e.g. ACL [10]) that is totally transparent to agents. The message content could be expressed in several different content languages (SL, KIF, RDF, ...); we chose to adopt RDF [11][12] and the PASSI supporting tool (PTK) offers a concrete aid in generating the RDF code from the designed ontology. Each communication explicitly refers to a piece of ontology (in the sense that information exchanged are concepts, predicates or actions defined in the ontology) and its flow of messages is ruled by an interaction protocol (AIP) that defines which communicative acts (the predefined semantic of the message content [13]) may be used in a conversation and in what order the related messages have to be sent to give the proper meaning to the communication.

The Implementation Domain describes the structure of the code solution in the chosen FIPA-compliant implementation platforms (like FIPA-OS or JADE) and it is essentially composed of three elements: (i) the FIPA-Platform Agent that represents the implementation class for the agent entity represented in the Agency domain; (ii) the FIPA-Platform Task that is the implementation structure available for the agent's Task and, finally, (iii) the Service element that describes a set of functionalities offered by the agent under a specific name that is registered in the platform service directory and therefore can be required by other agents to reach their goals. This description is also useful to ensure the system openness and the reusability of its components.

5   Comparison and Discussion

The three meta-models presented in the previous sections are very different and are a well representative example of the debate in the agent community about these strategic issues. In order to catch the essence of each of them we should consider the specific approach followed by the respective authors and the system structure pursued by them.

The ADELFE meta-model (Figure 1) clearly represents the aim of solving the problem with an adaptive MAS and therefore a great effort is done in order to study, through "cooperation rules", all the situations that could enable or inhibit the cooperation among agents. The cognitive and behavioral representations of the agent are performed in terms of its aptitudes, skills, characteristics, and representations (social or physical); agents interact via direct communications or the environment.

The Gaia meta-model (Figure 2) is mostly devoted to represent a MAS system as a social organization. For this reason, roles more than agents are the central subject of the model, as the basic building block of agents. While a Gaia role is characterized by an activity structure and by internal responsibilities, an organization is characterized by a structure - i.e., a set of roles interacting with each other according to specific protocols - and by "organizational responsibilities" or "organizational rules" - i.e., the constraints that the actual evolution of an organization mush adhere to. Little or no attention is paid to cognitive and representational issues.

The PASSI meta-model (Figure 3) aims at conciliating classical software engineering concepts like problem and solution domain with the potentiality of the agent-based approach while pursuing the goal of a traceability of the solution from requirements to the related code implementation. Authors clearly points to a FIPA-based implementation of their systems and therefore communications and implementation issues are typical of those specifications and most common related platforms (FIPA-OS, JADE). The convergence between agents and traditional issues of software engineering is obtained by introducing a new abstraction layer (agency domain) that complements the well-known problem-solution domain dichotomy.

Generally speaking, it is interesting to note that none of the discussed approaches explicitly refers to one of specific 'classical' agent architectures (like BDI or purely reactive agents) but these are seen as some kind of low level architectures that can be adopted during the MAS implementation. Only PASSI partially limits this range by referring to FIPA-compliant systems but this does not seem to be a real constraint since such systems have been used to implement all of the cited architectures.

In the following we will compare these meta-models by looking at some of their specific aspects; specifically we will consider:

- Agent structure: this means how each of the meta-models represents the agent and its most common elements (namely roles).
- Agent interactions: agents of different meta-models are supposed to interact using communications or the environment. Communications are sometimes specified by attributes like interaction protocols, content language and so on.
- Agent society and organizational structure: the goal of some of these meta-models is to model a specific society or an organizational infrastructure constrained by rules that enforce agents to some collective or individual behavior.
- Agent implementation: the code-level structure of the agent system.

Each of the cited categories will now be diffusely discussed and this study will be used to compose a new unifying meta-model that will try later to take the best of the different approaches.

5.1   Agent Structure

Looking at agent structure and specifically at agent and role definitions in the different meta-models, we can find that the ADELFE meta-model is quite different from the others because it tries to constrain the agent behavior with a cooperative attitude. In fact the ADELFE meta-model is not centered on the role notion because designers have to focus on the ability an agent possesses to detect and solve cooperation failures by observing cooperation rules. If a designer gives roles to agents, by describing a task or protocols, he/she will establish a fixed organization for these agents. However, a fixed organization in an AMAS is not welcomed because this organization must evolve to enable the system adaptation (cf. section 5.3).

The PASSI agent is the composition of some roles but each role is defined as the manifestation of the agent activity in some scenarios, it is associated with one or more communications and provides some services composing the capabilities offered by the agent's tasks (elementary agent behaviors). This structure can be regarded as the expected consequence of PASSI authors commitment in following the agent specifications provided by FIPA.

The Gaia agent is defined as a composition of roles. The specification of roles requires identifying the activities for which the role is responsible, including those activities that may require interactions with other agents, as well as the internal responsibilities of an agent. Once the abstract concept of role is translated into an actual agent, activities and responsibilities are translated into a set of services and a set of pragmatic activation and de-activation rules.

Goal and plan are other elements that should be considered in discussing the agent structure. None of the considered methodologies decidedly deal with them that are, conversely, central in other approaches (for instance goals are at the base of requirements analysis in the Tropos [14] methodology). In ADELFE, the notion of goal is only used to determine skills, but is not defined in a formal context. In the same way, plans are not modeled because usually, in complex and open applications, designers do not know plans. A plan will be built at runtime by the global system. However, if designers do know a plan, they can manage it by defining appropriate aptitudes. In Gaia, the concept of "goal" is implicit in roles, because a role in an organization (and thus the agent in charge of playing such a role) is by definition identified to achieve some specific application sub-goals. Plans play no explicit role in Gaia, although one can somehow consider that the activities of a role may include some sort of planning activities. In PASSI, goals are considered as non functional requirements and they are attached to agents according to their duties. As an example we can consider response or computational time constraints for agents operating in real-time contexts like robotics. They are usually described in the requirements analysis documentation in form of text. As regards agents' plans, they are not seen as a structural element of the PASSI meta-model, and they are usually modeled in a near algorithmic form (activity diagrams used as flow charts) during the Task Specification phase.

5.2   Agent Interaction Capabilities

In almost all the agent-based approaches, agents can interact with other agents or with the physical environment. About that, ADELFE, Gaia and PASSI are quite similar because in all of them agents are supposed to interact with others using communications ruled by some kind of interaction protocol (AIP) that could also ensure some level of interoperability among agents designed with different methodologies if they are all FIPA-compliant.

The most complete approach comes from ADELFE in which an agent can interact with other agents through direct communications but also in an indirect manner using the environment. An agent can perceive its environment and operate on it with its actions. Furthermore, ontologies have not to be modeled in ADELFE because if agents have to adapt themselves to their environment they are also able to adapt to the other agents. This adaptation can lead agents to learn to understand each other. For instance, if an agent does not understand a request made by another one, the former has to detect a NCS and solve it. May be it will be able to learn what the other wanted to say or it will find another manner to help it (e.g., by relaxing the request to another judged relevant agent).

In PASSI, agent perceptions (obtained by sensing the environment of by communicating with other agents) are not directly represented but they are shown in form of the knowledge that the agent acquires from them. Communications are designed as the composition of several messages according to the interaction rules defined by an AIP (Agent Interaction Protocol). Each message is purposeful since it expresses the precise intention specified by its communicative act (speech act theory [13]). In PASSI, communicating is a privilege of a role and therefore it significantly concurs in defining the PASSI concept of role as a communicational role.

In Gaia, communications are related to both AIP and mediated interactions via the environment. With regard to AIP, Gaia does not enter in details about ontologies and specific types of ACL messaging schemes: while Gaia developers' consider these as necessary concepts, they consider them as not very influential in the analysis and design processes. With regard to communications mediated by the environment, these are considered as a sort of side effect - due to the fact that different agents may influence and perceive overlapping portions of an environment. However, such an issue has never been analyzed in depth in Gaia.

5.3   Agent Society and Organizational Structure

Societies modeled in ADELFE are open. The society exists only by the representation an agent possesses about other agents and these representations may change at runtime. As a consequence the organization between agents is not predefined and fixed when the system starts and even less at the design stage. This organization emerges from the evolving interactions between agents and makes the system adapt. ADELFE agents have to obey cooperation rules at the (local) micro-level, to possibly change their relationships with others in order to ensure that the collective behavior is coherent at the macro-level. A large part of the ADELFE MAS meta-model is then devoted to model all the factors of that social attitude but not the society that the agents could form.

Gaia agent is particularly devoted to the creation of societal organizations, and recognizes organizations as a primary abstractions to be exploited in MAS analysis and design. For these reasons, Gaia considers a MAS organization more than a collection of agents somewhat interacting. Rather, Gaia considers an organization as an entity having a well-defined structure (the organizational "architecture") characterizing the position of each agent (better, of the agents playing specific roles) in it, as well as a set of "organizational rules". Organizational rules make explicit the fact that an organization as a whole cannot be simply assumed to work well because of the well-defined behavior of its individual components. Rather, supra-role and supra-agent specifications are required, expressing constraints on the inter-related activities of agents. Shifting to a societal metaphor, one can consider organizational rules as the social laws that have to drive all interactions in the organization and the evolution of the organization itself.

The PASSI model represents society aspects by defining services that can be provided/accessed by agents (specifically by some of their roles) and their participation in scenarios where they are supposed to interact via the already discussed communications. An agent is also supposed to have the availability of some resources that are explicitly modeled in order to identify its relevance for the remaining part of the society.

5.4   Agent Implementation

Even if the graphical modelling tool used within the ADELFE methodology (OpenTool) generates code skeletons, the problem of the system implementation is not treated yet and no platform is imposed.

Gaia totally abstracts from implementation tools. The key point is that - in the Gaia developers' intentions - the Gaia design specifications should be abstract enough that they could be used as guidelines to implement agents independently of the specific technology adopted.

In PASSI, a direct map exists among the most important elements of the model and their implementation; this is largely supported by a dedicated design tool (PTK, PASSI ToolKit) and the pattern reuse approach that is widely applied in the PASSI methodology. Each agent is coded using the base agent class of the selected implementation (FIPA-compliant) platform and it contains the tasks that are used by roles. A role has not a direct code level implementation since it is seen as an agent society domain element with only a virtual (not tangible) presence in the code. The service is described in a form that is suitable to be introduced in the deployment platform service directory in order to enable agents' collaborations.

6   Toward a Unifying Meta-model

After having analyzed the different MAS meta-models of ADELFE, Gaia and PASSI, we think that each of them has some very interesting features, but these are mainly located in different contexts (as discussed in section 5). This consideration brought us to design a new MAS meta-model that, including the most interesting aspects of each of the studied ones, could result in some kind of improvement to the state-of-the-art in this topic.

This model is presented in Figure 4 and we can see that it is quite a huge model. The fundamental choice that justifies it, is that we aim to create societies without (ADELFE) or with predefined organisations, in accordance with the growing interest for open systems in which an organization cannot always be given during the design phase. To achieve this result we enriched the generic agent with all the properties an agent may have, being cooperative or not. Fur-

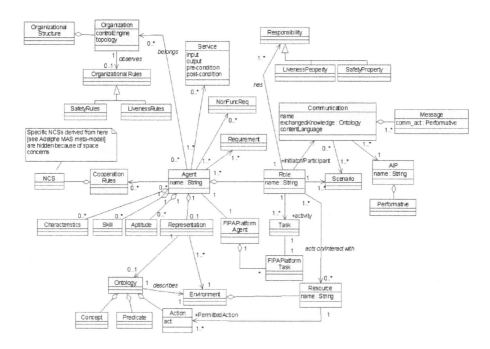

Fig. 4. A Unifying MAS Meta-Model - The new MAS meta-model is composed by merging the most significant contributions of ADELFE, Gaia and PASSI

thermore, this generic agent is composed of Gaia-like roles complemented by some PASSI features (tasks and a FIPA-compliant communication structure). This generic agent has two choices: belonging to an organisation or following cooperation rules (due to some lack of space in the figure above, inherited NCS such as incomprehension, uselessness have not been explicitly mentioned, see Figure 1). Agent are implemented (at code level) in the PASSI way. The proposed meta-model is also characterized by the possibility of identifying in it the three domains (problem, agency, solution) discussed in the PASSI approach.

From the experience of merging our three models we learnt that their composition adds some significant improvements to the new structure since they complement each other in several aspects, for example the ADELFE representation that the agent has of its environment, the Gaia environment and the PASSI ontology, naturally relates by representing the fact that an agent has a representation (possibly affected by errors or uncertainty) of the environment expressed in terms of an ontological model of it.

After identifying this extensive MAS meta-model the following natural step would be to define a methodology for designing systems according to it. Although we will move in this direction, we fear that probably such a great model could need a design methodology that is composed of too many activities to be really profitable. It is presumable that while several different methodologies could cover different parts of this model (e.g., some will produce cooperative agents while some others non cooperative ones), the presented model could be regarded as a unifying framework for the systems produced with different approaches thus enabling their interaction and providing a substantial step in the direction of a unique omni-comprehensive MAS meta-model.

7   Conclusion

A great number of agent-oriented methodologies exist nowadays; some are dealing with specific kinds of agents or multi-agent systems, like, for instance, the three ones that are depicted in this paper. ADELFE is devoted to cooperative agents and adaptive MAS, while Gaia aims more at creating social organisations and PASSI, the more general one, considers the whole life-cycle from the problem domain to the agent-based solution and the final level code implementation but limits the scope to FIPA-compliant systems. These differences are reflected by the meta-models elaborated by respecting authors to express the concepts used in the design activities and the resulting systems related to these three methodologies.

In this paper, these meta-models have been compared in order to begin a unification work that would be beneficial to the agent-oriented engineering domain. It has then appeared that all of the three models share common concepts such as the agent and interaction protocols ones while other elements are present only in some of them: this is the case of ADELFE and Gaia that share the communication and environment notions, and Gaia and PASSI that have notions like roles and services in common. Some concepts are only appearing in one of the three meta-models, for instance, responsibilities in Gaia, ontology in PASSI or representations (of others) in ADELFE. Putting these different meta-models together has enabled enriching them mutually as well as unifying the different used concepts. This preliminary unification has led methodologies authors to revise their respective meta-models to make choices and concessions to present the merged meta-model in Figure 4. Furthermore, we are sure that this unification would be useful to build tools in the OMG's MDA [15] spirit in order to automatically transform a meta-model into a model depending on a target platform.

This unification problem leads us to some interesting questioning that could represent (our) future works:

– Is it possible to identify a meta-model from which all the meta-models used in the multi-agent community could be derived? For instance, this latter could be defined from an extension of this unification work as well as FIPA Modelling TC standardisation activities.
– What description level has to be reached in the meta-model? For instance, skills and aptitudes in ADELFE are certainly used to implement the role notion of Gaia or PASSI.
– How may a designer choose meta-model elements he is interested in? What kind of tools can we provide him to ease his choices?

References

1. Saeki, M.: Software specification & design methods and method engineering. International Journal of Software Engineering and Knowledge Engineering (1994)
2. Kruchten, P.: The Rational Unified Process: An Introduction. Addison-Wesley (2000)
3. Bergenti, F., Gleizes, M.P., Zambonelli, F.: Methodologies and Software Engineering for Agent Systems. Kluwer (2004)
4. Bernon, C., Camps, V., Gleizes, M.P., Picard, G.: Tools for self-organizing applications engineering. In: First International Workshop on Engineering Self-Organising Applications (ESOA), Melbourne, Australia (2003)
5. Capera, D., Georg, J.P., Gleizes, M.P., Glize, P.: The amas theory for complex problem solving based on self-organizing cooperative agents. In: Proc. of the 1st International Workshop on Theory And Practice of Open Computational Systems (TAPOCS03@WETICE 2003), Linz, Austria (2003)
6. Wooldridge, M., Jennings, N.R., Kinny, D.: The gaia methodology for agent-oriented analysis and design. Journal of Autonomous Agents and Multi-Agent Systems **3** (2000) 285–315
7. Zambonelli, F., Jennings, N., Wooldridge, M.: Developing multiagent systems: the gaia methodology. ACM Transactions on Software Engineering and Methodology **12** (2003) 417–470
8. Cossentino, M., Sabatucci, L.: Agent System Implementation. In: Agent-Based Manufacturing and Control Systems: New Agile Manufacturing Solutions for Achieving Peak Performance. CRC Press (2004)
9. Chandrasekaran, B., Josephson, J.R., Benjamins, V.R.: What are ontologies, and why do we need them? IEEE Intelligent Systems (1999)
10. FIPA: Acl message structure specification. (Available online at http://www.fipa.org/specs/fipa00061/SC00061G.html)
11. FIPA: Rdf content language specification. (Available online at http://www.fipa.org/specs/ fipa00011/XC00011B.html)
12. W3C: Resource description framework (rdf) model and syntax specification. w3c recommendation. Available online at http://www.w3.org/TR/1999/REC-rdf-syntax-19990222/. (1999)
13. Searle, J.R.: Speech Acts. Cambridge University Press (1969)
14. Castro, J., Kolp, M., Mylopoulos, J.: Towards requirements-driven information systems engineering: The tropos project. Information Systems (2002)
15. Kleppe, A., Warmer, J., Bast, W.: MDA Explained: The Model Driven Architecture : Practice and Promise. Addison-Wesley (2003)

A Metamodel for Agents, Roles, and Groups

James Odell[1], Marian Nodine[2], and Renato Levy[3]

[1]Agentis Software, Inc., 3646 West Huron River Drive,
Ann Arbor, MI 48103-9489, USA
email@jamesodell.com
http://www.jamesodell.com
[2] Telcordia Technologies, Inc., 106 East 6th Street, Suite 415,
Austin, TX 78733, USA
nodine@research.telcordia.com
[3] Intelligent Automation Inc., 7519 Standish Place, Suite 200
Maryland, MD 20855, USA
rlevy@i-a-i.com

Abstract. Societies need patterned behavior to exist. Large-scale agent societies may contain a diversity of agents, each with differing abilities and functionalities. When such an agent system is given a task, it must dynamically muster together a group of agents that collectively have the capability to accomplish the task. To do this, the agent society needs to be able to understand its agents and their potential interactions.

This paper contains a proposed superstructure specification that defines the user-level constructs required to model agents, their roles and their groups. These modeling constructs provide the basic foundational elements required in multi-agent systems to foster dynamic group formation and operation. As agent systems scale beyond the point where an individual organization can track and control their behavior, the use of these concepts within the society will facilitate dynamic, controlled, task-oriented group formation. This in turn will enhance the predictability, reliability and stability of the agent system as a whole, as well as facilitating the analysis of both group and system behavior.

1   Introduction

"We simply have hardly any real experience building truly heterogeneous, realistically coordinated multi-agent systems that work together, and … almost no basis for systematic reflection and analysis of that experience." [Gasser, 2001].

Societies need to employ patterned behavior to exist. The behavior of each individual is determined to a great extent by the requirements of these patterns [Katz, 1978]. However, the current practice of Multi-Agent System (MAS) design tends to be limited to individual agents and small face-to-face groups of agents that operate as closed systems. We have little principled understanding for:

- organizing sophisticated, interactive, heterogeneous agent-based systems.
- grouping the agents in such systems into very large-scale aggregates that exhibit predictable, stable, and reliable behavior.

J. Odell et al. (Eds.): AOSE 2004, LNCS 3382, pp. 78–92, 2005.
© Springer-Verlag Berlin Heidelberg 2005

- achieving economies of scale and scope within a large MAS.
- building and operating such systems in situ.

From a scientific standpoint, the foundations for constructing large multi-agent systems have a long history. Although researchers have been explicitly thinking about MAS/DAI (Multi-Agent System/Distributed Artificial Intelligence) organizations and attempting to link organization theory with MAS/DAI models for decades, the idea of organization, *per se*, has been only a peripheral theme. MAS/DAI researchers have focused on specific coordination techniques, rather than the central issues involved in MAS organization. Yet, without considering organizational issues for MAS, MAS designers will not be able to leverage benefits that can be gained from such social constructs and patterns, such as emergence and scalability. Therefore, any discussion of agent classification metamodels must also address organizational elements. At a minimum, this includes agent classifiers, roles and groups—and the structural and behavioral patterns defined by such constructs.

This paper contains a proposed superstructure specification[1] for modeling agents, agent roles, and agent groups. This architecture addresses simple homogeneous agent systems as well as those that require complex and heterogeneous social interaction. Furthermore, this specification is based on—and extends—the Unified Modeling Language (UML) superstructure [OMG, 2003]. It also contains a few suggested notations for some of these structures. Developing a notation to express these structures more fully is an on-going effort in several standards organizations including the Foundation for Intelligent Physical Agents (FIPA) and the Object Management Group's (OMG's) Agent SIG.

2   The Essential Class Model

Figure 1 illustrates the essential class model being proposed in this document. UML defines *class diagram* as follows: "A diagram that shows a collection of declarative (static) model elements such as classes, types, and their contents and relationships" [Booch, 1999]. Due to the relative complexity of agent design and the many differences that exist between an agent and an object [Odell, 2002], the agent class structure must extend UML class specifications to accomplish this. The complete notation for the extensions described in this paper may be found in [FIPA, 2004].

Starting from the left of Fig. 1, the Agent Classifier is a classifier specifically for classes of agents. An *Agent Classifier* defines the various ways in which agents will be classified and is subclassed in two ways: *Agent Physical Classifier* and *Agent Role Classifier*. *Agent Physical Classifier* defines the primitive, or basic, classes that define the core requirements of an agent. In general, an agent is implemented using some specific physical platform, such as JADE [Bellifemine, 2001] or Cybele [Cybele, 2000][Aronson, 2003]. The physical agent platform itself engenders certain properties and capabilities on its agents, regardless of any other agents that they are collaborating with. These properties remain throughout the lifetime of the agent. *Agent Role Classifier* classifies agents by the various kinds of roles agents may

---

[1] A *modeling superstructure* specifies user-level constructs for modeling. In general, a *modeling infrastructure* provides the foundational constructs for the modeling language.

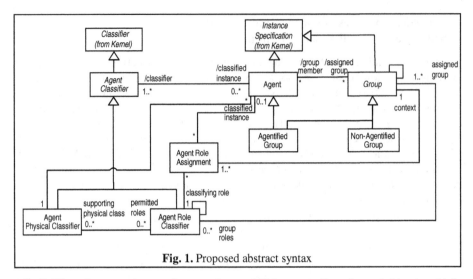

Fig. 1. Proposed abstract syntax

"play". These in turn relate to the agent's capabilities as well as the activities in which it may become involved. The set of roles that an agent is playing may vary over time. Section 3 provides a more detailed explanation of the agent classifiers.

In the middle of Fig. 1 are the Agent instances. The class called *Agent* defines the set of all agents that populate a system. Each instance of an Agent is associated with one or more Agent Classifiers that define its necessary features. Agents are discussed further in Section 3.

To the right in Fig. 1 are the *Groups*, or sets of agents that have been collected together for some reason. Within a group, its member agents interact according to the roles that they play. Thus, each instance of a Group is defined by a set of roles and, by transitivity, its collection of agents. Groups are partitioned into Agentified Groups and Non-Agentified Groups according to whether or not they are addressable as an agent and can act as an agent in their own right. Groups are discussed further in Section 4.

Lastly we consider the associations between Agents and their Agent Role Classifiers and Agent Physical Classifiers (Section 5). The association of an Agent to an Agent Physical Classifier gives the agent its primitive, core capabilities and requirements. Every Agent must be associated with one Agent Physical Classifier. The association between an Agent and the Agent Role Classifiers determine what sorts of activities that the Agent is participating in. An Agent may have no associated Agent Role Classifiers; however, such an agent is not involved in any *Group*.

Key to understanding this figure is a crisp notion of the distinction between a UML Classifier and a UML Class. The two UML notions *Classifier* and *Class* are different elements in UML. A UML Classifier is:

- a *Namespace* whose members can include features.
- a *Type*, thereby making it possible to define generalization relationships to other Agent Classifiers.
- a *RedefinableElement*, meaning that it can be redefined more specifically or differently in the context of another classifier that specializes (directly or indirectly) the context classifier.

UML Classifiers do not have attributes, interfaces, inheritance, or any of the basic features that are associated with an object-oriented class. In contrast, the UML class called *Class* has these features. Class is a specialization of Classifier and possesses those additional features that are required for objects. (For more information on the differences between Classifier and Class, see [OMG, 2003]). This is important because agent classification will be based on an extension of Classifier, not Class. The reason for this is that we do not wish to develop a superstructure that is based on object orientation. To do so would mean that agents would necessarily support object-oriented-based messaging and polymorphism. Instead, by extending Classifier, we can add in those features that object-oriented classes possess that are useful for agents (e.g., attributes), while omitting features that are problematic for agents.

3   Agents and Agent Classifiers

Agent Classifier is a UML Classifier that specifically provides a way to classify *Agent* instances by a set of features that they have in common. Its associated instances are the Agents that it classifies. Classification is important because it enables the definition of a set of entities that share one or more capabilities and/or features in common. For example, Agent Classifiers named "Buyer" or "Seller" could be defined to represent the collection of agents that possess capabilities for buying and selling resources. Further-more, Agent Classifiers facilitate the definition of those features that entities of a particular classification

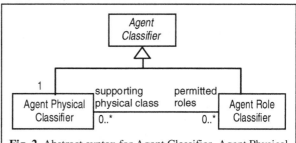

Fig. 2. Abstract syntax for Agent Classifier, Agent Physical Classifier and Agent Role Classifier

can have. For example, the "Buyer" Agent Classifier could define properties relating to what a Buyer can buy, and what its spending limit is.

Figure 2 shows Agent Classifier and its two specializations: Agent Physical Classifier and Agent Role Classifier. The default notation for an Agent Classifier is a solid-outline rectangle containing the classifier's name. Abstract Agent Classifiers are shown in italics.

3.1   Agent Role Classifier

The Agent Role Classifier is an Agent Classifier that classifies according to the kinds of *roles* the agent is capable of playing at a given time. Within a MAS, roles define normative repertoires of behavior and other features, contextualized according to the group in which the role is being played. Agents can be associated with more than one Agent Role Classifier at the same point in time (multiple classification) and can change roles over time (dynamic classification).

The notion of *role* is fundamentally a thespian concept, and attention to how it functions in the theater can reinforce our intuitions and provide useful metaphors for application to multi-agent systems.

> All the world's a stage,
> And all the men and women merely players:
> They all have their exits and entrances;
> And one man in his time plays many parts.
> –W. Shakespeare, *As You Like It*, Act II, Scene 7.

The similarities between the Shakespeare's characterization and our present-day usage of *role* in role theory [Biddle, 1966] and organization psychology [Katz, 1978] are noteworthy. The *role perspective* [Odell, 2003] consists of those factors presumed to be influential in governing human behavior. It assumes that performance results from social proscriptions and individual behavior and that the individual variations in performance are expressed within the framework created by these factors. An individual's behavior is shaped by the demands and roles of others, the individual's own understanding of appropriate behavior, and the individual's competence in the performance.

Roles provide both the building blocks for agent social systems and the requirements by which agents interact. Each agent is linked to other agents by the roles it plays by virtue of the application's functional requirements—which are based on the expectations that the application has of the agent. Also, all Agent Role Classifiers must be associated with one or more groups, because the role is qualified by and given meaning by the group context. For example, the role of President for the United States is different that the role of President for IBM. The group context, therefore, provide a namespace for terms such as "President" so that unique role features can be specified for each context.

Agent Role Classifiers form a generalization hierarchy. Figure 3 illustrates a small hierarchy of Agent Role Classifiers, where the Broker and Matchmaker roles are sub-classifiers of the Facilitator role. In the UML extension for agents, Agent Role Classifiers are indicated using the stereotype «agent role»; non-agent classes which represent object classes

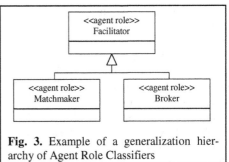

Fig. 3. Example of a generalization hierarchy of Agent Role Classifiers

will not have a stereotype designation. Please note that using a generalization relationship between classifiers does *not* necessarily imply inheritance. Generalization specifies inclusion which implies that whatever can be said of a classifier can also be said of its sub-classifiers. Generalization, therefore, can be implemented using various techniques—inheritance is only one. For agent-based systems, current wisdom suggests that using inheritance is not considered to be a good practice.

3.2   Agent Physical Classifier

The purpose of an Agent Physical Classifier is to define those sets of core, or primitive, features that all agents possess—*independent* of any role they may play.

Every agent must be classified according to some Agent Physical Classifier. Also, an agent always will remain in the same basic Agent Physical Classifier that created it and bestowed its basic features.

An Agent Physical Classifier describes the set of basic (i.e., primitive, core) features that all agents possess. Certain features are basic to all agents, such as the possession of a unique name (from the namespace in the UML Classifier). Others are dependent on the implementation of the agent, such as how an agent sends and receives messages, maintains its attributes (i.e., its state, or beliefs), interacts with its particular environment or software package, and so on. In this way, Agent Physical Classifier could also be called "Agent Primitive Classifier" or "Agent Core Classifier" because its purpose is to define those classes that describe the set of basic features that all agents of a particular kind possess.

Figure 4 depicts several instances of Agent Physical Classifier (Cybele Agent Classifier, JADE Agent Classifier, and FIPA Agent Classifier) in a hierarchy. Any agents associated with the Cybele Agent classifier would possess all the features required and provided by the Cybele software environment (for example, the ability to possess state variables and to receive and send communications, create and refer to clocks and timers of various kinds).

As stated earlier, agents can be associated with more than one role at the same point in

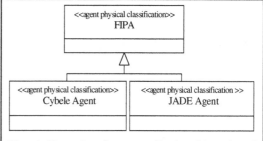

Fig. 4. Example of a generalization hierarchy of Agent Role Classifiers

time and can change roles over time. However, an agent is quite likely considered to remain in the same basic Agent Physical Classifier that created it and bestowed its basic features. Therefore, the Agent Physical Classifier provides the required features for all agents, whereas, roles supplement these basic features by providing additional sets of features on an "as needed" basis.

3.3   Agents

For agent-based design, the primary fundamental modeling constructs, or *elements*, are Agent Classifier and Agent (Fig. 5). These elements are considered fundamental because they enable agent-based systems to define both the instances of agent for a system and the enabling classifications for those agents. The instances of Agent specify the autonomous, interactive entities known as an "agent" in a modeled agent-based system. That is, they are important because those are the *actual* functioning entities thought of as agents within a system; the classifications are necessary as they provide the underlying features for each and every agent. In other words, each instance of Agent Classifier specifies those features that its associated Agents may possess (such as state and provided services).

Agent is a concrete class and its description may include:

- Classification of the agent by one or more Agent Classifiers of which the agent is a classified instance (multiple classification).

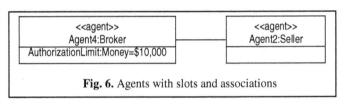

Fig. 5. Association of Agents with Agent Classifiers

- Specification of features of the agent, independently of those specified by associated Agent Classifiers.

- Specification of how to compute, derive or construct the agent (optional).

An Agent instance specification describes the agent. These details can be incomplete. The purpose of an Agent instance specification is to show what is of interest about an agent in the modeled system. The agent conforms to the specification of each Agent Classifier that classifies it, and has features with values indicated by each slot of the Agent instance specification.

Figure 6 illustrates two linked Agent instances. Agent instances represent the agent at a specific point in time (a snapshot). Each Agent is depicted using the same notation as its classifier, but in place of the classifier name appears an underlined concatenation of the instance name (if any), a colon (':')

<<agent>> Agent4:Broker	<<agent>> Agent2:Seller
AuthorizationLimit:Money=$10,000	

Fig. 6. Agents with slots and associations

and an optional comma-separated list containing the classifier name or names. Slots may be shown textually as a feature name followed by an equal sign ('=') and a value specification. Other properties of the feature, such as its type, also may be shown. Agents may be linked by the roles they play. In this situation, Agent4 is a Broker, and is brokering something for Seller Agent2.

3.4 Associations Between Agent Physical Classifiers and Agent Role Classifiers

The association between an Agent Physical Classifier and an Agent Role Classifier specifies those Agent Role Classifiers that are permitted for any given Agent Physical Classifier. Figure 7 depicts instances of Agent Physical Classifier ("JADE". "Cybele") and Agent Role Classifier ("Manager", "Buyer", "Trust Manager"). For any of the roles of "Buyer", "Broker" and "Trust Manager" can be taken on by Agents with the Agent Physical Classifier "Cybele". Similarly, either of the roles "Manager" or "Broker" can be taken on by Agents with the Agent Physical Classifier "JADE".

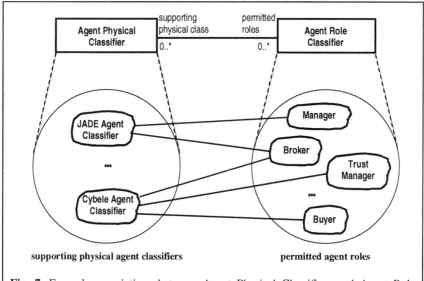

Fig. 7. Example associations between Agent Physical Classifiers and Agent Role Classifiers

The associations between Agent Physical Classifiers and Agent Role Classes restrict the roles that specific agents may take on, independent of the capabilities of the individual Agents themselves. In the following section, we discuss Agents and their associations with Agent Classifiers, based on both these restrictions and the capabilities of the individual Agents.

3.5   Association of Agents with Agent Classifiers

The association of an Agent with its Agent Classifiers establishes the features and behavior for each agent. Each Agent Classifier classifies of agent instances according to a common set of physical or role-based features that they have in common. Figure 8 depicts instances of Agent Physical Classifier ("Cybele" and "JADE"), instances of Agent Role Classifier "Buyer", "Seller", "Broker", "Trust Manager") as well as a set of instances of Agent ("Agent1", "Agent2", "Agent3", and "Agent4"). The links indicate classification; e.g., Agent1 is a classified instance of both the "JADE" Agent Physical Classifier and the "Seller" Agent Role Classifier.

Note that a given agent can be classified with more than one role at the same point in time (e.g., Agent2). Also, Agents can change roles over time, as the needs of the applications change.

4   Group, Agentified Group, and Non-agentified Group

A *group* is a set of agents that are related via their roles, where these links must form a connected graph within the group. Another way to look at this is that a group is a composite structure consisting of interrelated roles, where each of the group's roles has any number of agent instances. This definition implies not only that a group is a function of the roles contained within it, but also that roles have no meaning without their group referent. Hence, our ability to understand roles is limited by our ability to understand the groups of which they are a part.

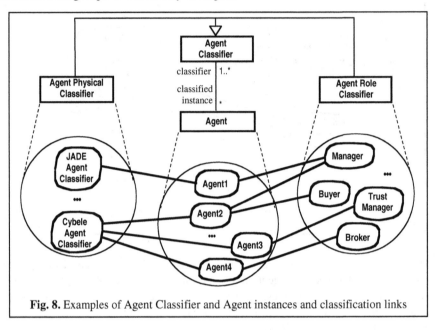

Fig. 8. Examples of Agent Classifier and Agent instances and classification links

A group can be formed to take advantage of the synergies of its members, resulting in an entity that enables products and processes that are not possible from any single

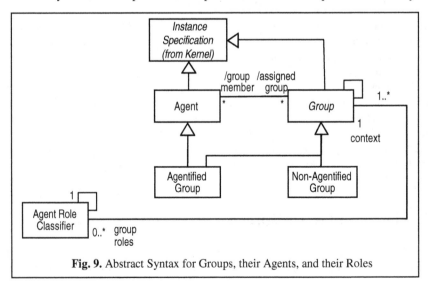

Fig. 9. Abstract Syntax for Groups, their Agents, and their Roles

individual. As with roles, groups may be deliberately established (i.e., by a system designer) or they may be emergent. In human organization terms, a deliberately established group could be a department or other workgroup that has been defined by some organizational authority. In contrast, an emergent group might be a social group that forms when several individuals decide to go out for a beer after work. Over time, they define themselves as a group ("My Friday Afternoon Drinking Buddies").

Groups are commonly formed to regulate, foster, or support the interaction of those agents *within* the group; so the group provides a place for a limited number of agents to interact among themselves via roles. In this way, intra-group associations encourage resource sharing, promote internal coordination. establish common supervision, and provide a degree of safety in numbers.

4.1   Metamodel for Group

Figure 9 presents the abstract syntax for Groups, their Roles and their Agents. The Group class extends the UML Instance Specification. However, each Group could be defined as a composite structure. In UML, structured classifiers can be thought of structured collection of classifiers. Groups could then become structured collections of Agent Role Classifiers. Group is an abstract class.

Conceptually, a group consists of a set of Agents playing roles. The roles that the Agents may play within the group are represented by one or more Agent Role Classifiers that are associated with the Group. The set of Agents within the Group, according to the model, can be derived from the Group via the Agent Role Classifiers (which will be discussed in Section 5).

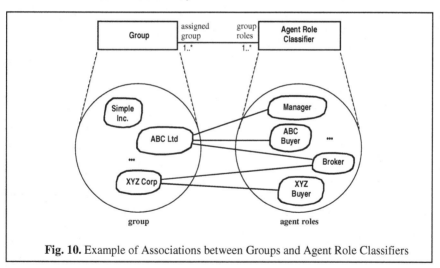

Fig. 10. Example of Associations between Groups and Agent Role Classifiers

4.2   Relationships Between Groups and the Roles That Agents Play in Them

Figure 10 illustrates the necessary association between groups and the roles that are played in groups (by Agents). Roles are only meaningful in a context; therefore, all roles must be assigned to a group. For example, the "Broker" role is used by the

"ABC Ltd." and "XYZ Corp" groups. Notice also that both groups have a "Buyer' role. However, since the buyer role for "ABC Ltd." has different features than for "XYZ Corp.", two different roles are defined, "ABC Buyer" and "XYZ Buyer".

4.3   Agentified and Non-agentified Groups

A group can take on the qualities of being an agent in its own right, with its own interactive capability. Such groups can be thought of as sets of agents that interact with other agents or sets of agents. Inter-group associations are important and appropriate, because they encourage a basis for input and output standardization. This in turn facilitates interaction between groups, promotes patterns of interaction between groups, and establishes standard interaction points for each group.

An *Agentified Group* possesses all the features that any agent might possess. For example, it can send and receive messages directly and take on roles. Such a group is an agent in its own right, and therefore is a subclass not only of Group but also of Agent. In contrast, Non-Agentified Groups are still first-class entities; however, these entities do not possess agent properties. Thus, they are as objects, rather than agents.

Figure 11 represents the Group "ABC Ltd" as a composite structure with three associated roles, "Manager", "Broker" and "ABC Buyer". The "Manager" interacts directly with the "ABC Buyer" and the "Broker". In this situation, it is possible to interact with the agent "ABC Ltd." without knowing directly about any specific "Manager", "Broker" or "ABC Buyer" within the department; thus, this group is Agentified. The stereotype "<<agent>>" indicates that the group is Agentified.

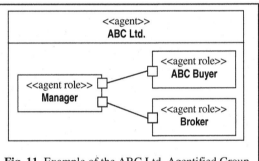

Fig. 11. Example of the ABC Ltd. Agentified Group and its associated Roles

Groups can also be formed simply to establish a set of agents for purposes such as intra-group synergies or conceptual organization. A *Non-Agentified Group* is a Group that is not a subclass of Agent. Figure 12 shows a Non-Agentified version of "ABC Customer Sales Dept". It has the same associated Roles; however, it does not have the "<<agent>>" stereotype. In order to interact with this Department, you must interact directly with one of its members -- a "Manager", an "ABC Buyer" or a "Broker".

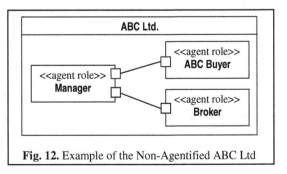

Fig. 12. Example of the Non-Agentified ABC Ltd

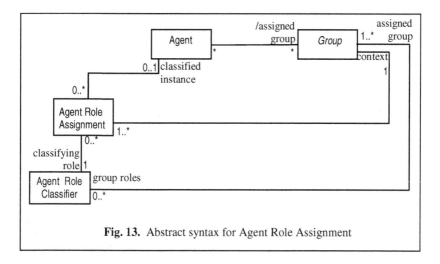

Fig. 13. Abstract syntax for Agent Role Assignment

5 Agent Role Assignment

Section 3 describes the association between Agents and their Agent Role Classifiers. However, the assignment of Agents to Roles is dynamic. This assignment is modeled by the Agent Role Assignment. Figure 13 shows the Agent Role Assignment and its associations. This section describes how Agent Role Assignment supports the dynamic association of Roles to Agents.

5.1 Agent Role Assignment as a Ternary Association

A direct association between Agent and Agent Role Classifier would represent that Agents play particular Roles, or Roles are played by specific Agents. However, this distinction is not sharp enough, because an Agent could play a given Role in one Group and not another. In Fig. 14, Agent2 plays the role of Broker in GroupB, but not in GroupC; furthermore, Agent3 is a Broker in GroupC, but not in GroupB. This situation illustrates that a role assignment between an agent and its role must be qualified by a group context. For example, the Broker role is used by GroupB and GroupC. The Broker for GroupB is Agent2, and the Broker for GroupC is Agent3.

Agent Role Assignments, then, are three-way, or ternary, associations. An Agent Role Assignment is a Class whose associated instances associate Roles and Groups and Agents. Each instance of the ternary Agent Role Assignment, associates a role, group, and an agent.

Contextualizing roles to groups has the additional advantage that it allows for a greater diversity of situations. For example, GroupB has two associated roles, Seller and Broker, played by Agent1 and Agent2, respectively. Agent1 is also a Buyer for Group A. This is allowed, even though Agent1 is now both a Buyer and a Seller, because Agent1 is a Buyer in one Group and a Seller in the other; thus, there is no conflict of interest.

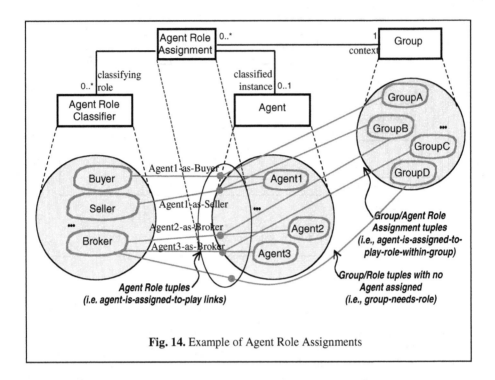

Fig. 14. Example of Agent Role Assignments

5.2   Positions

While each Agent Role Assignment must have a Role and Group, it might not have an associated agent. Agent role assignments without agents can be called *positions*. For example in Fig. 14, there is an assignment that links the "Broker" role with "GroupD", but no Agent is assigned. This means that a slot, or *position*, has been assigned for some yet-to-be-defined agent to be empowered to play a "Broker" role in "GroupD". In other words, no agent has been assigned to "fill" the position. This approach is useful when "requisitioning" role assignments that must be filled at some point in the future to accomplish some task.

The set of all Agent Role Assignments that have agent assignments can be expressed as an association in its own right. These links are considered as part of the derivation of the association between Agent and Agent Classifier, as expressed in Figs. 1 and 5.

6   Conclusions

Agent-based systems are increasing both in size and diversity. This growth is pushing agent-based systems beyond a size that is manageable by individual organizations. Thus, there is a growing need for agents to be able to organize themselves according to their assigned tasks. Since these tasks may be complex, and beyond the abilities or knowledge of individual agents, this capacity to self-organize must be based on a solid metamodel. This metamodel needs to take into account individual agents, how they can interact, and how they can and do fit into groups.

This paper presents general metamodeling constructs for large-scale multi-agent systems. These concepts are anchored in the modeling and classification of agents according to both the capabilities that they have from their physical implementation (Agent Physical Classifiers) and from their current activities (Agent Role Classifiers). Agent activities are done in the context of *groups*. Furthermore, within the group their behavior conforms to specific patterns, and these patterns of behavior are enacted by the agents via the *roles* that they play in the group. For example, a group involved in a purchase may include an agent taking on the role of "Buyer", an agent taking on the role of "Trust Manager", and an agent taking on the role of "Seller". Within this group, the role of "Buyer" specifies the capabilities and governs the operations that are allowed for the agent that is playing it.

Using this metamodel within an agent system as a basis for understanding, regularizing and controlling agent behavior has many advantages. While the agent itself may be both large and diverse, the scoping of tasks within groups increases the predictability, stability, and reliability of the entire agent system. It also facilitates the monitoring and analysis of operations within the multi-agent system. This in turn means that the multi-agent system itself can scale to a greater size while still retaining properties of stability and controllability.

Acknowledgement

We would like to acknowledge the FIPA Modeling Technical Committee members for their contribution to this work. Also, this work was funded in part by NASA contract # NAS2-02093.

References

[Bellifemine, 2001] Bellifemine, Fabio, Agnstino Poggi, and Giovanni Rimassa, "JADE: A FIPA2000 Compliant Agent Development Environment," *Proceedings of the International Conference on Autonomous Agent*, Montreal, Canada, ACM, 2001.

[Biddle, 1966] Biddle, Bruce J., and Edwin J. Thomas, *Role Theory: Concepts and Research*, John Wiley and Sons, New York, 1966.

[Booch, 1999] Booch, Grady, James Rumbaugh, Ivar Jocobson, *The Unified Modeling Language User Guide*, Addison-Wesley, Reading, MA, 1999.

[Cybele, 2000] *OpenCybele User's Manual*, Intelligent Automation, Inc, http:www.opencybele.org/docs/Users.pdf, 2000.

[FIPA, 2004] Odell, James, Renato Levy and Marian Nodine, *FIPA Modeling TC: Agent Class Superstructure Model*, http://www.auml.org/auml/documents/CD2-04-21.doc, 2004.

[Gasser, 2001] Gasser, Les, "Perspectives on Organizations in Multi-Agent Systems," *Multi-Agent Systems and Applications*, Michael Luck *et al.* eds., Springer-Verlag, Berlin, pp. 1-16, 2001.

[Aronson, 2003] Aronson, J., Manikonda V., Peng W., Levy R. and Roth K.. *An HLA Compliant Agent-based Fast-Time Simulation Architecture for Analysis of Civil Aviation Concepts.* Spring SISO Simulation Interoperability Workshop, Orlando, Florida, April 2003.

[Karageorgos, 2003] Karageorgos, A., *Using Role Modeling and Synthesis to Reduce Complexity in Agent-Based System Design*, in *Dept. of Computation*, doctorate thesis, University of Manchester Institute of Science and Technology, Manchester, 2003.

[Katz, 1978] Katz, Daniel, and Robert L. Kahn, *The Social Psychology of Organizations*, (2nd ed.), John Wiley and Sons, New York, 1978.

[Mintzberg, 1993] Mintzberg, Henry, *Structure in Fives: Designing Effective Organizations*, Prentice Hall, Englewood Cliffs, NJ, 1993.

[Moreno, 1960] Moreno, J.L. ed., *The Sociometry Reader*, The Free Press, Glencoe, IL, 1960.

[Odell, 2002] Odell, James, "Objects and Agents Compared," *Journal of Object Technology*, Vol 1, Number 1, May, 2002.

[Odell, 2003] Odell, J., H.V.D. Parunak, and M. Fleischer, *The Role of Roles in Designing Effective Agent Organizations*, in *Software Engineering for Large-Scale Multi-Agent Systems*, A.F. Garcia *et al.*, Eds., Springer-Verlag: Berlin. pp. 27-38, 2003.

[OED, 1992] Oxford English Dictionary, (2nd ed.), Oxford University Press, Oxford, 1992.

[OMG, 2003] OMG, *UML 2.0 Superstructure Specification*, OMG document ptc/03-08-02, September 2, 2003.

Bridging the Gap Between Agent-Oriented Design and Implementation Using MDA[*]

Mercedes Amor, Lidia Fuentes, and Antonio Vallecillo

Dpto. Lenguajes y Ciencias de la Computación,
Universidad de Málaga. Campus de Teatinos,
s/n, 29071 Málaga, Spain
{pinilla, lff, av}@lcc.uma.es

Abstract. Current agent-oriented methodologies focus mainly on multi-agent systems analysis and design, but without providing straightforward connections to the implementation of such systems on any of the existing agent platforms (e.g. FIPA-OS, Jade, or Zeus), or just forcing the use of specific agent platforms. In this paper we show how the Model Driven Architecture (MDA) can be effectively used to derive agent implementations from agent-oriented designs, independently from both the methodology used and the concrete agent platform selected. Furthermore, this transformation process can be defined in an scalable way, and partly automated thanks to the use of a platform-neutral agent model, called *Malaca*.

1 Introduction

Software agents are becoming a widely used alternative for building open and distributed applications, developed as Multi-Agent Systems (MAS). This recognition has led to consider agent technology as a promising paradigm for software development [1]. As a result, several agent-oriented methodologies for developing MAS have been recently proposed [2], with the aim to provide tools, practical methods, and techniques for developing MAS.

The variety of methodologies may become a problem for the software developer when it comes to select the best-suited methodology for a given application domain. Selection criteria may include aspects such as the effort required to learn and to use, completeness, documentation, and suitability. Recent works (e.g., [3, 4, 5, 6]) provide comparison studies between the different agent-oriented methodologies, showing the weaknesses and strengths of each one, with the aim to help the software engineer select the most suitable methodology in each case. The results clearly show that there is not a single unified and unique general-purpose methodology. FIPA [7] and OMG [8] have also created some technical committees focused on the identification of a general methodology for the analysis and design of agent-oriented systems, embracing current agent-oriented methodologies such as GAIA [9], MaSE [10], Tropos [11, 12] or MESSAGE [13]. The idea is to identify the best development

---

[*]This research was funded in part by the Spanish MCYT under grant TIC: 2002-04309-C02-02.

J. Odell et al. (Eds.): AOSE 2004, LNCS 3382, pp. 93–108, 2005.
© Springer-Verlag Berlin Heidelberg 2005

process for specific MAS. This work is being complemented with the definition of an agent-based unified modelling language (FIPA AUML work plan [14]).

One of the main problems of these methodologies is that they cover the analysis and design phases of MAS development, but do not address the implementation phase, i.e., they do not completely resolve how to achieve the model derivation from the system design to a concrete implementation [9, 10, 13]. Thus, the software engineer is forced to either somehow select one of the existing agent platforms for implementing the agent-oriented design, or to use a concrete agent platform because it is the only one supported by the design methodology —which demands specialized skills from the developer. In the former case, the problem is that the criteria usually considered for choosing an agent platform are mainly based on the developer expertise, the programming language, available tools, or its recognition in the agent community. However, these criteria do not take into account the methodology used to design the MAS, for instance.

Besides, this transformation process —which is not a trivial task, and could be, in some cases, quite complex to achieve— has to be defined in an ad hoc manner in each case, for each methodology and for each agent platform. Thus, every single developer has to define and implement the mappings and transformations from the design produced by the selected agent-oriented methodology, to the API's provided by the particular agent platform, without any guidance or help.

Our goal in this paper is to study how such gap can be bridged, thus covering the complete life cycle of MAS. Furthermore, we also analyze how much of this process can be automated, independently from the original methodology used to analyze and design the MAS, and from the agent platform selected to implement the system.

In order to achieve such goal we will use the concepts provided by OMG's Model Driven Architecture (MDA). MDA is a modelling initiative that tries to cover the complete life cycle of software systems, allowing the definition of machine-readable application and data models, which permit long-term flexibility of implementation, integration, maintenance, testability and simulation [15]. MDA defines platform-independent models (PIM), platform-specific models (PSM), and transformations between them.

In this paper we will show how our problem can be naturally expressed in terms of the MDA, and then how the MDA mechanisms can be used for defining (and partially automating) the mappings. By applying the MDA ideas, the design model obtained as the result of applying an agent-oriented methodology can be considered as a PIM, the target agent platform for the MAS as the PSM, and the mappings between the two can be given by the transformations defined for the particular agent platform selected. The target models needs to be expressed in terms of their corresponding UML profiles, as indicated by the MDA.

However, when we initially tried to use this approach, we saw that it could work for some individual cases, but that it did not scale well for the ever-increasing number of agent-oriented methodologies and agent platforms: somebody had to define and automate the mappings between every agent-oriented methodology and every agent platform. This is not affordable at all. However, we then discovered that the use of a platform-neutral agent architecture could greatly simplify this task, since the numbers of mappings was significantly reduced. Thus, we propose the use of the agent model [16, 17] *Malaca.*). One of the most outstanding features of this agent architecture is that it is possible to execute a Malaca agent on top of any FIPA-compliant agent platforms, i.e., it was designed to be independent from the underlying agent platform. Therefore we define mappings from agent-oriented methodologies to Malaca, and from Malaca to the different agent platforms. Consequently, with just one transformation between an agent-oriented methodology and the Malaca agent model, the resulting MAS could run in any agent platform. The developer could then deploy the MAS in any agent platform, depending on the availability, price, tools provided, etc.

Moreover, as we will show later, the mappings and transformations from agent-oriented methodologies such as Tropos to Malaca are very simple, and most of them can be easily automated due to the use of UML and AUML, a big step towards bridging the gap between agent-oriented design and MAS implementation. A significant feature of this architecture is that any Malaca agent can be "programmed" simply by editing XML documents. Since most of the UML diagrams can be expressed easily in XML, the transformations between agent-oriented methodologies and Malaca are direct. This architecture reduces the development time, cost and effort, and simplifies the implementation of multi-agent systems.

In order to validate our proposal, mappings from one of the most representative agent-oriented methodologies to Malaca have been defined, namely from Tropos. They will be used throughout the paper for illustrating our approach.

The structure of this paper is as follows. Section 2 provides a brief overview of Tropos methodology. Section 3 introduces the Malaca agent architecture, and its underlying agent model. Section 4 describes our main contribution, by showing how to use the MDA approach for mapping MAS designs into the Malaca model, which can be then run into any agent platform. Section 5 outlines some of the problems and limitations of our approach, as well as further research work that could help address such limitations. Finally, Section 6 draws some conclusions.

2 Agent-Oriented Methodology Overview

Agent-Oriented methodologies provide a set of mechanisms and models for developing agent-based systems. Most agent-oriented methodologies follow the approach of extending existing software engineering methodologies to include abstractions related to agents. Agent methodologies capture concepts like conversations, goals, believes, plans or autonomous behaviour. Most of them take advantage of software engineering approaches to design MAS, and benefit from UML and/or AUML diagrams to represent these agent abstractions.

There are many methodologies with different strengths and weakness and different specialized features to support different applications domains. Clearly there is not a widely used or general-purpose methodology, but we took into account some issues like the modelling diagrams used, the kind of application domain it is appropriated for, and above all, the level of detail provided at the design phase and the available documentation. Some methodologies were not considered in this first approach because of their lack of public documentation or the level of detail achieve at the design phase. After examining current research in this area, and despite there were other good candidates, such as Mase [10], we only use Tropos [11,12] for illustrating our proposal.

2.1 Tropos

Tropos [11] is an agent-oriented methodology created by a group of authors from various universities in Canada, Italy, Belgium and Brazil. Tropos is founded on the concepts of actor and goal and strongly focus on early requirements. The development process in Tropos consists in five phases: *Early Requirements*, *Late Requirements*, *Architectural Design*, *Detailed Design* and *Implementation*.

The first phase identifies actors and goals represented by two different models. The actor diagram depicts involved roles and their relationships, called dependencies. These dependencies show how actors depend on each other to accomplish their goals, to execute their plans, and to supply their resources. The goal diagram shows a analysis of goals and plans regarding a specific actor in charge of achieving them. This analysis is based upon reasoning techniques such as AND/OR decomposition, means-end and contribution analysis. These models will be extended in the second phase, which models the system within its environment.

The third phase is divided in three steps. In the first one, new actors, which are derived from the chosen architectural style, are included and described by an extended actor diagram. These actors fulfil non-functional requirements or support sub-goals identified in the previous phase. The second and third steps identify the capabilities, and group them to form agent types, respectively. The last step defines a set of agent types and assigns each of them a set of capabilities. This assignment, which is not unique and depends on the designer, is captured in a table.

The *Detailed Design* phase deals with the detailed specification of the agents' goals, belief and capabilities. Also communication among agents is specified in detail. This phase is usually strictly related to implementation choices since it is proposed within specific development platforms, and depends on the features of the adopted agent programming language. This step takes as input the specification resulting from the architectural design and generates a set of UML activity diagrams for representing capabilities and plans, and AUML sequence diagrams for characterizing agent interaction protocols. AUML is an extension of UML to accommodate the distinctive requirements of agent, which results from the cooperation established by FIPA and the OMG. This is achieved by introducing new classes of diagrams into UML such as *interaction protocol diagrams* and *agent class diagrams*.

Finally, the implementation phase follows the detailed design specification given in the previous phase. Tropos chooses a BDI platform for the implementation of agents, namely JACK Intelligent Agent [18], an agent-oriented development environment built on top of Java. The main language constructs provided by this platform (agents, capabilities, database relations, events and plans) have a direct correspondence with the notions used in the Tropos design phase. In addition, Tropos provides guidelines and heuristics for mapping Tropos concepts into BDI concepts, and BDI concepts into JACK constructs. However, Tropos does not impose the use of JACK, and the developer can implement the design in any other agent platform.

3 The Malaca Agent Model

Most existing agent architectures focus on the type of agent (BDI, reactive), but do not provide direct support for handling and reusing properties and functionality separately. This approach results in agent design and implementations being quite complex, brittle, and difficult to understand, maintain, and reuse in practice.

The Malaca agent architecture is based on the definition and reuse of software components, let they be either in-house or commercial-off-the-shelf (COTS) components. In addition, by applying the separation of concerns principle promoted by aspect-oriented software development [19], we separate into different and decoupled entities the distribution of messages through FIPA-compliant platforms, the codification of exchanged messages in FIPA ACL formats, and also the agents functionality from their coordination. By "componentizing" agents in such way, they can be reused and replaced independently to build specific agent architectures independently from the underlying agent platform(s) used. This also enables dynamic composition of agent at runtime, allowing the dynamic reconfiguration and adaptation of the agents' behaviour to support new interaction protocols and functionality, to access to different agent platforms, or to use different ACL formats. Besides, when treated as components, Malaca agents are simply configured using XML documents that contain the agents' descriptions.

Fig. 1 shows the meta-model of the Malaca agent model (a part of its UML profile), where all these entities are explicitly represented. This diagram also represents the basic structure of the XML agent description that is used to create an agent since there is a direct correspondence between the UML model shown there and the XML representation of the agent: meta-model classes and association represent the XML elements, and class attributes represent XML element attributes.

In order to produce agents able to be executed in any FIPA-compliant agent platform, we have separated everything related with the use of Message Transport Service (MTS), bundling it into a "distribution aspect". This distribution aspect will be later bound to the particular adaptors (*plug-ins*) of the corresponding agent platforms on which the agent instance will be run. Then, the actual distribution of messages using a particular message transport service offered by a FIPA-compliant agent platform is performed by an independent entity, the *adaptor*. Such adaptor defines a common interface, which will be realized by each concrete adaptor instance of the target agent platform(s), which will deal with the specific services of such platform(s). Since agent platform dependencies are encapsulated as an external plug-ins, our agents can be adapted to engage in any FIPA-compliant agent platform, and even be used in more than one agent platform simultaneously (for additional details see [17]).

As stated before, the encoding format of messages exchanged by the agent within an interaction is also bundled in a separated entity. Thus, the codification of ACL messages in a concrete FIPA format is merged neither with the agent platform access, nor with the behavior of the agent. In our agent architecture, parsers deal with different ACL representations. Each parser has to realize a common interface to code and decode output and input messages. In the model, for each different ACL format supported, we provide an *ACLParser* plug-in that parses ACL messages formatted according to the value of the *format* attribute. Once again, the agent could support more that one ACL format at the same time.

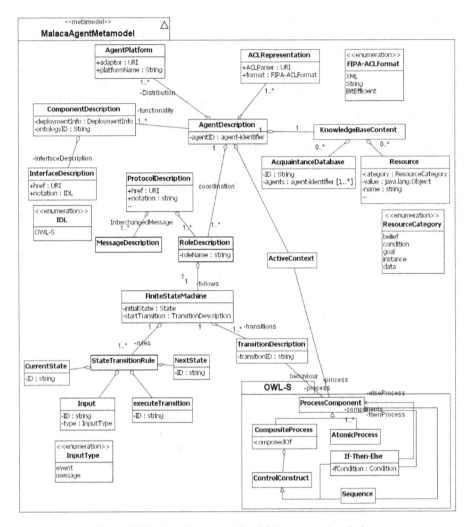

Fig. 1. UML class diagram with a Malaca agent description

The behaviour of a Malaca agent is given by its functionality and by the way it interacts with other agents (i.e., its *coordination* aspect). In our model, agent functionality is provided by reusable software components, which offer the set of core services, and also the application-dependent functionality. Components that are initially plugged into the agent architecture are packaged into the functionality element of the agent description. Each component is described in a *ComponentDescription* class, which provides information about its provided interface and its implementation. The component interface describes the set of offered services in an XML document in the format specified by the *notation* element (by default, OWL-S [20]). The *deploymentInfo* attribute points to a XML document with the description, using the *notation* format (by default, the CCM *softpackage* format [21]), of the component implementation. This information includes the kind of implementation (e.g. Java, CORBA, Web service), how to locate and deploy the component, etc.

Coordination is also modelled by using an independent entity called *connector*, which decouples the agent functionality from its interactions. Every time a new conversation starts, a new connector is created to control it. For this task, the connector uses a description of the interaction protocol followed. The set of roles of interaction protocols supported is given by the *coordination* element. Each role description is part of an interaction protocol is described by a XML document using the *notation* format (by default, the *ProtocolDescription* XML schema [16]).

The UML class diagram in Fig. 1 also depicts the structure of a protocol description. Agent interaction protocols are described by the set of message description, interchanged during the interaction and by a set of finite state machines for representing the behavior of each participant role. The description of a message, in a *MessageDescription* element, should include the performative and should contain at least some description of the message content. The value of any other message field can also be specified. A separate finite state machine within the *RoleDescription* class, identified by an attribute *roleName*, describes each side of a conversation (at least the initiator and the responder). Each finite state machine is represented by a set of state transition rules enclosed by the *FiniteStateMachine* class and each rule is defined in a *StateTransitionRule* class.

The transition from a state to another carries out the execution of the agent functionality (defined in the *StateTransitionRule* by the attribute *executeTransition*). The *TransitionDescription* class encloses the set of agent actions that are invoked during protocol execution. Instead of a simple sequence of invocations to the agent internal functionality, it is possible to use more complex control structures to coordinate the execution of the agent functionality. OWL-S provides the basis for the definition of agent functionality as services. As part of the DARPA Agent Markup Language [22] program and within the OWL-based framework, OWL-S is an ontology for describing Web services that gives a detailed description of a service's operation, and provides details on how to interoperate. The control structures defined in the *Process Model* of OWL-S are used to encompass a set of agent actions in a transition description.

Finally, the agent description also contains the initial content of the agent Knowledge Base, expressed in terms of beliefs, goals, and conditions; the acquaintance database, defined as a set of the identifiers of the agents with which the agent will interact; and an active context of the agent upon start up. Within an *ActiveContext* class, it is possible to specify the initial behaviour the agent will execute (expressed in OWL-S by a sequence of actions, a set of protocols executed in parallel, etc.).

The Malaca UML Profile, which is derived from its metamodel, defines *stereotypes* for each metamodel element and also defines *constraints*, associated to stereotypes, which impose restrictions on the corresponding metamodel elements. Constraints can be used, for instance, to state that the attribute *transitionID* has a unique value for all the elements in the *transitions* collection of a *FiniteStateMachine*. The abovementioned restriction can be expressed by the following OCL [23] constraint:

Context MalacaAgentMetamodel::FiniteStateMachine
Inv: self.transitions -> isUnique(transitionID)

The Malaca agent model is implemented in Java, and currently provides adaptors for Jade [24], Zeus [25], and FIPA-OS [26] agent platforms. It also supports String and XML ACL encodings. One of the benefits of this model is that the only artifacts that should be provided by the developer to define a MAS in Malaca are the XML documents with the agent descriptions, the components provided interfaces, and the protocol descriptions. We shall see in the next section how these artifacts can be even automatically generated from the MAS designs produced by Tropos. This will allow a direct connection between the MAS design and its implementation in any of the agent platforms.

4 Applying MDA to MAS Design to Produce Implementations

The problem of transforming the design diagrams produced by a given agent-oriented methodology to a set of implementation classes of an agent platform API, such as the ones provided by FIPA-OS, Zeus, or Jade, can be addressed by expressing such designs and agent platforms as *models*, and then expressing the transformations between them in terms of *mappings* between models. The OMG Model Driven Architecture (MDA) provides the right kind of mechanisms for expressing such kind of models, the entities of each one, and for defining transformation between them.

MDA is an approach to system development based on the use of models, which are descriptions of a system and its environment for some certain purpose. A model is often presented as a combination of drawings and text (the text may be in a modelling language or in natural language). Regarding a set of models, MDA sets down how those models are prepared, and the relationships between them. In MDA, a platform is a set of subsystems and technologies that provides a set of functionality through interfaces and specified usage patterns, which any application supported by that platform can use without concern for the details of how the functionality provided by the platform is implemented. MDA distinguishes between platform-independent models (PIM) and platform-specific models (PSM).

The general MDA model transformation is depicted by the MDA pattern, shown in Fig. 2(a). The PIM and some other information are combined by the transformation to produce a PSM. MDA defines many ways in which such transformations can be done. A MDA mapping provides specifications for transformation of a PIM into a PSM for a particular platform. A model type mapping specifies a mapping from any model built using types. Another approach to mapping models is to identify model elements in the PIM, which should be transformed in a particular way, given the choice of a specific platform for the PSM. However, most mappings will consist in some combination of type and instance mappings. A mapping may also include templates to specify particular kinds of transformations. In order to apply these concepts to agent technologies, we need to define agent-oriented PIMs and PSMs, and mappings between them. Here, the design model of a MAS produced by an agent-oriented methodology will constitute the PIM, that needs to be marked using the UML profile, or the metamodel expressed in UML, MOF or any other language, of the target agent platform to produce a PSM.

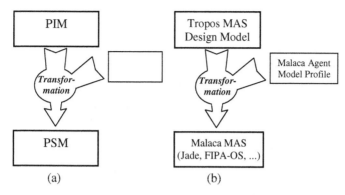

Fig. 2. (a) The MDA pattern for model transformation, and (b) The MDA model transformation from Tropos design model to the Malaca MAS specification using the Malaca Agent Model UML Profile

To illustrate this approach, in this paper we will apply MDA to transform Tropos design model to the Malaca agent model. An important benefit of our agent model is that it does not depend on the target agent platform on which it will be executed, and therefore there is no need to develop different implementations for each FIPA-compliant agent platform. This fact greatly simplifies the process of providing an implementation for each different agent platform. Fig. 2(b) graphically shows the process that will be described in detail in the next sections. The transformations are illustrated using UML, AUML diagrams produced by Tropos, the agent-oriented methodology used here. The MDA transformation process shown here is based on marking the Tropos design model. The developer performs this step manually. After that, the marked model is transformed into a Malaca model applying some transformation rules. This process can be automated.

4.1 Applying MDA: From Tropos to Malaca

Now we will show through an example how the set of models resulting from applying Tropos can be transformed in a set of Malaca agents using the MDA mechanisms.

To illustrate the transformation for the Tropos design model, we will use the diagrams supplied in [11], which provides a case study. Unfortunately, available literature of Tropos does not provide a complete example, and also the process that explains each phase varies from paper to paper.

Marking Tropos Detailed Design Model. As stated before, in Tropos, the design phase deals with the detailed specification of the agents, capabilities and communications. More precisely, the design phase in Tropos produces:

- Agent assignments, expressed as a table resulting from the architectural design phase, that defines the agent types and the capabilities assigned to each agent. An agent can have assigned capabilities that are associated to different actors.
- Agent Interaction Diagrams. AUML sequence diagrams are used to model basic interactions between agents. In [12], interactions are described by introducing additional interactions, together with constraints on the exchanged messages.

– Capability Diagrams. One UML activity diagram models each capability. External events, such as input messages, define the starting state of a capability diagram; activity nodes model plans, transition arcs model events, and beliefs are modelled as objects. UML activity diagrams can further specify each plan node of a capability at the lowest level. In this case, the activity nodes correspond to simple or complex actions.

Now we will show how the Tropos detailed design given in [11], can be transformed into a Malaca Model. In order to define this transformation we will "mark" the Tropos design model using the classes defined in the Malaca metamodel showed in Fig. 1. A *mark* represents a concept stereotyped in the Malaca profile and is applied to an element of the Tropos design model to indicate how it should be transformed. Thus, we will mark Tropos design elements (agents, interactions, messages, capabilities, plans and so on), with the corresponding Malaca entities that will implement them (AgentDescription, ProtocolDescription, TransitionDescription, OWL-S processes, etc). Agent types are marked as *AgentDescription*. Each capability is marked as a *TransitionDescription*, and each interaction (represented in UML sequence diagram) is marked as a *ProtocolDescription*.

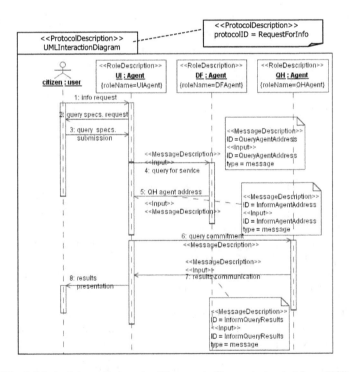

Fig. 3. Marked Agent Interaction Diagram in Tropos (extracted from [10])

The elements of each UML diagram can also be marked. Fig. 3 shows the marked agent interaction diagram given in [11]. Every agent (object) in the agent interaction diagram (UML interaction diagram) is marked as a *RoleDescription*, and every communicative act between agents is marked as a *MessageDescription*, but also as an *Input* (an element of a *StateTransitionRule*). Also, we specify the value of the tagged value (that corresponds to an attribute of the metamodel class) associated to the stereotype element including notes that show the corresponding stereotype, the name of the tagged value, and the value assigned to it.

Fig. 4 displays the marked diagram of the capability *Present Query results*. The external event is marked as a *MessageDescription* and every plan —activity node— is marked as an *Atomic* or a *Composite* OWL-S process. If the plan node is not further specified in another UML activity diagram it is marked as an Atomic process (see *Present Empty Result* and *Present Query Results* node s). Otherwise, it is marked as a Composite process, as occurs with the *Evaluate Query Result* plan, since it is further specified in another UML activity diagram. Plan diagrams are also marked.

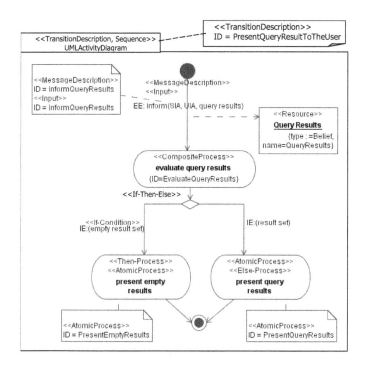

Fig. 4. Marked Capability Diagram (extracted from [10])

Tropos to Malaca Mappings and Transformations. After applying the marks defined in the Malaca profile, we obtain a set of marked UML and AUML diagrams. The transformation process applies mapping rules for the same mark depending on the marked element. The result of the application of such mapping rules is, in this case, a set of XML documents that specify the PSM of the system for the Malaca platform.

In order to illustrate the mapping rules, we will describe here, as example, some rules that have been applied to a few elements marked in the diagram of Fig. 4.

- When a mark <<TransitionDescription>> is applied to a UML activity diagram the transformation produces an XML instance of the complex type TransitionDescription (defined in a XML schema). The value of the XML attribute is taken from the value assigned to the tagged value ID in the note (in the example is *PresentQueryResultToTheUser*).
- When a mark <<Sequence>> is applied to a UML activity diagram the transformation produces the definition of a *CompositeProcess* XML description attached to the TransitionDescription element produced by the application of the previous rule. The components of the *Sequence* are derived from the application of the following transformation rules.
- When a mark <<AtomicProcess>> is applied to an action state element within a UML activity diagram the transformation produces the XML description of an *AtomicProcess*, which is included as a *component* of the *ControlConstruct* element produced by the application of the previous rule.
- When a mark <<CompositeProcess>> is applied to an action state element within a UML activity diagram the transformation produces the XML description of an *CompositeProcess*, which is included as a *component* of the *ControlConstruct* element produced by the application of the previous rule.
- When a mark <<If-Then-Else>> is applied to a junction element within a UML activity diagram the transformation produces the XML description of an *If-Then-Else* control construct which is included as a *component* of the *ControlConstruct* element produced by the application of the previous rule.
- When a mark <<IfCondition>> is applied to a transition element within a UML activity diagram that depart from a junction marked as <<If-Then-Else>>, the transformation produces the XML description of a condition ,which is included as a *ifCondition* element of the *If-Then-Else* element produced by the application of the previous rule.
- When a mark <<thenProcess>> or <<elseProcess>> is applied to a action state element, marked also as a <<AtomicProcess>>, within a UML activity, the transformation produces the XML description of an atomic process, which is included as a *then* (or *else*) element of the *If-Then-Else* element produced by the application of a previous rule.

The application of these transformation rules to the diagram of Fig. 4 produces the XML description of a transition identified as *PresentQueryResults* as depicted in Fig. 5.

Also, we can apply the constraints expressed in OCL to ensure that the identifier of the transition is unique within the collection of transitions identifiers.

This is only a very brief example of how MDA can be applied to transform elements of the Tropos design model into a Malaca agent description, using marks and transformation rules. Again, once we count with a Malaca description of the MAS, it can be implemented in any FIPA-compliant agent platform. Then, we can obtain a straightforward implementation from that design by applying MDA mappings and transformations again.

```
-<TransitionDescription ID="PresentQueryResultsToTheUser">
 -<CompositeProcess>
  -<composedOf>
   -<Sequence>
   -<components>
    +<CompositeProcess ID="EvaluateQueryResult">
    -<If-Then-Else>
     -<ifCondition>
        <IsTrue resource="emptyResultSet" />
      </ifCondition>
     -<then>
        <AtomicProcess ID="presentEmptyResults" />
      </then>
     -<else>
       -<AtomicProcess ID="presentQueryResults"/>
      </else>
     </If-Then-Else>
    </components>
   </Sequence>
  </composedOf>
 </CompositeProcess>
</TransitionDescription>
```

Fig. 5. Present Query Result XML description (complete)

MAS metamodel are becoming relevant in the context of MDA. Using metamodels, the transformation can be automated from the beginning to the end. Regarding the example followed here, the Tropos metamodel, provided in [11], could be used to define general transformations from elements of the source metamodel into elements of the target metamodel. The developer has not to mark manually the Tropos design model elements before to transform them. Instead, transformations are automatically applied to instances of the elements of the metamodel. However, for this purpose, the Tropos metamodel has to provide a more detailed and accurate description of the Tropos design model elements and concepts (their relationships, attributes, constraints, etc) in order to derive and automate the transformation process as much as possible.

5   Limitations and Further Extensions to Our Work

One of the problems found when trying to implement multi-agent systems directly from their high-level designs and descriptions appear when the designer describes *what* needs to be done, but gives no indication on *how* (for instance, using heuristics, guidelines and examples rather than algorithms). In such cases, the transformations cannot be automated, since such algorithms have to be provided. In general, the level of detail provided in the design phase determines the accuracy of the implementation, and therefore its potential automated implementation. Thus, an important aspect in selecting a methodology is the level of detail provided.

Second, the diagrams and texts used in the design phase have to be interpreted and mapped during the transformation process. Since one of our goals is to automate such mappings, it is very important for diagrams and texts used in agent-oriented methodologies to follow standard notations (such as UML), allowing its automatic processing. Besides, AUML diagrams should also allow for some kind of automated support, currently inexistent —although the advent of UML 2.0 and its new extensions mechanisms can alleviate this if AUML gets aligned with UML 2.0.

Finally, MDA seems a very attractive and powerful approach for automated development. However, it also has many unresolved issues, and still lacks tool support. The availability of MAS metamodels [27, 28], the use of UML 2.0, the advent of QVT [29] and the emergence of new modelling tools that support the MDA principles can also help MDA get more mature and consolidate its ideas.

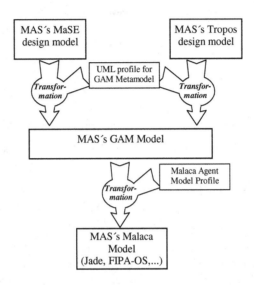

Fig. 6. Derivation of MAS implementations using a middle GAM model

Apart from these shortcomings, there are further extensions to our work. First, we plan to develop some tools for automating the transformations described in this paper. Apart from providing a proof-of-concept to our work, we think they can be of great value to any MAS developer that follows MaSE or Tropos
methodologies. They will also assist uncover some more issues of our proposal, helping us make it more robust.

A second line of work is related to the interesting idea by FIPA and the OMG to define a common agent model to most agent-oriented methodologies. Here we have seen the benefits of using a neutral model (Malaca) for MAS implementation purposes, which provides the common mechanisms provided by FIPA-compliant agent platforms. In this way, any design model of the MAS produced using an agent-oriented methodology can be implemented by mapping it (using the MDA mechanisms) into its corresponding Malaca model. But this means that a different transformation is needed for every methodology into the Malaca model. Instead, a better solution is to identify and standardize the commons elements of the existing agent-oriented methodologies at the design phase, as pursued by FIPA and the OMG. The common elements could form a generic agent model (GAM) on which specialized features of every agent-oriented methodology might be based. Thus, we could introduce an intermediate model that semantically can cope with the concepts managed at design time by agent-oriented methodologies. With this, MAS design models could be naturally mapped to a new design model conforming the element defined in the GAM. From there, we will count with a general and common model for MAS designing purposes, a common model for implementation purposes, and the only thing that needs to be done is to define (just) one MDA transformation from the GAM to Malaca, as shown in Fig. 6.

6   Conclusions

In this paper we have presented how MDA can be effectively applied to agent technologies, providing a partially automated support for the derivation of MAS implementations right from their designs, independently from the methodology used to realize the design, and the target agent platform selected.

Our main contributions have been the definition of a common and neutral agent model that implements all the concepts required by FIPA-compliant agent platforms, and the use of the MDA mechanisms for defining the transformations between the design models produced by existing agent-oriented methodologies and the Malaca model. From there, the MAS implementation is quite straightforward. We have presented our experience in deriving and applying these transformations to a well-known methodology, Tropos.

References

1. M. Wooldridge, P. Ciancarini, "Agent-Oriented Software Engineering: The State of the Art", in *First Int. Workshop on Agent-Oriented Software Engineering*, LNAI 1957, 2000. pp. 1-28.
2. C.A. Iglesias, M. Garijo, J.C. Gonzalez, "A Survey of Agent-Oriented Methodologies", in *Intelligent Agents V – Proceedings of the Fifth International Workshop ATAL 98*, Springer-Verlag, 1998.
3. S. A. O'Malley, S.A. DeLoach, "Determining When to Use an Agent-Oriented Software Engineering Paradigm", in *Second International Workshop On Agent-Oriented Software Engineering*, 2001.
4. Sturn, O. Shehory, "A Framework for Evaluating Agent-Oriented Methodologies", in *International Workshop On Agent-Oriented Information Systems*, 2003.
5. K.H. Dam, M. Winikoff, "Comparing Agent-Oriented Methodologies", in *International Workshop On Agent-Oriented Information Systems*, 2003.
6. J. Sudeikat et al. "Evaluation of Agent-Oriented Software Methodologies – Examination of the Gap Between Modeling and Platform", in Proceedings of AOSE 2004.
7. FIPA, "FIPA Methodology Technical Committee", Foundation for Intelligent Physical Agents http://www.fipa.org/activities/methodology.
8. OMG, "OMG Agent Working Group", in Object Management Group http://www.objs.com/agent/
9. F. Zambonelli, M. Wooldridge, and N. R. Jennings, "Developing Multiagent Systems: The Gaia methodology", in ACM Transactions on Software Engineering and Methodology, Vol.12 , Issue 3, pp. 317 – 370, 2003

10. S. A. DeLoach, M. F. Wood, C. H. Sparkman, "Multiagent System Engineering", in *International Journal of Software Engineering and Knowledge Engineering*, vol. 11, n. 3, pp. 231-258. July 2001.

11. P. Bresciani, P. Giorgini, F. Giunchiglia, J. Mylopoulos, and A. Perini. "Tropos: An Agent-Oriented Software Development Methodology", in *International Journal of Autonomous Agents and Multi-Agent Systems*, Vol. 8, Issue 3, pp. 203 - 236, May 2004.

12. J. Castro, M. Kolp, J. Mylopoulos, "Towards Requirements-Driven Information Systems Engineering: The Tropos Project", in *Information Systems*, vol. 27, Issue 6, 2002. pp. 365-389.

13. MESSAGE: Methodology for Engineering Systems of Software Agents. Deliverable 1. Initial Methodology. July 2000. EURESCOM Project P907-GI.

14. B. Bauer, J. P. Muller, J. Odell, "Agent UML: A Formalism for Specifying Multiagent Software Systems", in *International Journal of Software Engineering and Knowledge Engineering*, vol.11, n.3, 2001. pp 207—230.

15. OMG, "Model Driven Architecture. A technical Perspective", Object Management Group, OMG Document ab/2001-01-01, 2001. Available from www.omr.org.

16. M. Amor, L.Fuentes, J.M. Troya, "Training Compositional Agents in Negotiation Protocols", next publication in *Integrated Computer-Aided Engineering International Journal*, 2004.

17. M. Amor, L.Fuentes, J.M. Troya, "A Component-Based Approach for Interoperability Across FIPA-Compliant Platforms", in *Cooperative Information Agents VII*, LNAI 2782, 2003. pp. 266—288.

18. The Agent Oriented Software Group, "Jack Development Environment", http://www.agent-software.com

19. Aspect-Oriented Software Development, in http://www.aosd.net

20. The DAML Services Coalition, "OWL-S: Semantic Mark-up for Web Services" available at http://www.daml.org/services/

21. OMG, "CORBA Components. Packaging and Deployment", in Object Management Group, OMG Document formal/02-06-74, June 2002.Available from www.omg.org.

22. The DARPA Agent Markup Language Homepage, http://www.daml.org/

23. Object Management Group. Object Constraint Language Specification, OMG document ad/02-05-09, 2002. Available from www.omg.org.

24. F. Bellifemine, G. Caire, T. Trucco, G. Rimassa, "Jade Programmer's Guide", 2003, available at http://sharon.cselt.it/projects/jade/

25. J. Collis, D. Ndumu, C. van Buskirk "The Zeus Technical Manual", Intelligent Systems Research Group, BT Labs. July 2000.

26. Emorphia, "FIPA-OS Developers Guide", Nortel Networks' Agent Technology Group, 2002, available at http://sourceforge.net/projects/fipa-os/

27. C. Bernon, M. Cossentino, and M.P. Gleizes, "A Study of some Multi-Agent Meta-Models", in Proceedings of AOSE 2004.

28. J. Odell, M. Nodine, and R. Levy," A Metamodel for Agents, Roles, and Groups", in Proceedings of AOSE 2004.

29. OMG, "MOF 2.0 Query/View/Transformation RFP", in Object Management Group, OMG Document ad/03-08-03. 2003. Available from www.omg.org.

A Design Process for
Adaptive Behavior of Situated Agents

Elke Steegmans, Danny Weyns, Tom Holvoet, and Yolande Berbers

AgentWise, DistriNet, Department of Computer Science, K.U.Leuven
Celestijnenlaan 200 A, B-3001 Leuven, Belgium
{Elke.Steegmans, Danny.Weyns, Tom.Holvoet,
Yolande.Berbers}@cs.kuleuven.ac.be

Abstract. Engineering non-trivial open multi-agent systems is a challenging task. Our research focusses on situated multi-agent systems, i.e. systems in which agents are explicitly placed in an environment which agents can perceive and in which they can act. Situated agents do not use long-term planning to decide what action sequence should be executed, but select actions based on the locally perceived state of the world and limited internal state. To cope with change and dynamism of the system, situated agents must be able to adapt their behavior. A well-known family of agent architectures for adaptive behavior are free-flow architectures. However, building a free-flow architecture based on an analysis of the problem domain is a quasi-impossible job for non-trivial agents. To tackle the complexity of designing adaptive agent behavior based on a free-flow architecture, suitable abstractions are needed to describe and structure the agent behavior. The abstraction of a role is obviously essential in this respect. A modeling language is needed as well to model the behavior of the agents. We propose a statechart modeling language to support the design of roles for situated agents. In this paper we describe a design process for adaptive behavior of situated agents as part of a multi-agent oriented methodology. The design process integrates the abstraction of a role with a free-flow architecture. Starting from the results of analysis of the problem domain, the designer incrementally refines the model of the agent behavior. The resulting class diagram serves as a basis for implementation. We illustrate the subsequent design steps with a case study on controlling a collection of automated guided vehicles.

1   Introduction

Dealing with the increasing complexity of developing, integrating and managing open distributed applications is a continuous challenge for software engineers. In the last fifteen years, multi-agent systems have been put forward as a key paradigm to tackle the complexity of open distributed applications. In our research we focus on situated multi-agent systems[1](situated MASs) as a generic approach to develop self-managing open distributed applications.

---

[1] Alternative descriptions are behavior-based agents [5], adaptive autonomous agents [14] or hysteretic agents [10][9].

J. Odell et al. (Eds.): AOSE 2004, LNCS 3382, pp. 109–125, 2005.

In situated multi-agent systems, agents and the environment constitute complementary parts of a multi-agent world that can mutually affect each other. Situatedness places an agent in a context in which it is able to perceive its environment and in which it can (inter)act. Situated agents do not use long-term planning to decide what action sequence should be executed, but select actions based on the locally perceived state of the world and limited internal state. Contrary to knowledge-based agents, situated agents do not emphasize internal modeling of the environment. Instead, they favor to employ the environment itself as a source of information. The environment can serve as a robust self-revising common memory for agents. This can unburden the individual agents from continuously keeping track of their knowledge about the system. Intelligence in a situated MAS originates from the interactions of the agents in their environment rather than from the capabilities of the individual agents. Agents interacting form an organization in which they all play and execute their own role(s). Situated MASs have been applied with success in numerous practical applications over a broad range of domains, e.g. manufacturing scheduling [20], network support [3] or peer-to-peer systems [2]. The benefits of situated MAS are well known, the most striking being flexibility, robustness and efficiency.

To cope with change and dynamism of the system, situated agents must be able to adapt their behavior according to the changing circumstances. A well-known family of agent architectures for adaptive behavior are free-flow architectures [21][23][6]. Free-flow architectures allow adaptive behavior, yet from our experiences we learned that it is unrealistic to assume that -starting from the analysis of the problem domain- software engineers build a complex free-flow architecture for complex applications, where agents can perform many actions. For such applications, the architecture quickly becomes unmanageable, it is no longer possible to have an overall view of the architecture. To tackle the complexity of designing adaptive agent behavior based on a free-flow architecture suitable abstractions are needed to describe and structure the agent behavior. The abstraction of a role is obviously essential in this respect, as roles provide the building blocks for social organization of a MAS. A modeling language is needed as well to model the behavior of the agents. We propose a statechart modeling language to support the design of roles for situated agents.

In this paper we describe a design process for adaptive behavior of situated agents as part of a multi-agent oriented methodology. The design process integrates the abstraction of a role with a free-flow architecture. We illustrate the subsequent design steps with a case study on controlling a collection of automated guided vehicles.

This paper is structured as follows. In section 2 we introduce free-flow architectures and outline the design process for adaptive agent behavior. Section 3, the core of the paper, explains in detail the different steps of the design process for roles proposed in this paper. We illustrate our design process with an example application. Finally, in section 4 we conclude the paper and give some future work.

2 Free-Flow Architectures and Designing Adaptive Behavior

In this section we start with a brief introduction of free-flow architectures and illustrate the complexity of developing a free-flow architecture for non-trivial agents. Then we outline the design process for adaptive agent behavior we propose in this paper.

2.1 Free-Flow Architecture for Adaptive Agent Behavior

Open multi-agent systems are characterized by dynamism and change: new agents may join the system, others may leave, the environment may change, e.g. its topology or its characteristics such as throughput and visibility. To cope with such dynamism the agents must be able to adapt their behavior according to the changing circumstances. A well-known family of agent architectures for adaptive behavior are free-flow architectures.

Free-flow architectures are first proposed by Rosenblatt and Payton in [21]. In his Ph.D thesis, T. Tyrrell [23] demonstrated that hierarchical free-flow architectures are superior to flat decision structures, especially in complex and dynamic environments. The results of Tyrrell's work have been very influential, for a recent discussion see [6]. An example of a free-flow architecture is depicted in Fig. 1.

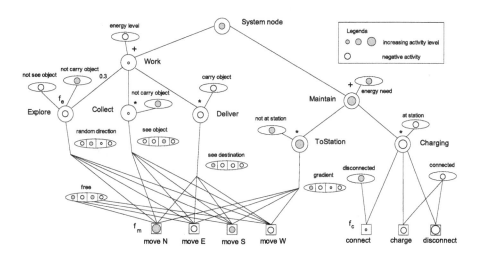

Fig. 1. An example of a free-flow architecture

The hierarchy is composed of *nodes* which receive information from internal and external stimuli in the form of *activity*. The nodes feed their activity down through the hierarchy until the activity arrives at the *action nodes* (i.e. the leaf nodes of the tree) where a winner-takes-it-all process decides which action is selected. The main advantages of free-flow architectures are:

- Stimuli can be added to the relevant nodes avoiding the 'sensory bottleneck' problem. In a hierarchical decision structure, to make correct initial decisions, the top level has to process most of the sensory information relevant to the lower layers.
- Decisions are made only at the level of the action nodes; as such all information available to the agent is taken into account to select actions.
- Since all information is processed in parallel the agent can take different preferences into consideration simultaneously. E.g. consider an agent that moves to a spotted object but is faced with a neighboring threat. If the agent is only able to take into account one preference at a time it will move straight to the spotted object or move away from the threat. With a free-flow decision tree the agent avoids the threat *while* it keeps moving towards the desired object, i.e. the agent likely moves around the threat towards the spotted object.

Fig. 1 depicts a free-flow tree for action selection of a simple robot. This robot lives in a grid world where it has to collect objects and bring them to a destination. The robot is supplied with a battery that provides energy to work. The robot has to maintain its battery, i.e. when the energy level of the battery falls below a critical value the robot has to recharge the battery at a charge station. The left part of the depicted tree represents the functionality for the robot to search, collect and deliver objects. On the right, functionality to maintain the battery is depicted. The *System node* feeds its activity to the *Work* node and the *Maintain* node. The *Work* node combines the received activity with the activity from the *energy level* stimulus. The '+' symbol indicates that the received activity is summed up. The negative activity of the *energy level* stimulus indicates that little energy remains for the robot. As such the resulting activity in the *Work* node is almost zero. The *Maintain* node on the other hand combines the activity of the *System node* with the positive activity of the *energy need* stimulus, resulting in a strong positive activity. This activity is fed to the *ToStation* and the *Charging* nodes. The *ToStation* node combines the received activity with the activity level of the *not at station* stimulus (the '*' symbol indicates they are multiplied). In a similar way the *Charging* node combines the received activity with the activity level of the *at station* stimulus. This latter is a binary stimulus, i.e. when the robot is at the charge station its value is positive, otherwise it is negative. The *ToStation* node feeds its positive activity towards the action nodes it is connected to. Each moving direction receives an amount of activity proportional to the value of the *gradient* stimulus for that particular direction. *gradient* is a multi-directional stimulus, i.e. a compound stimulus with a value of the stimulus for each direction. The values of the *gradient* stimulus are based on the sensed value of the gradient field that is transmitted by the charge station. In a similar way, the *Charging* node and the child nodes of the *Work* node (*Explore*, *Collect* and *Deliver*) feed their activity to the action nodes they are connected to. Action nodes that receive activity from different nodes combine that activity according to a specific function. The action nodes for moving actions use a function f_m

to calculate the final activity level. A possible definition of this function is the following:

$$A_{moveD} = \max \left[(A_{Node} + A_{stimulusD}) * A_{freeD} \right]$$

Herein is A_{moveD} the activity collected by a move action, D denotes one of the four possible directions, i.e. $D \in \{N, E, S, W\}$. A_{Node} denotes the activity received from a node. The move actions are connected to four nodes: $Node \in \{Explore, Collect, Deliver, ToStation\}$. With each node a particular *stimulus* is associated. *stimulus* $\in$ {*random direction, see object, see destination, gradient*} are multi-directional stimuli with a corresponding value for each moving direction. Finally, *free* is a multi-directional binary stimulus that indicates whether the way to a particular direction is free (or not free) for the robot to move to.

When all action nodes have collected their activity the node with the highest activity level is selected for execution. In the example, the *ToStation* node is clearly dominant over the other nodes connected to actions nodes. Currently the East and West directions are blocked (see the *free* stimulus), leaving the robot two possibilities to move towards the charge station: via North or via South. In the depicted situation, the robot will move northwards according to the values of a guiding gradient field.

2.2 Designing Adaptive Behavior

For the simple robot example discussed in the previous section, the free-flow tree is already fairly complex. For a non-trivial agent however, the overall view of the tree quickly becomes very cluttered. When a change is made in one part of such a tree it becomes unclear how this affects the other parts. Although free-flow trees are at best developed with a focus on a particular functionality of the agent, the architecture itself does not support any structuring. From our experiences we learned that it is unrealistic to assume that software engineers build a complex free-flow architecture for complex applications, where agents can perform many actions. For such applications, the architecture quickly becomes unmanageable, it is no longer possible to have an overall view of the architecture.

To tackle the complexity of designing adaptive agent behavior based on a free-flow architecture suitable abstractions are needed to describe and structure the behavior of the agent. The software engineer as a designer needs a comfortable modeling language that guides him or her in the process of designing the behavior of non-trivial agents.

Several agent-oriented methodologies acknowledge the abstraction of a role as a core abstraction for designing multi-agent systems, examples are Gaia [26], MESSAGE [8] or SODA [19], see also [18]. In these methodologies the design process is described independent of a particular multi-agent architecture, for a recent discussion see Chapter 4 of [13]. When it comes to building a concrete multi-agent application however, the gap between the high level design models and the chosen multi-agent architecture that is used to implement the multi-agent system has to be filled, see also [1]. In this paper we aim to bridge this gap enabling designers to build concrete multi-agent systems applications. In particular, we propose a design process that enables a designer to incrementally refine the model of the agent behavior from a high level role model toward a concrete agent architecture for adaptive behavior, in casu a free-flow architecture.

In previous work, we already proposed statecharts as a formalism to describe roles, see [11]. In that work the focus was on reusing roles in different applications and the statecharts notation was extended with new concepts, such as pre-action and post-action. Although a statechart specification of agent behavior is simple to design and to understand, it is typically a static, rigid model in that it leaves little room for adaptive and explorative behavior. In this paper we revise the statechart modeling language, i.e. we refrain from considering a statechart description of agent behavior as a kind of sequence chart, but use statecharts to describe role composition and to structure related actions in roles only.

To design adaptive behavior for agents, the designer needs to go through a number of subsequent design steps as depicted in Fig. 2. In the first step, the adaptive behavior is designed in a *high level model* making use of the role abstraction and the proposed role statechart modeling language. The diagrams of this high level model serve as a basis for structuring the free-flow tree in the next design step, resulting in a skeleton of the *free-flow architecture*. As the name indicates, it is a skeleton of the free-flow tree and thus it still needs to be refined by the designer. The refined free-flow architecture serves on its turn as a basis for the *class diagram* model in the last step of the design process. In the next section we elaborate in detail on each of the steps of the design process and illustrate them with a concrete example. Note that in practice the design process is typically not a one way pass through the indicated design steps. The designer may iterate a number of times over the different steps of the design process.

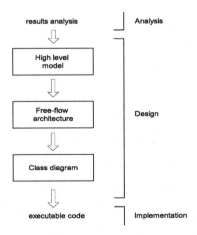

Fig. 2. Design process for adaptive behavior of situated agents

3   A Design Process for Roles

In this section we discuss the design process for adaptive agent behavior. We start with a brief introduction of the example application. Then we zoom in and discuss the subsequent steps of the design process in detail.

3.1   Example Application

In a current research project with an industrial partner we investigate how the paradigm of situated multi-agent systems can be applied to the control of logistic machines. Traditional systems use one central controller that instructs the machines to perform jobs based on a preceding calculated plan. Increasing demands with respect to adaptability and scalability faces the centralized approach with a number of limitations. By looking at machines as agents of a situated multi-agent system, we aim to convert the centralized control system into a self-managing distributed system, improving adaptability and scalability.

For the case in this paper we limit the discussion to the Automated Guided Vehicle (AGV) transport system. The AGV transport system is typically one part, yet a crucial part, of an integral logistic warehouse system. AGVs are unmanned vehicles that transport goods from one place to another. AGVs can supply basic/raw materials to a production department, serve as a link between different production lines or store goods between different processes and connect to the dispatch area. In a centrally controlled approach, the functionality of the individual AGVs is rather limited. Each AGV is provided with basic infrastructure to ensure safety. Besides, a typical AGV is able to perform pick and drop functions autonomously. The distribution of jobs, the routing through the infrastructure, collision avoidance at junctions etc. are all handled by the central control system.

In the research project we apply a decentralized approach to tackle the problem of controlling the AGVs. In this paper we look at a number of basic roles for an AGV to deal with jobs autonomously. We take into account functionality for the AGV to find a job, to handle a job, to park when no more work has to be done and finally to ensure that the battery is charged in time.

3.2   High Level Model: Role Model

Before we elaborate on the design of the role model we first clarify what we mean by the role abstraction. We regard a role as an agent's functionality in the context of an organization. Roles provide the building blocks for social organization of the MAS. Agents are linked to other agents by the roles they play in the organization. The links can be explicit, e.g. a set of agents that pass objects along a chain; or implicitly, e.g. in an ant colony a dynamic balance exists between ants that supply the colony with food and ants that maintain the nest.

In the first step of the design process, the high level role model of the agents is designed. High level modeling is supported by two diagrams and one schema. The *role diagram* structures the agent roles and their interdependencies. We distinguish two kinds of interdependencies: roles can be related in a hierarchy and

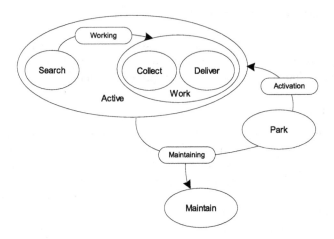

Fig. 3. The role diagram of the AGV

roles can be related through situated commitments. The role hierarchy expresses the behavior of the agent at different levels of abstraction. A situated commitment expresses an agent's preference of one role in relation to one or more other roles. The *action diagrams* structure the related actions within the roles. Finally a *commitment schema* defines the activation and deactivation conditions for a situated commitment.

Role Diagram. The roles and their interdependencies that describe the behavior of an agent are described in a role diagram. Fig. 3 depicts the role diagram of an AGV. A role diagram consists of a hierarchy of roles of which some are related through situated commitments.

A *role* is represented by a white oval and the name of the role is written in the oval. A role can consist of a number of sub-roles, and sub-roles of sub-sub-roles etc. As such the role diagram is typically composed of a hierarchy of roles. Roles at the bottom of the hierarchy are denoted as *basic roles*. The first role of the AGV is the *Active* role consisting of two sub-roles, *Search*, i.e. a basic role, and *Work*. The *Work* role is further split up in two sub-roles, *Collect* and *Deliver*. This latter too are two basic roles. In the *Search* role the AGV searches for a new job. Once the AGV finds a job it will *Collect* the good associated with the job and subsequently *Deliver* the good at the requested destination. Besides the *Active* role, the AGV has the *Maintain* role and the *Park* role. The AGV executes the *Park* role when it has no more work to do. In this role the AGV simply moves to the nearest parking place. The *Maintain* role ensures that the AGV keeps its battery loaded. When the energy level crosses a critical value, the AGV finishes its current job and moves towards the nearest charging station. To find its way to the charging station an AGV uses an internal gradient map. At regular time intervals all charging stations broadcast their current status. AGVs use these messages to keep their gradient maps up to date.

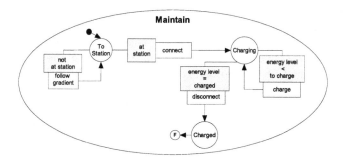

Fig. 4. The action diagram of the Maintain role

A *situated commitment* is represented by a rounded rectangle and the name of the situated commitment is written in the rectangle. A situated commitment defines a relationship between one role (the goal role) and a non-empty set of other roles (the source roles) of the agent. When a situated commitment is activated the behavior of the agent tends to prefer the goal role of the commitment over the source role(s). Favoring the goal role results in more consistent behavior of the agent towards the commitment. An agent can commit to itself, e.g. when it has to fulfill a vital task. However, in a collaboration agents commit relatively to one another, typically via communication. We elaborate on situated commitments below, references that explain the concept in detail are [25][24][22]. In Fig. 3, the *Maintaining* commitment ensures that the AGV maintains its energy level. Since energy is vital for the AGV to function, all roles (except the *Maintain* role of course) are connected as source roles to the *Maintaining* commitment. The *Activation* commitment is activated when the AGV starts to work. This commitment ensures that the AGV remains active once it decides to start working. The *Working* commitment is activated once the AGV accepts a job. This commitment ensures that the AGV acts consistently with the job in progress.

Action Diagram. Action diagrams are defined for the basic roles. An action diagram describes the structure of the related actions for a basic role. In Fig. 4 the action diagram of the *Maintain* role of the AGV is depicted.

A *state* is represented by a white circle in the diagram. In Fig.4 three states can be distinguished: *ToStation*, *Charging* and *Charged*. Besides these states there are two special states: the *initial state* and the *final state*. The initial state, represented by a black circle, indicates the typical start state of the action sequence of the modelled role. The final state, depicted by a circle with an F written in it, indicates the typical end state of the action sequence of the modelled role.

A *transition* connects two states with each other. A transition expresses a change of state due to the execution of an action. An *action*, which is added to a transition, models the functionality that must be performed by an agent to achieve a new desired state from an old state. An action is represented by a white rectangle in which the name of the action is written and which is attached to a transition. To fulfill the *Maintain* role, the AGV has to perform four different actions: *follow gradient* to find the charge station, and *connect*, *charge* and *disconnect* to charge its battery (see Fig. 4). The execution of an action may be constrained by a *precondition*. Only when the precondition is satisfied the attached action can be executed. A precondition is represented by a gray rectangle in which the precondition is written and which is attached to an action. In Fig. 4 the gray rectangle with *not at station* denotes that the AGV keeps following the gradient until it reaches the charge station. At that time the precondition *at station* becomes true and that enables the AGV to *connect* to the charge station. As long as *energy level < to charge* is true, the AGV keeps charging. Finally when condition *energy level = charged* becomes true, the AGV *disconnects* and that finishes the *Maintain* role.

Commitment Schema. For each situated commitment a commitment schema is defined that describes the source roles and the goal role of the commitment as well as its activation and deactivation conditions. Activation and deactivation conditions are boolean expressions based on internal state of the agent or perceived information, or information received from messages. Activating situated commitments through communication enable situated agents to setup explicit collaborations in which each participant plays a specific role. In this paper we do not elaborate on this latter scenario, for a detailed discussion we refer to [24][22]. Fig. 5 depicts the commitment schema for the situated commitment *Maintaining*.

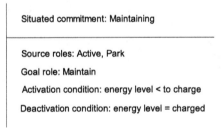

Fig. 5. The commitment schema for the situated commitment Maintaining

This commitment schema expresses that when the *energy level* of the AGV falls below the threshold *to charge*, the situated commitment *Maintaining* is activated. This will urge the AGV to prefer to execute the *Maintain* role over the *Active* and *Park* roles. Once the battery is recharged the condition *energy level = charged* becomes true and this deactivates the *Maintaining* commitment.

3.3   Free-Flow Architecture

The role and action diagrams, together with the commitment schema serve as a basis to design the free-flow architecture in the second design step. First the

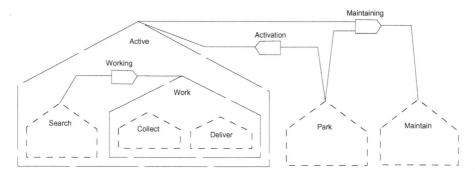

Fig. 6. Skeleton structure of the free-flow tree according to the role diagram of Fig. 3

high level models are used to build a skeleton of the free-flow architecture which then can further be refined.

Skeleton of Free-Flow Tree. The free-flow tree describes the behavior of the agent in detail. The high level diagrams for roles and situated commitments described in the previous section serve as a basis for structuring the free-flow tree. The role structure as described in the role diagram (see Fig. 3) is reflected in the skeleton structure of the tree. Fig. 6 depicts the skeleton structure for the AGV example.

Roles match to trees in the free-flow tree, sub-roles to sub-trees etc. Situated commitments on the other hand correspond to connectors that connect the source roles of the situated commitment with the goal role. When a situated commitment is activated, extra activity is injected in the goal role relative to the activity levels of the source roles. Details are discussed shortly.

The action diagrams and commitment schemas enable the developer to refine the skeleton tree. Fig. 7 depicts the refined sub-tree for the *Maintain* role and the *Maintaining* commitment. States in the action diagram correspond to activity nodes in the tree. Preconditions correspond to binary stimuli connected to the corresponding nodes. Examples are the stimuli *at station* or *connected* (compare Fig. 4 and Fig. 7). Each action in the action diagram of the basic role corresponds with an action node in the tree. A number of other analog stimuli in the tree represent data in the action diagram that determines the action selection. An example is the stimulus *gradient* that guides the AGV to move towards the station.

The activation and de-activation conditions of the situated commitments, described in the commitment schema correspond to the conditions associated with the corresponding connectors in the free-flow activity tree. Fig. 7 illustrates this for the *Maintaining* commitment.

Refining the Free-Flow Tree. Next the developer can refine the free-flow tree, integrating all details needed for action selection. Fig. 8 depicts the refined subtree of the *Maintain* role and the situated commitment *Maintaining*.

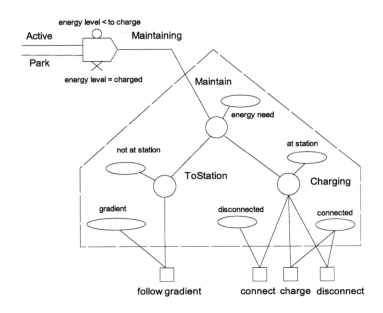

Fig. 7. Detailed skeleton of Maintain role and Maintaining commitment

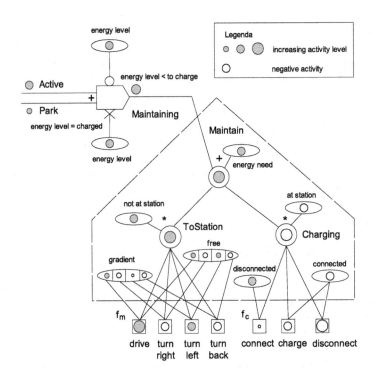

Fig. 8. Maintain role and Maintaining commitment after refinement

The abstract action node *follow gradient* in Fig. 7 is refined towards the different moving actions of the AGV. The stimulus *gradient* is split up in a multi-directional stimulus. Each segment represents the tendency (based on the value of the gradient field) of the AGV to move in a particular direction. Besides, a couple of extra stimuli represent data that influences the action selection. An example is the multi-directional stimulus *free* that denotes in which direction the AGV is able to drive.

Stimuli needed to verify the activation and deactivation condition are connected to the situated commitment. The *Maintaining* commitment is activated when the value of the *energy level* crosses the threshold value *to charge*. The commitment then calculates the extra activity to inject in the *Maintain* role. For the *Maintaining* commitment this extra activity is calculated as the sum ('+' symbol) of the activity level of the *Active* and *Park* role, i.e. the activity levels of the top nodes of these roles. As soon as the battery level reaches the threshold value *charged* the *Maintaining* commitment is deactivated and it no longer injects extra activity in the *Maintain* role.

3.4   Class Diagram: Free-Flow Framework

In the last design step, the refined free-flow tree is mapped onto a class diagram. For this class diagram we distinguish two parts, a *framework* and the application specific part for each *hot spot* that instantiates the framework.

Framework. We have designed a framework [16] for the free-flow architecture and implemented it in .NET. In Fig. 9 only a part of the framework is depicted, i.e. the classes and associations drawn above the dotted line[2] belong to the framework. The framework consists of a set of related classes that model the concepts of the free-flow architecture as described in the previous section. The concept of a *situated commitment* with its activation and deactivation conditions is modeled by the `SituatedCommitment` class which subclasses the `FunctionNode` class and which has an `activationCondition` and a `deactivationCondition` association with the `SituatedCommitmentFunction` class. In the free-flow architecture two kinds of *stimuli* are distinguished, a *binary stimulus* and an *analog stimulus*. This is modeled in the framework by the class hierarchy `Stimulus`, `BinaryStimulus` and `AnalogStimulus`. The concept of a *link* in the free-flow architecture represents a path along which activity can flow. A link is modeled as the `Link` class in the framework. `Link` has two associations, a `sourceNode` association with the class `GenericNode` and a `goalNode` association with the `FunctionNode` class.

Instantiating the Framework. For a concrete free-flow tree, the generic framework has to be instantiated, i.e. the the application specific part for each *hot spot* has to be instantiated in the framework. The part of the class diagram under

---

[2] For clarity, details such as the method names of the classes are not depicted. For all the details of the framework see [4].

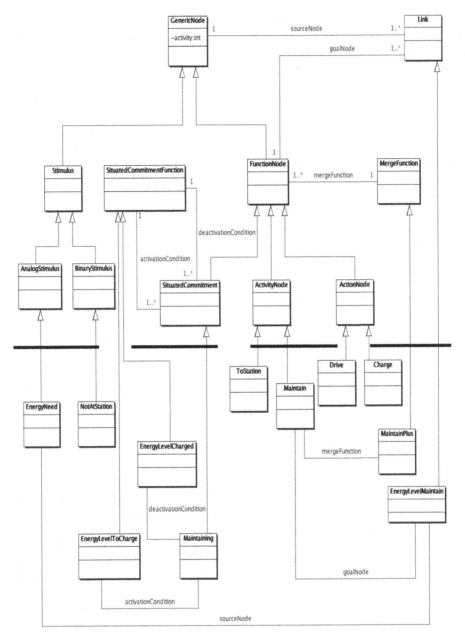

Fig. 9. The Maintain role and Maintaining commitment in the framework (partial)

the dotted line in Fig. 9 depicts a partial instantiation of the framework for the *Maintain* role and the *Maintaining* commitment. The situated commitment *Maintaining* is translated to the `Maintaining` class which subclasses the `SituatedCommitment` class of the framework. The `activationCondition` association of the `Maitaining` commitment is modeled as the `EnergyLevelToCharge` class while the `deactivationCondition` association is modeled as the `EnergyLevelCharged` class (both are a subclass of `SituatedCommitmentFunction`). The link between the binary stimulus *energy need* and the *Maintain* activity node is translated to the `EnergyLevelMaintain` class which subclasses the `Link` class of the framework. The `EnergyLevelMaintain` class has a `goalNode` association with the `Maintain` class (a subclass of the `ActivityNode` class) and a `sourceNode` association with the `EnergyLevelStimulus` class (a subclass of the `AnalogStimulus` class). A number of other examples are depicted in the figure, but are not further explained here.

4   Conclusion and Future Work

Designing non-trivial open multi-agent systems is a challenging task. In this paper we focussed on designing adaptive behavior of situated agents.

Most existing agent-oriented methodologies describe the design process independent of a particular agent architecture, however when it comes to building a concrete multi-agent application, the gap between the high level design models and the chosen multi-agent architecture has to be filled. In this paper we proposed a design process for adaptive agent behavior as part of a multi-agent oriented methodology. The design process bridges the gap between high level role modeling and a free-flow architecture for adaptive agent behavior.

Starting from the results of analysis of the problem domain, the designer incrementally refines the model of the agent behavior. At the highest level, roles and their interdependencies are caught into a high level model. This model is used as a basis for designing a skeleton of the free-flow architecture. Next the skeleton is refined such that it contains all details needed for action selection. Finally, the free-flow tree is mapped onto a class diagram that serves as a basis for the implementation of the agent's behavior. Throughout the paper we illustrated the role design process for a case study on controlling a collection of automated guided vehicles.

The phased design process proposed in this paper is in line with the paradigm of Model Driven Architecture [17]. In the successive design steps, the agent behavior is specified at subsequent lower levels of abstraction, each level introducing more detail. The highest level model is independent of the architecture chosen at the medium level. Likewise, the free-flow architecture is independent of the chosen framework at the lowest design level. In future work we intend to elaborate on this vision and extend the design process towards other abstractions [15] that need to be engineered in situated MASs such as agent communication and interaction (see also [12] and [7]), and the design of the environment of the MAS.

Acknowledgements

This research is supported by the K.U.Leuven research council (AgCo2) and the Flemish Institute for Advancement of Research in Industry (EMC2). We also would like to express our appreciation to Nelis Boucké for his contribution to the work presented in this paper.

References

1. M. Amor, L. Fuentes and A. Vallecillo. *Bridging the Gap Between Agent-Oriented Design and Implementation.* In Proceedings of the 5th International Workshop on Agent-Oriented Software Engineering (AOSE 2004), pp.1-16.
2. O. Babaoglu, H. Meling and H. Montresoret. *Anthill: A Framework for the Development of Agent-Based Peer-to-Peer Systems.* International Conference on Distributed Computing Systems, Vienna, Austria 2002.
3. E. Bonabeau, F. Hnaux, S. Gurin, D. Snyers, P. Kuntz and G. Theraulaz. *Routing in Telecommunications Networks with Ant-Like Agents.* IATA, 1998, pp.60-71.
4. N. Boucké. Situated Multi-Agent Approach for Distributing Control in Automatic Guided Vehicle Systems. Master Thesis, 2004.
5. R. A. Brooks. *Intelligence without representation.* Artificial Intelligence Journal, 1991, Vol. 47, pp.139-159.
6. J. J. Bryson. *Intelligence by Design, Principles of Modularity and Coordination for Engineering Complex Adaptive Agents.* PhD Dissertation: MIT, 2001.
7. L. Cabac and D. Moldt. *Formal Semantics for AUML Agent Interaction Protocol Diagrams.* In Proceedings of the 5th International Workshop on Agent-Oriented Software Engineering (AOSE 2004), pp.97-112.
8. G. Caire and others. *Agent Oriented Analysis Using MESSAGE/UML.* Agent-Oriented Software-Engineering II, Vol. 2222 of LNCS, New York: Springer, 2001, pp.119-135.
9. J. Ferber. *An Introduction to Distributed Artificial Intelligence.* Addison-Wesley, 1999.
10. M. R. Genesereth and N. Nilsson. *Logical Foundations of Artificial Intelligence.* Morgan Kaufmanns, 1997.
11. T. Holvoet and E. Steegmans. *Application-Specific Reuse of Agent Roles.* Software Engineering for Large-Scale Multi-Agent Systems, 2003, Vol. 2603 of LNCS, Springer Verlag, pp.148-164.
12. M. Ph. Huget and J. Odell. *Representing Agent Interaction Protocols with Agent UML.* In Proceedings of the 5th International Workshop on Agent-Oriented Software Engineering (AOSE 2004), pp.65-80.
13. M. Luck, R. Ashri and M. D'Inverno. *Agent-Based Software Development.* Artech House, 2004.
14. P. Maes. *Modeling Adaptive Autonomous Agents.* Artificial Life Journal, Vol. 1(1-2), 1994, pp.135-162.
15. X. Mao and E. Yu. *Organizational and Social Concepts in Agent Oriented Software Engineering.* In Proceedings of the 5th International Workshop on Agent-Oriented Software Engineering (AOSE 2004), pp.49-64.
16. M. E. Markiewicz and C. J. P. Lucena. *Object Oriented Framework Development.* ACM Crossroads Xrds7-4, 2001. See www.acm.org/crossroads/xrds7-4/frameworks.html
17. Model Driven Architecture (MDA): http://www.omg.org/mda/
18. J. Odell, M. Nodine and R. Levy. *A Metamodel for Agents, Roles, and Groups.* In Proceedings of the 5th International Workshop on Agent-Oriented Software Engineering (AOSE 2004), pp.131-146.

19. A. Omicini. *SODA: Societies and Infrastructures in the Analysis and Design of Agent-Based Systems.* Agent-Oriented Software Engineering, Vol. 1957 of LNCS, New York: Springer, 2001, pp.185-193.
20. V. Parunak. *The AARIA Agent Architecture: From Manufacturing Requirements to Agent-Based System Design.* Integrated Computer-Aided Engineering, Vol. 8(1), 2001, pp.45-58.
21. K. Rosenblatt and D. Payton. *A fine grained alternative to the subsumbtion architecture for mobile robot control.* International Joint Conference on Neural Networks, IEEE, 1989.
22. E. Steegmans, D. Weyns, T. Holvoet and Y. Berbers. *Commitment-Driven Collaboration in Situated Multi-Agent Systems: A Case Study.* Technical CW Report.
23. T. Tyrrell. *Computational Mechanisms for Action Selection.* Ph.D thesis, University of Edinburgh, 1993.
24. D. Weyns, E. Steegmans and T. Holvoet. *Protocol Based Communication for Situated Multi-Agent Systems.* In Proceedings of the Third International Conference on Autonomous Agents and Multi-Agent Systems (AAMAS 2004), ed. N. Jennings, C. Sierra, L. Sonenberg and M. Tambe, pp.118-126, New York, 2004.
25. D. Weyns, E. Steegmans and T. Holvoet. *Towards Commitments for Situated Agents.* Role-Based Collaboration at IEEE SMC 2004, International Conference on Systems, Man and Cybernetics, The Hague, The Netherlands, 2004.
26. M. Wooldridge, N. Jennings and D. Kinny. *The Gaia Methodology for Agent-Oriented Analysis and Design.* Autonomous Agents and Multi-Agent Systems, Vol. 3(3), 2000, pp.285-312.

Evaluation of Agent–Oriented Software Methodologies – Examination of the Gap Between Modeling and Platform

Jan Sudeikat[1], Lars Braubach[2], Alexander Pokahr[2], and Winfried Lamersdorf[2]

[1] University of Applied Sciences Hamburg,
Berliner Tor 3, 20099 Hamburg, Germany
Jan.Sudeikat@hamburg.de
[2] Distributed Systems and Information Systems,
Computer Science Department, University of Hamburg,
Vogt–Kölln–Str. 30, 22527 Hamburg, Germany
Tel. +49-40-42883-2091
{braubach, pokahr, lamersd}@informatik.uni-hamburg.de

Abstract. More and more effort is made to provide methodologies for the development of agent–based systems. Awareness has grown that these are necessary to develop high quality agent systems. In recent years a number of proposals have been given. Based on our experiences we argue that a complete evaluation of methodologies cannot be done without considering target platforms, because the differences between available implementations are too fundamental to be ignored. In order to conduct a suitable comparison we present a flexible evaluation framework that takes platform specific criteria into account. Part of this framework is a procedure to derive relevant criteria from the evaluated platforms and methodologies. In combination with a set of platform dependent and independent criteria our framework allows evaluation of the appropriateness of methodologies with respect to platforms. As a consequence, also the suitability of methodologies for an individual platform, or vice versa of several platforms for an individual methodology can be examined. To show the usefulness of our proposal, we evaluate the suitability of different methodologies for an example platform.

1   Introduction

Besides the necessity of reliable agent platforms, the need for the methodical development of applications has been noticed (as described in [20], [21]) and is addressed by a number of proposed methodologies for building agent–based software applications (surveyed in [40], [18]). According to [34] a methodology aids development through (1) guidance by a life cycle process, (2) a set of predefined techniques (guidelines, heuristics, etc.) and (3) allows modeling by providing a suitable notation. What these three elements comprise is different in the specific proposals. This makes it difficult for organizations to decide which one to use.

J. Odell et al. (Eds.): AOSE 2004, LNCS 3382, pp. 126–141, 2005.

The selection of the right methodology is crucial for the success of a large software project, because developers will need guidance how to use this new paradigm. According to [23], suitable methodologies are a key factor in introducing agent–orientation as an engineering approach to the industry. Since a number of methodologies have been proposed, there exists a need for structured means to select appropriate ones with respect to a concrete setting. Organizations will need guidance to select one to adopt for their own development.

To address these needs, different comparison frameworks have been proposed. These use feature–based evaluations of numerous criteria to identify superior ones. However, none of the proposed approaches takes the target agent platform into consideration. Platforms imply different concepts of agency in different peculiarities. Since the support for agent oriented concepts differs between concrete implementations, our proposal stresses that there are both platform dependent and independent criteria to evaluate. In the following pages we identify a set of aspects to take into account and show how to derive platform dependent criteria from target platforms.

To guide evaluation regarding these criteria, we present a flexible framework to examine the match between platform and methodology. It allows to examine the appropriateness of methodologies for a preselected platform or vice versa the appropriateness of different platforms for an individual methodology. This flexibility is advantageous, because software producing organizations are seldom free to choose tools and methodologies as they like. Often there will be certain restrictions, e.g. industry projects may have to focus on a single platform because a client demands its usage, or universities may favor a special methodology and need to find a suitable software environment.

The usage of our approach is clarified by an example evaluation of the appropriateness of prominent methodologies for a concrete platform, implementing the BDI architecture [31]. Following our framework we derive a number of platform dependent criteria from this implementation, and, together with platform independent criteria we examine the match between pairs of platform and methodology.

The next section gives a brief overview of proposed methodologies, and examines the comparisons of agent–oriented methodologies that have already been conducted. Section three presents our framework. First we describe the modus operandi of our approach and present thereafter the set of criteria to examine. The fourth section shows an example evaluation of a set of methodologies for a concrete platform. Finally, we conclude and give prospects for further work.

2   Background

In [16] a number of different methodologies have been arranged in a genealogy. Figure 1 gives an overview of current proposals in a similar way. It illustrates the main influences on the individual methodologies. We found Object–Orientation (OO), Knowledge Engineering (KE) and Requirements Engineering (RE) as ancestors, which have been extended by agent programming abstractions (denoted

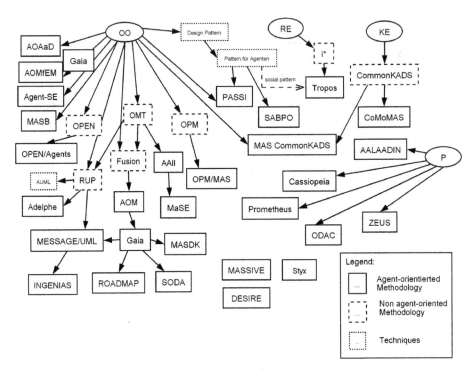

Fig. 1. Genealogy of proposed methodologies

by ovals). *P* denotes a coarse category of sources. Associated methodologies were inspired by experiences with specific agent platforms or architectures. Intermediate forms (dotted rectangles) have been extended to truly agent–oriented methodologies (rectangles). A complete list of references to these methodologies is omitted here for the sake of brevity, it can be found in [38].

A small amount of work has been conducted to compare agent–oriented methodologies. These approaches found two sources of features to examine. First, they adopt general software–engineering criteria, which have been found relevant to the evaluations of methodologies according to various paradigms. Secondly, they identified specific criteria that are needed to support agent–oriented concepts in development. All of them gather a set of criteria, which is supposed to be independent from the field of application or platform. They point out what is needed for a comprehensive methodology, together with individual drawbacks and advantages.

O'Malley and DeLoach [25] collected a set of criteria to guide organizations in making the decision, whether an AOSE methodology should be adopted, or if an object–oriented methodology is appropriate for a particular project. They distinguish between *Management Issues* and *Project Requirements*. The criteria have been validated by a survey [25]. Management issues examine the consequences, an adoption of a methodology causes for the (software producing) organization. Aspects like cost and suitability for the organization are examined. Project requirements concentrate on the technical issues. The authors found a set of aspects that need to be modeled (such as interactions, distribution, etc.). These criteria are rated and a weighted mean value is calculated. Kitchenham [22] describes the vagueness and shortcomings of these approaches.

Cernuzzi and Rossi [8] proposed a qualitative analysis followed by a quantitative rating. They constructed a so called *Attributes Tree*, which organizes the found criteria in weighted branches. After rating the leafs the value of the root can be calculated and compared to other methodologies.

The authors identified three kinds of criteria. *Internal Attributes* characterize the internal structures of the agents, *Interaction Attributes* describe how the interactions inside the system can be modeled. Finally, the *Other Process Requirements* judge the design and development–process, proposed by the methodologies.

The above described proposals compared the methodologies by a screening of the criteria, which should be compared as unbiased as possible. Dam and Winikoff [10] evaluated methodologies by surveying inventors of the selected methodologies and developers, who modeled a case study. They divided their found criteria into *Concepts & Properties*, *Modeling & Notation*, *Processes* and *Pragmatics*.

The concepts and processes are suitable for a feature–based analysis. They examine the extent to which specific concepts are supported and the coverage of different stages in development. Besides requirements, architectural/detailed design, implementation and testing, these also include deployment and maintenance. The other two categories examine the notation and the general management and technical characteristics of the methodologies. Judging the appropriateness of a notation and the mentioned characteristics is a challenging task. Dam and Winikoff successfully addressed it by a survey approach.

Shehory and Sturm [35] developed a catalog of criteria for feature–based analysis of AOSE methodologies. They distinguished between *Software–Engineering Criteria* and *Agent–Based Characteristics*. Their performed analysis identified areas of improvement, to meet the needs of developers.

In [37] they recently adopted the classification from [10] and combined the criteria from this work with their own. They give a sound overview of what a mature methodology should offer in the field of agent–oriented software engineering. Their set of criteria is appropriate to show the drawbacks of currently proposed methodologies and therefore gives suggestions for further development.

3   A Platform Dependent Comparison Framework

All of the approaches characterized in section 2 focus on the identification of a superior methodology among a group of candidates. These are influenced by previous work, examining methodologies of various paradigms. The spread of e.g. object oriented methodologies was possible, because there was a sound un-

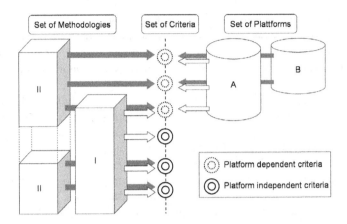

Fig. 2. Modus Operandi for the Evaluation Framework

derstanding of the object–oriented paradigm in itself. For agent systems we lack this sound foundation to build methodologies upon (also described in [2]). There is ongoing research on how to bridge the gap between agent oriented design and it's actual implementation, as demonstrated at the session *From Design to Implementation* of the AOSE–2004 Workshop ([1], [36] and [24]). Even if we look at a particular architecture - like BDI - we still see a lot of differences between the available implementations and theories. These denote conceptual differences in the expressiveness for the properties of individual agents. We conclude that, in opposition to other software engineering paradigms, which may be language independent, the use of agent–oriented methodologies is to a certain extent dependent from the used platform. Different implementations of agent architectures need different levels of expressiveness. The suitability of a methodology is highly influenced by the support for this expressiveness.

Having noted this, we present a framework to evaluate the appropriateness of methodologies in relation to platforms. Figure 2 gives a visual description of our approach. Two kinds of criteria are evaluated. Platform independent criteria can be examined in a feature analysis, for platform dependent ones the properties of the implemented concepts need to be compared to properties supported in the methodology. The match between them is examined to show their appropriateness. As Figure 2 depicts, not all features of a methodology will match properties of all platforms. For our purposes it is important to identify the differences. The shared absence of properties is regarded as a match, since it also identifies appropriateness.

This approach allows an important adjustment to evaluation for different purposes. As stated earlier, software producing organizations are seldom free to choose tools and methodologies unbiasedly. Industry projects may have to focus on a single platform because their client demands a dedicated platform, universities may favor a special methodology and thus, need to find a suitable software environment. Premises of this kind are regarded by our approach. There are three possible relations for evaluation. Evaluations of one methodology to many

Table 1. Overview of the evaluated criteria[1]

1st Phase: screening		2nd Phase: examination	
Concepts	Process	Notation	Pragmatics
Internal Architecture*	Coverage of Workflows	Usability	Tool Support
Social Architecture*	Management	Expressiveness	Connectivity*
Communication*	Complexity	Refinement	Documentation
Autonomy	Properties of Process	Dependency of Models	Usage in Projects
Pro–activity		Traceability	
Distribution*		Clear definition	
		Modularity	

platforms (1:n), several methodologies for one specific platform (n:1; see the later given example) and a n:m scenario where n methodologies are rated to m platforms (see Figure 2). All of these can be conducted in the same modus operandi. Evaluations of the latter relations force the conductor to deliberate about match vs. quality of the methodology. A good matching methodology may not comprise all the platform independent criteria. Desirable is a methodology that matches a given platform and supports as many of the independent criteria as possible.

3.1   Criteria

Before an examination following our approach can take place the relevant criteria need to be identified. The selection is based on the above described directions of comparison, but we have found a set of aspects that every evaluation has to take into account. For our framework we adopted the classification of these criteria from [10]. Therefore, the criteria are separated into four groups. *Concepts*, *Notation*, *Process* and *Pragmatics*. Table 1 lists our selection of criteria.[1] The concepts are mostly platform dependent, because even for a concrete agent architecture (e.g. BDI), there is no sound foundation for the properties of the single concepts. For example, the representation and expressiveness of goals varies greatly among different implementations. The notation and process are independent from the platform. These aspects describe the usage of a methodology. Also the pragmatics concentrate on an examination of the support for a methodology. The following sections will give a further explanation of the listed criteria.

The Agent–Oriented Concepts. These Criteria have to be supported by suitable methodologies.

Internal Architecture*. The concepts which describe the internals of an agent vary greatly between the proposed architectures. For example, BDI architectures [15] describe agents with notions of mental attitudes, other approaches use different internal representations (e.g. Subsumption-architecture [5], Soar [39]).

---

[1] Platform dependent criteria are marked with an asterisk.

Social Architecture*. These concepts describe, which social models are used to organize the multi agent systems. Prominent models are the notions of *groups*(e.g. AALAADIN [12]) or *teams* [17], others allow agents to offer services, e.g. via a yellow pages directory [13].

Communication*. Different Communication models have been proposed. Prominent models are message based (e.g. speech acts using ontologies [14] or event based message exchange), others use memory based (e.g. blackboard [9]) architectures.

Autonomy. The abilities of an agent to solve problems in an autonomous way, is illustrated by the modeling of functionalities or tasks an agent can execute on its own authority. In addition, it is helpful to express the mechanisms used to make decisions about which actions to take.

Pro–activity. It is needed to express the proactive abilities of a agent.

Distribution*. It is desirable to be able to express the allocation of agents to places in the environment.

The Notation. The notation defines abstract views on the most important aspects of the developed system. It comprises symbols, syntax and semantic. The **Usability** is supported by a clearly defined and intuitively comprehensible notation that is easy to draw. To support the requirements analysis, the analysis and design of the system to build, an **expressive** notation supports several views on the system to develop. It allows to express the functional, structural and dynamic properties, where the structure includes the data and the flow of data inside the system.

Furthermore, these models should support some technical criteria to allow convenient usage. During development, the **refinement** and **modularity** of the single models should be supported. Models should **depend** on each other and single artifacts should be **traceable**. It is indispensable that syntax and semantic are **clearly defined**.

The Process. To evaluate the proposed development processes we compare them to the "Unified Process" (UP) [19]. In [37] it is already proposed to evaluate the **coverage** of the 5 basic workflows from the UP. The selection of the UP is arbitrary. It is suitable as a well known reference to ease comparison. Many more complete methodologies have been developed (e.g. the Rational Unified Process [32]), but an illustration of the coverage of these 5 basic activities is suitable, due to the immaturity of current proposals. The individual workflows are: *Requirements* (gathering and documentation of necessities), *Analysis* (further examination of the problem domain), *Design* (defining how the software will be implemented), *Implementation* (conversion of design into executables) and *Testing* (development of test–cases, their execution and debugging). Furthermore, we consider the support for the **management** of an agent–oriented software project. Currently this support mainly consists of heuristics and guidelines. The **complexity** of the process measures the necessary effort to learn and to use it. Favorable is one where the tasks of the single development steps and the sequence of them is easy to understand and to comprehend. Finally, **proper-ties of process** note special properties, e.g. whether it is an iterative approach or not, top–down or bottom–up, etc.

The Pragmatics. The pragmatics are dominated by the impressions of the available (CASE–)**tool support**. Evaluating these tools is a difficult task itself. Their usability is influenced by many aspects, in our evaluation we tried to give consideration to ergonomic aspects. Tools should be easy to use and support the whole development cycle. The currently available tools allow drawing the notations and checks for consistency. The **connectivity** describes the platform dependent aspects of the tool support. When tool support is available it is desir-able to have a connection between the design artifacts and the target platform to use it seamlessly in development. In the most convenient case there will be the possibility to directly generate code for target platforms. Another impor-tant aspect is the available **documentation** which has a great impact on the usability and understanding of a methodology. Also the documentation of the tools is important here. Reported experiences with the **usage in projects** is an important factor for judging the maturity of a methodology.

3.2   Evaluation Process

The actual evaluation takes place in two steps. First, the abstract concepts set need to be concretized with respect to methodologies and target platform(s). Second, they can be examined together with our proposed platform independent criteria.

In opposition to the properties of notations and pragmatics, the support of concepts and the properties of a proposed process can be examined by a simple screening of the single methodologies. Evaluating the notations and pragmatics is a challenging task itself. It has to take objective criteria as well as ergonomic aspects into consideration. Also the usability of CASE–Tools (an important part of the pragmatics) is influenced by them. The work of Wood et al. [41] gives hints how to examine a notation, and Kitchenham [22] is also taking the examination of tools into account. But differences are subtle and subjective to the conductor screening specific candidates. For our example, we made a case study to evaluate these. Other possibilities are formal experiments or surveys according to the available resources and purposes.

4   Example Evaluation

To give an example for an evaluation following our framework, we will evaluate how the methodologies *MaSE* [11], *Tropos* [4] and *Prometheus* [27] (see Figure 1) match up the *Jadex* [29], [3] agent platform. Jadex, developed at the Distributed Systems and Information Systems group at the Computer Science Department of the University of Hamburg, is an add–on to the popular JADE[2] agent plat-

---

[2] http://sharon.cselt.it/projects/jade/

form. It extends JADE with sophisticated BDI mechanisms and is under busy development.

The Multiagent Systems Engineering Methodology (MaSE) proposes a complete life cycle methodology for multi agent systems. It guides the developer from the specification of the system to the final implementation. Agents are described as finite state machines.

Tropos has been influenced by the i^* framework from Yu [43] for analysis of the *early requirements* of a software system. It leads the developers to an understanding of an agent–oriented system as an organization of actors. These seek to achieve goals by means of plans and have dependencies on other actors.

Prometheus has been influenced by the JACK[3] agent platform. Static structures of multi agent systems are clearly illustrated. This methodology allows very detailed modeling by descriptors, which hold design specific properties.

These preselected methodologies are well documented, most mature, support BDI–concepts and CASE–tools are available (in [10] the same selection has been found).

We are here evaluating the suitability for only one platform. Note that this forms an *3:1* relation (three methodologies are rated to one platform). According to the modus operandi we first derive the relevant platform dependent criteria from the target platform. Thereafter, the concepts and process are rated by a screening, and finally, the notations and tools are evaluated using a case study. The presented considerations are based on our own evaluation of a suitable methodology for this BDI platform, which has been conducted in the context of a diploma thesis [38].

4.1   Selection of Criteria

Considering only one platform makes it fairly easy to identify the internal, social architectures and the communication concepts. Finding the relevant criteria means to examine the platforms and methodologies in order to find aspects of the platforms, which need to be supported by methodologies and vice versa. For our example evaluation we found:

- **Internal Architecture:**
    Goals, Plans, Beliefs (BDI–Architecture). Since Jadex is focused on the use of BDI–concepts, these have to be supported by the methodology. It is needed to be able to describe how goals (by which plans) can be achieved and which beliefs these plans have to access. Properly described elements allow appropriate modeling of properties to implement using Jadex.
    Capabilities. This is a concept to unitize BDI systems into functional modules, as described in [6].
    Events. These express the reactiveness of agents. It should be possible to model changes in the environment of single agents by events. Jadex also

---

[3] http://www.agent-software.com

supports internal events to express changes inside an agent. The kind of event should be exactly describable, to allow inferring the filters Jadex uses to distinguish events.

- **Social Architecture:**
  Roles. Some methodologies use Roles as a concept to structure a multi agent system and to identify single agent classes. Therefore, we need to examine how Jadex supports their implementation.
- **Communication:**
  Protocols. These characterize the communication between the agents and are supported by the underlying JADE platform.
  Messages. In Jadex, the exchanged messages follow the FIPA model of agent communication [14].

4.2 Examining the Concepts and Process

Table 2 summarizes our results for the concepts and processes. All three methodologies develop a system coming from the identified goals. As opposed to MaSE, Tropos and Prometheus use the BDI–notions throughout the whole development cycle. In all methodologies, the modeled goal concepts differ from the ones used in Jadex. In Prometheus and MaSE agents are associated to system goals. Tropos is more suitable, because both system and individual goals in addition to the contribution/decomposition of plans are described. Modeled plans in all methodologies lack Jadex specific properties. Only Prometheus describes the individual beliefs of agents in detail, but the structures of the beliefbases differ, causing a slight mismatch. Tropos and Prometheus support the concept of capabilities. Only in Prometheus, events are stated explicitly. It is also distinguished between *percepts* (recognized changes in the environment) and the resulting relevant events (*incidents*) for the system. Jadex is not aware of this distinction. The other methodologies describe events implicitly in their UML–based models for design.

Roles are supported by MaSE and Tropos. Roles are used as means to identify the different types of agents the system will be composed of. Roles are not explicitly supported by Jadex, they can be implemented using services. Since neither Prometheus nor Jadex support this specific concept, they match closely. Protocols between agents are described in Tropos and Prometheus by the sequence of transmitted messages. Instead MaSE describes the exchange of messages in relation to the processing inside the agents. However, these representations are of the same suitability for Jadex. In MaSE and Tropos, the content of a message is not explicitly described. Only Prometheus defines special descriptors to describe properties of messages. These are not compliant to FIPA ACL messages and are therefore slightly mismatching the messages used in Jadex.

The autonomy is described in Tropos through associations between agents, their goals and the available plans. In addition, the dependencies between the agents are described. MaSE describes the autonomy by *tasks*, which an agent is capable to execute on its own responsibility. Prometheus supports a similar concept, *functionalities* are at the agent's disposal to achieve goals. Therefore,

Table 2. Evaluation results: Concepts and Process

		MaSE	Tropos	Prometheus
Concepts:				
Internal Architecture	Goals*	$+|\neq|+$	$+|\approx|+$	$+|\neq|+$
	Plans*	$+|\approx|+$	$+|\approx|+$	$+|\approx|+$
	Beliefs*	$+|\approx|+$	$+|\approx|+$	$+|\approx|+$
	Capabilities*	$-|\neq|+$	$+|\approx|+$	$+|=|+$
	Events*	$+|\approx|+$	$+|\approx|+$	$+|\approx|+$
Social Architecture	Roles*	$+|\neq|-$	$+|\neq|-$	$-|=|-$
Communication	Protocols*	$+|\neq|-$	$+|\neq|-$	$+|\neq|-$
	Messages*	$+|\approx|+$	$+|\approx|+$	$+|\approx|+$
	Autonomy	$++$	$++$	$++$
	Pro–activity	$+$	$++$	$++$
	Distribution*	$+|=|+$	$-|\neq|+$	$-|\neq|+$
Process:				
	Coverage of Workflows	3/5	4/5	4/5
	Management	n.a.	n.a.	n.a.
	Complexity	$++$	$++$	$++$
	Properties of Process	for all iterative and top-down		
Support		$--$: poor $-$: not well n.a.: not available +: well $++$: very well		
Match		**Left hand side:** methodology supports property: $+$ / - **Middle:** match between the properties no match: $\neq$ coarse match: $\approx$ good match: $=$ **Right hand side:** platform supports property: $+$ / -		

autonomy is clearly expressed by all methodologies. The expressiveness of pro–activity is closely related to the BDI concepts. Tropos and Prometheus are taking advantage of their comprehensive support for BDI notions. The distribution and mobility of agents is only displayed by MaSE, matching Jadex. The other methodologies just model the acquaintance and communicational relationships between agents.

In [4] the development phases of Tropos are shown in relation to other methodologies by comparing the coverage of different development phases. Figure 3 displays the coverage of the different workflows from the UP in a similar way. To guide grading, other prominent approaches are included (Gaia [42] and MESSAGE/UML [7] along with the AUML–Notation[4]). MaSE supports the development from requirements analysis to implementation. In Tropos, the analysis of the requirements is more comprehensive. The so called early requirements of the system are modeled according to the i* framework by Yu [43]. Prometheus is also taking testing into account [30]. Guidance in management of an agent oriented software project is fairly small. For the most part, merely heuristics

---

[4] http://www.auml.org

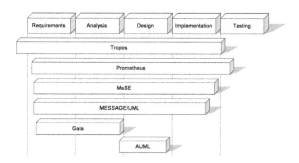

Fig. 3. Coverage of the different workflows from the UP (according to [4])

are given. In the examined methodologies, the proposed progression in development is clearly described and easy to comprehend. They all propose an iterative approach and develop top–down, from the analysis of the requirements to the identification and description of the single agents.

4.3   Examining the Notation and Tools – Modeling a Case Study

Beginners are guided in the usage of Jadex with a tutorial [3]. In small examples the implementation of agent–oriented concepts is presented. We modeled the last and most complex of these examples that combines the core concepts to a small and therefore easy to comprehend multi agent system. Aim of this system is to translate sentences by forwarding requests for the translation of single words to a dedicated agent, which has access to a dictionary. This translation service is registered at a Directory Facilitator (see [3] for details).

The made experiences in the usage lead to an impression on the expressiveness of notations and usability of the methodology in itself (including the tools).

Another promising approach to gain more experiences is modeling a *Challenge Exemplar* as proposed in [44], which leads to a sounder understanding of the strengths and weaknesses of the different methodologies.

MaSE. Usage of this methodology showed its focus on modeling the communications. Also the flow of control inside a plan is very obviously displayed. The *pragmatics* are dominated by the CASE–Tool *agentTool* 2.0,[5] which is freely available and comfortable to use. We used it merely as a drawing tool, because connectivity is only given for agent platforms which differ fundamentally from Jadex. Methodology and tool are well documented in conference proceedings. According to [10], this methodology has been most widely used in university projects, no industrial use is known.

Tropos. Examining the early requirements has not been suitable for our small case study. These are more concentrated on the situation in which the system

---

[5] http://www.cis.ksu.edu/ sdeloach/ai/agentool.htm

to develop is needed. Process and models lead the developers to understand the agent based application as an organization of dependent individuals. This is especially valuable for inexperienced users to get used to this new paradigm. While lacking a specialized CASE-Tool, conventional support for UML is suitable during design. For the earlier phases of development, specialized tools supporting the notation from i* can be used.[6] There is no known connectivity to agent platforms from these tools. Documentation is nearly exclusively available as conference submissions, but [4] gives a comprehensive description. Tropos has been used in a few projects (according to [10]).

Prometheus. On the design level Prometheus describes implementation related details using descriptors. Central elements are the System and Agent Overview Diagrams. They give an intuitive overview of the system and the agents. This unusual and exceptional non–UML based notation is supported by the *Jack Development Environment*, an integrated development environment for the commercial JACK agent platform. Code is directly generated, which means best connectivity for this platform. In addition, the *Prometheus Design Tool*[7] (PDT) is freely available. It is a drawing and documentation tool (no connectivity), which is easy to use and very helpful for the use of the notation. The diagrams give a general impression, but the associated descriptors hold the relevant information. Being able to navigate these descriptors by the visual representations is most valuable and allows to get a quick impression on the single elements. Besides conference contributions, there are also useful tutorial notes available [26]. Like in MaSE, this methodology has been used in a number of university projects [10].

Result of Evaluation. All three evaluated methodologies are basically capable to support the development of applications using Jadex. A big disadvantage of MaSE is that it does not use BDI concepts throughout the whole development cycle. Prometheus is unique in its detailed description of the individual components forming the agent system and the freely available CASE–Tool. In addition, the used criteria are matching to the greatest extent, the process is nearly as extensive as in Tropos and the modeling language is slightly more comprehensive.

Therefore, it is concluded to propose the use of Prometheus for development with Jadex. This leads to considerations how to include Prometheus in development efforts. Since Jadex is a fairly new development, there is currently no connectivity between Prometheus and Jadex. Therefore, we evaluated the possible exchange of detailed design information between the above mentioned PDT and the Jadex platform. Agents in Jadex are defined by so called *Agent Definition Files* (ADF). These are XML descriptions of their properties, and a set of Java classes (referenced in the ADF) to implement the desired behavior. In [38] a prototype has been developed to transform PDT project files into a set of ADFs

---

[6] Overview of available tools at: http://www.troposproject.org/

[7] http://www.cs.rmit.edu.au/agents/pdt/

and vice versa. The match is not comprehensive enough to allow automatic trans-formation, the developers need to add a number of implementation dependent details to get fully functional ADFs. Since the match between methodology and platform has been examined, areas of further improvement which allow transfer of detailed design information between modeling and platform (connectivity) are indicated by the evaluation itself. The discovered mismatches identify, which im-provements of agent oriented concepts are needed (in methodology or platform) to cover a common expressiveness. As a partial result of the described evalu-ation, we adopted the Prometheus methodology for a larger research project, which proposes an agent oriented approach to the problem domain of hospital logistics [28].

5   Conclusions

In this paper we presented a flexible framework for evaluation of agent–oriented methodologies that takes platform specific criteria into account. This frame-work is based on the observation that available agent platforms imply differ-ent concepts of agency in different peculiarities. Therefore, the match between methodologies and platforms is examined. A methodology is well suited for a platform if the properties of a methodology match the properties of the plat-form used for development. The framework stresses that there are both plat-form dependent and independent criteria to evaluate. The dependent ones need to be derived from the proposed list of abstract concepts with respect to the candidates before they can be examined. Evaluation has to take the nature of criteria into account. Some are suitable for a simple feature–analysis, others are more subtle and subjective, their assessment is therefore a difficult task in itself. Case studies, formal experiments and surveys are appropriate for their consideration.

Considering the above described match makes it possible to evaluate different scenarios. It is possible to compare one methodology to many platforms (1:n), several methodologies for one specific platform (n:1) and n:m scenarios where n methodologies are rated to m platforms. This flexibility fits the needs of most software producing organizations. To interpret the evaluation results correctly, it is needed to deliberate about the match vs. quality of proposals. A well suited methodology is not only perfectly matching a target platform, but also support-ing a wide range of platform independent criteria.

The usage of our framework was illustrated by an example evaluation of a group of well known methodologies for their suitability to support development using the Jadex platform. This example usage also illustrated how to derive platform dependent criteria from the proposed abstract concepts set.

Future improvements to the presented framework may result from an ex-amination whether it is useful to consider *application dependent* criteria. For software producing organizations, the problem domain according to a concrete project may have impact on the selection of platforms and methodologies.

References

1. Amor M., Fuentes L. and Vallecillo A. "Bridging the gap Between Agent–Oriented Design and Implementation Using MDA", In Proc. of AOSE 2004 Workshop, 2004.
2. Bernon C., Cossentino M. and Gleizes M. P. "A Study of some Multi–Agent Meta–Models", In Proc. of AOSE 2004 Workshop, 2004.
3. Braubach L. und Pokahr A. *Jadex Tutorial* - Release 0.9, 2003.
4. Bresciani P., Giorgini P., Giunchiglia F., Mylopoulos J., Perini A. *Troops: An agent-oriented software development methodology*, Technical Report DIT-02-0015, University of Trento, 2002.
5. Brooks R. "Elephants Don't play chess". Robotics and Autonomous Systems, 6:3-15, 1990.
6. Busetta P., Howden N., Rönnquist R. und Hodgson A. "Structuring BDI Agents in Functional Clusters". in N. R. Jennings and Y. Lesperance, Intelligent Agents VI. Springer Verlag, Berlin, 1999.
7. Caire G., Leal F., Chainho P., Evans R., Garijo F., Gomez J., Pavon J., Kearney P., Stark J. and Massonet P. "Agent oriented analysis using message/uml". In Agent-Oriented Software Engineering (AOSE), 2001.
8. Cernuzzi L. und Rossi G. "On the evaluation of agent oriented modeling methods", In Proc. of Agent Oriented Methodology Workshop, Seattle, 2002.
9. Corkill D. D. "Blackboard Systems", AI Expert, 6(9):40-47, September, 1991.
10. Dam K. H. and Winikoff M. "Comparing Agent-Oriented Methodologies", In Proc. of the Fifth Int. Bi-Conference Workshop on Agent-Oriented Information Systems (at AAMAS03), 2003.
11. DeLoach S. A. "Analysis and design using MaSE and agentTool". In Proc. of the 12th MAICS, 2001.
12. Ferber J. und Gutknecht O. "A Meta-Model for the Analysis and Design of Organizations in Multi- Agent Systems", In Proc. of the Third Int. Conf. on Multi-Agent Systems (ICMAS98) Paris, France, 1998.
13. Foundation for Intelligent Physical Agents. *FIPA Abstract Architecture Specification*, SC00001L, 2002. http://www.fipa.org/specs/fipa00001/
14. Foundation for Intelligent Physical Agents. *FIPA ACL Message Structure Specification*, SC00061G, 2002. http://www.fipa.org/specs/fipa00061/
15. Georgeff M. and Lansky A. "Reactive Reasoning and Planing: An Experiments With a Mobile Robot", in Proc. of the 1987 National Conference on Artificial Intelligence (AAAI 87), 1987.
16. Henderson–Sellers B. and Gorton I. "Agent-based Software Development Methodologies", White Paper, Summary of Workshop at the OOPSLA 2002, 2003.
17. Hodgson A., Rönnquist R., Busetta P. *Specification of Coordinated Agent Behavior (The SimpleTeam Approach)*, Technical Report 99-05, Agent Oriented Software Pty. Ltd., 1999.
18. Iglesias C.A., Garijo M. und González J.C. "A Survey of Agent-Oriented Methodologies". In Intelligent Agents V – Proc. of the Fifth Int. Workshop on Agent Theories, Architectures, and Languages (ATAL-98), 1999.
19. Jacobson I., Booch G., Rumbaugh J. *The Unified Software Development Process.* Object Technology Series. Addison Wesley, 1999.
20. Jennings N.R. "On Agent–Based Software Engineering", Artificial Intelligence, 117(2), 2000:277.
21. Jennings N.R. und Wooldridge M. *Agent-Oriented Software Engineering*, Handbook of Agent Technology AAAI/MIT Press, 2000.

22. Kitchenham B. *DESMET: A method for evaluating Software Engineering methods and tools*, Technical Report TR96-09, ISSN:1353-7776, 1996.
23. Luck M., McBurney P. und Preist C. *Agent Technology: Enabling Next Generation Computing: A roadmap for agent–based computing*. AgentLink report, ISBN 0854 327886, 2003. http://www.agentlink.org/roadmap/index.html
24. Mao X., Yu E. "Oranisational and Social Conceps in Agent Oriented Software Engineering", In Proc. of AOSE 2004 Workshop, 2004.
25. O'Malley S. A. and DeLoach S. A. "Determining When to Use an Agent-Oriented Software Engineering Paradigm", In Proc. of the AOSE-2001, 2001.
26. Padgham L. "Design of Multi Agent Systems", Tutorial at Net.ObjectDays, October 7-10, 2002, Erfurt, Germany, 2002.
27. Padgham L. und Winikoff M. "Prometheus: A Pragmatic Methodology for Engineering Intelligent Agents", in Proc. of the workshop on Agent-oriented methodologies at OOPSLA 2002.
28. Paulussen T. O., Zöller A., Heinzl A., Pokahr A., Braubach L., Lamersdorf W.: "Dynamic Patient Scheduling in Hospitals" in: Agent Technology in Business Applications (ATeBA-04), 2004.
29. Pokahr A., Braubach L. and Lamersdorf W. *Jadex: Implementing a BDI-Infrastructure for JADE Agents*, EXP – in search of innovation, 3(3):76-85, 2003.
30. Poutakidis D., Padgham L., Winikoff M.: "Debugging multi-agent systems using design artifacts: The case of interaction protocols". In Proc. of the First Int. Joint Conf. on Autonomous Agents and Multi Agent Systems (AAMAS'02), 2002.
31. Rao A. und Georgeff M. "BDI-agents: from theory to practice". In Proc. of the First Intl. Conf. on Multiagent Systems, 1995.
32. Rational Software White Paper. *Rational Unified Process: Best Practices for Software Development Teams*, 2001.
33. Rumbaugh J., Jacobson I. und Booch G. *The Unified Modeling Language Reference Manual*, Addison-Wesley, 1999.
34. Rumbaugh J., Blaha M., Premerlani W., Eddy F. und Lorensen W. *Object–Oriented Modeling and Design*, Prentice–Hall, 1991.
35. Shehory O. and Sturm A. "Evaluation of modeling techniques for agent-based systems". In Proc. of the 5th Int. Conf. on Autonomous Agents, ACM Press, 2001.
36. Steegmans E., Weyns D., Holvoet T. and Berbers Y. "Designing Roles for Situated Agents", In Proc. of AOSE 2004 Workshop, 2004.
37. Sturm A. and Shehory O. "A Framework for Evaluating Agent-Oriented Methodologies", Workshop on Agent-Oriented Information System (AOIS), 2003.
38. Sudeikat J. "Betrachtung und Auswahl der Methoden zur Entwicklung von Agentensystemen", diploma thesis, in German, HAW Hamburg, 2004.
39. Tambe M. "Agent Architectures for Flexible, Practical Teamwork". In Proc. of the Nat. Conf. on Artificial Intelligence, AAAI, 1997.
40. Tveit A. "A survey of Agent-Oriented Software Engineering". In: NTNU Computer Science Graduate Student Conference, 2001.
41. Wood B., Pethia R., Gold L.R. and Firth R. *A guide to the assessment of software development methods*, Technical Report 88-TR-8, 1988.
42. Wooldridge M. J., Jennings N. R. und Kinny D. "The Gaia methodology for agent-oriented analysis and design". Autonomous Agents and Multi-Agent Systems, 3(3):285–312 , 2000.
43. Yu, E. "Towards Modelling and Reasoning Support for Early-Phase Requirements Engineering". Proc. of 3rd IEEE Int. Symp. on Requirements Engineering, 1997.
44. Yu E. and Cysneiros L. M. "Agent-Oriented Methodologies - Towards A Challenge Exemplar". CEUR Workshop Proceedings, 2002.

A Formal Approach to Design and Reuse Agent and Multiagent Models

Vincent Hilaire[1], Olivier Simonin[1], Abder Koukam[1], and Jacques Ferber[2]

[1] Université de Technologie de Belfort Montbéliard., 90010 Belfort Cedex, France
vincent.hilaire@utbm.fr
(33) 384 583 009
[2] LIRMM Université Montpellier II - CNRS, 161 rue Ada
34392 Montpellier Cedex 5 - France

Abstract. While there are many useful models of agents and multi-agent systems, they are typically defined in an informal way and applied in an ad-hoc fashion. Consequently, multi-agent system designers have been unable to fully exploit these models commonalities and specialise or reuse them for specific problems. In order to fully exploit these models and facilitate their reuse we propose a formal approach based upon organisational concepts. The formal notation is the result of the composition of Object-Z and statecharts. The semantics of this multi-formalisms is defined by transition systems. This operational semantics enables validation and verification of specifications. We present this approach through the specification of the satisfaction-altruism model which has been used to design situated multi-agent systems. We put the emphasis on the specification of a mobile robot architecture based on the refinement of this model. The availability of such generic models is a fundamental basis for reuse. We also show how to analyse the specification by validation and verification.

1 Introduction

While there are many useful models of agents and multi-agent systems, they are typically defined in an informal way and applied in an ad-hoc fashion. Consequently, multi-agent system designers have been unable to fully exploit these models commonalities and specialise or reuse them for specific problems. We believe, and the experience bear this out, that formal specification can be used to describe model concepts which can be refined to fulfil a particular system needs.

A whole range of methodological efforts relating to MAS have been undertaken, and can be divided into those that are based upon semi-formal models [2, 4, 22] on the one hand, and those that are based on formal models [17, 11, 24]. A drawback of semi-formal methods is that they do not allow validation or verification of MAS. Among formal models many impose specific agent architecture like the BDI one and are not well fitted to enable reuse of concepts. The aim of this paper is to present a formal approach for the specification of MAS models and their reuse. This formal approach allows validation and verification and is presented through a case study. First a formal specification of a multi-agent model is given then it is refined for a specific application.

J. Odell et al. (Eds.): AOSE 2004, LNCS 3382, pp. 142–157, 2005.

The specification approach is based on a formal notation OZS [7] and an organisational framework [12]. The organisational framework gives methodological rules in order to specify a system in terms of an organisational meta-model named RIO which stands for Role, Interaction and Organisation [13]. This point of view is the basis of several other specification approaches such as [24, 6, 23]. The OZS notation is the result of the composition of Object-Z [5] and state-charts [9]. This multi-formalisms notation allows the modelling of systems with both reactive and functional aspects. Indeed, the basic construct of this notation is an Object-Z class which encapsulates a statechart. The Object-Z class specify attributes and operations in a set-theoretic fashion and the statechart specifies how the class react to external and internal events. This notation allows the prototyping and the verification of produced specifications. The prototyping and verification processes enable the production of correct specifications which can be refined downto executable code as shown in the figure 1. Each concept of the RIO meta-model is specified by an OZS class which may encapsulates a statechart in order to specify behaviours.

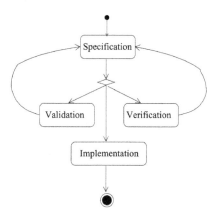

Fig. 1. Specification refinement process

We present this approach through the formal specification of a multi-agent architecture: the satisfaction-altruism model [20, 21]. This model is based on a behaviour-based architecture as [1] and introduces a cooperation mechanism. This one is defined as reactions to the perception of simple signals broadcasted by agents. We illustrate the refinement of the resulting formal model in order to specify a mobile robot application. However, the specification approach isn't limited to behaviour-based architecture. Indeed, in [8] we have specified a mentalistic based architecture.

The paper is organised as follows : section 2 introduces the OZS notation. Section 3 abstracts the satisfaction-altruism model. Section 4 presents the formal specification of the satisfaction-altruism model with the OZS notation and section 5 the mobile robots extension. Section 6 illustrates prototyping and verification on this case study. Eventually, section 7 concludes.

2   OZS Notation

Many specification formalisms can be used to specify entire system but few, if any, are particularly suited to model all aspects of such systems. For large or complex systems, like MAS, the specification may use more than one formalism or extend one formalism.

Our choice is to use Object-Z to specify the transformational aspects and statecharts to specify the reactive aspects. Object-Z extends Z [17] with object-oriented specification support. The basic construct is the class which encapsulates state schema and operation schemas which may affect its variables.

Statecharts extend finite state automata with constructs for specifying parallelism, nested states and broadcast communication for events. Both language have constructs which enable refinement of specification. Moreover, statecharts have an operational semantic which allows the execution of a specification.

We introduce a multi-formalisms notation that consists in integrating statecharts in Object-Z classes. The class describes the attributes and operations of the objects. This description is based upon set theory and first order predicates logic. The statechart describes the possible states of the object and events which may change these states. A statechart included in an Object-Z class can use attributes and operations of the class. The sharing mechanism used is based on name identity. Moreover, we introduce basic types [*Event*, *Action*, *Attribute*]. *Event* is the set of events which trigger transitions in statecharts. *Action* is the set of statecharts actions and Object-Z classes operations. *Attribute* is the set of objects attributes.

The *LoadLock* class illustrates the integration of the two formalisms. It specifies a *LoadLock* composed of two doors which states evolve concurrently. Parallelism between the two doors is expressed by the dashed line between *DOOR*1 and *DOOR*2. The first door reacts to *activate*1 and *deactivate*1 events. When someone enter the *LoadLock* he first activate the first door enter the *LoadLock* and deactivate the first door. The transition triggered by *deactivate*1 event execute the *inLL* operation which sets the *someoneInLL* boolean to true. Someone which is between the first and the second door can activate the second door so as to open it.

```
_ LoadLock _____

  |  _____
  |  someoneInLL : 𝔹
  |  _____

  |  _ INIT _____
  |  | ¬ someoneInLL

  |  _ inLL _____   _ outLL _____
  |  | ΔsomeoneInLL                | ΔsomeoneInLL
  |  | _____          | _____
  |  | someoneInLL'                | ¬ someoneInLL'
  |
```

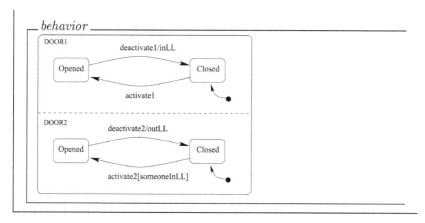

The notation for attribute modification consists of the modified attributes which belongs to the Δ-list. In any operation sub-schema, attributes before their modification are noted by their names and attributes after the operation are suffixed by '.

The result of the composition of Object-Z and statecharts seems particularly suited in order to specify MAS. Indeed, each formalism has constructs which enable complex structure specification. Moreover, aspects such as reactivity and concurrency can be easily dealt with.

3   Overview of Satisfaction-Altruism Model

The satisfaction-altruism model has been developed to integrate intentional cooperative behaviours into the collective solving problem approach. Assume the system is composed of simple self-organised entities (reactive agents) working for a common goal. Intentional cooperation is integrated thanks to three concepts.

The first concept is personal satisfaction. It is a value computed continuously by each agent (noted P), representing the evolution of the current task. At each step of the decision cycle, the agent computes a variation v of the value P, which can be a positive value if it progresses or a negative value if it regresses or stagnates (see details in [20]). The cycle action-perception-update of P is shown in figure 2 for one agent.

The second concept is dynamical influences. They are simple attractive or repulsive signals locally emitted by the agents towards their neighbours (represented by Signal arrows in figure 2). An influence is released when an agent perceives conflicts or possibilities to cooperate with its neighbours (represented by the constraints evaluation box in figure 2). The influences are coded by values defined in the same interval as P, with positive values for attraction and negative ones for repulsion.

The last concept is altruistic behavior. Each agent computes in its action-selection module a comparative test between the values of the perceived influences and its personal satisfaction (P). If the intensity of an external influence is

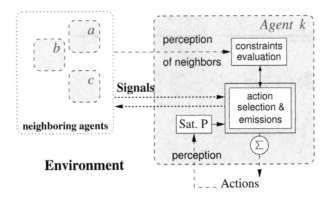

Fig. 2. Satisfaction Altruism principle

greater than P then the agent stops its current task and executes a predetermined altruistic behavior. It is a response to the strongest influence: a displacement to go towards the emitter or to move away. Note that agents executing an altruistic behavior can propagate the signal they perceive. It is useful to solve conflicts involving several close agents [21].

This model constitutes an extension of the Artificial Potential Field (APF) approach in the sense that agents emit dynamical signals which are perceived by others as environmental influences. These dynamical influences can be then combined to other classical perceptions, for instance the repulsions from the close obstacles. This combination is represented by the sum operation in figure 2.

Different distributed problems have been efficiently solved by this model. On the one hand with simulation tools: foraging tasks [20], navigation conflicts solving [21], cooperation for box-pushing and box-cutting in heterogeneous multi-robot systems [3]. On the other hand with real autonomous mobile robots: navigation conflicts solving [16].

4   Satisfaction-Altruism Kernel Specification

The satisfaction-altruism model is now detailed through its formal specification, using the previously introduced approach. The analysis of the satisfaction-altruism model using RIO is out of the scope of this paper. We only present the classes we obtained.

The class *DiscreteSensor* specifies a discrete sensor device. The first line of the class introduces the *Intensity* abbreviation by the == symbol. *Intensity* denotes $[-P_{max}, P_{max}]$ interval where P_{max} is a real constant. The next unnamed sub-schema specifies the state space of the class. Such a device takes as input a discrete number of signals which are represented by the *stimulus* sequence. Each different sensor, indexed by a number i in $\mathbb{N}$, gives a different signal, $stimulus(i)$. One can select the greater signal received by the *getMax* operation. An operation is enclosed in named sub-schema and is divided in two parts. The first part, above a short line is a declaration part and the second part below the short line is a predicate part. To include output (resp input) parameters the name of the variable should end with an exclamation (resp question) mark. In the *getMax* operation there is an output variable s. The predicate part specifies the s domain. It belongs to the *stimulus* sequence range. It also states that s is the greater stimulus perceived in terms of greater absolute value of signal intensity.

```
┌─ DiscreteSensor ─────────────────────────────────────────
│  Intensity == [−P_max, P_max]
│  ┌──────────────────────────────────────────────────────
│  │  stimulus : seq Signal
│  └──────────────────────────────────────────────────────
│  ┌─ getMax ─────────────────────────────────────────────
│  │  s! : Intensity
│  │  ┌───────────────────────────────────────────────────
│  │  │  s ∈ ran stimulus
│  │  │  ∄s′ ∈ ran stimulus • |s′| ≥ |s|
└──┴──┴───────────────────────────────────────────────────
```

With the *SAAgent* class we introduce an agent based upon the satisfaction-altruism kernel. Its attributes, operations and behaviour are defined according to the satisfaction-altruism model. The class *SAAgent* inherits from Agent defined in the RIO framework [12] and specifies the Satisfaction/Altruism behavior model. The *altruismTest* boolean decides if the agent must be in individual state or altruism state. It is defined as a λ-expression which evaluates the condition included in the predicate part.

The agent attributes are first an action it currently undergo : *current*. Then the agent is described by weights attached to the actions it can do *weight*. These different weights can be modified by the agents evolution and their initial values are defined by *initialWeight*.

The *progressionReward* function maps each action to a 3-uplet giving the bonus or penaltypenalty values for agents satisfaction when it is respectively in progression, in regression or locked.

The statechart included in the behavior sub-schema specifies the behavior of *SAAgent*. It consists of two exclusive-or states. These states specify the individual and altruistic behaviours. By default an agent is in individual state and if the altruism test becomes true then it is in altruistic state. Each superstate is divided in two parts. First an action part which is the reaction to events and second a communication part which emits a I valued signals.

The operations of the class are P which computes the personal satisfaction of the agent according to the Satisfaction Altruism model and I_{ext} which selects the perceived signal with the maximum intensity. Eventually, *actionSelection* decides for the individual state which action is to be achieved. This operation modifies the state space of the class. Specifically it modifies the *current* and *weight* variables. These variables are listed in the Δ-list of the operation. The mechanism of action selection isn't described further here since we restrict actions to movements in the sequel.

SA Agent

Agent

$altruismTest : \mathbb{B}$

$altruismTest \Leftrightarrow |I_{ext}()| \geq P() \wedge |I_{ext}()| \geq |I|$

$BMValue == [-\Delta s, \Delta s] \times [-\Delta s, \Delta s] \times [-\Delta s, \Delta s]$

$current : Action$
$initialWeight, weight : Action \rightarrow [0, 1]$
$progressionReward : Action \rightarrow BMValue$
$s : DiscreteSensor$
$satisfaction, I : [-P_{max}, P_{max}]$

$current \subseteq actions$
$dom\ initialWeight = dom\ weight \subseteq actions$
$\forall\ v \in ran\ progressionReward \bullet v =$
$(n, m, f) \wedge \Delta s \leq f \leq n \leq 0 \leq m \leq \Delta s$

_P_

$satisfaction! : [-P_{max}, P_{max}]$

$progression(current) \Rightarrow satisfaction' = satisfaction + v.m$
$regression(current) \Rightarrow satisfaction' = satisfaction + v.n$
$locked(current) \Rightarrow satisfaction' = satisfaction + v.f$

_I_{ext}_   _actionSelection_

$ext! : \mathbb{R}$ $\Delta(current, weight)$

$ext! = s.getMax()$

behavior

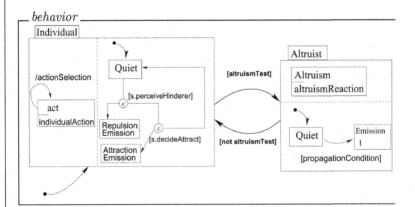

5   Mobile Robots Extension

5.1   Principle of Robots Behavior

In the previous section we have presented the kernel of the satisfaction-altruism model. To apply it on concrete problems it is necessary to refine the agent perceptions and to clarify the satisfaction computation. Here we aim to define a mobile robot architecture using the model to allow agents cooperation for navigation. In order to treat navigational conflicts the satisfaction-altruism kernel is refined by adding the key concepts of : displacement, perception and satisfaction.

When an agent tries to move towards a direction its displacement is defined by a vector (V). This vector represents the current task of the agent. When the agent gets the altruist state this vector becomes equal to the predetermined reaction to signals. In any case the vector V integrates obstacles avoidance.

An agent blocked by the fault of others emit a repulsive signal when its satisfaction becomes negative (the value emitted is then equals to P). When an agent perceives such a signal and the intensity of the signal is higher than its personal satisfaction the agent tries to move away from the transmitting agent. It is the altruistic reaction.

Each agent is equipped with sensors allowing the detection of walls and robots, towards different directions (into $[0°,360°]$). When the agent can progress towards its goal the variation of satisfaction v is positive (equal to $m > 0$). When it moves away v is a negative value (equals to $n \leq 0$). If the agent is locked (paralysed) the variation of P is equal to f, with $f < n \leq 0$. The value f is computed in function of the elements surrounding the agent. Each element has a negative weight: value θ for robots, θ' for walls as $\theta' < \theta < 0$ because walls are stronger constraints than mobile robots. v is then computed as the sum of these weights over all the directions. In other words, the more an agent is surrounded by walls the faster its satisfaction will decrease. As a consequence, there is an induced emergent phenomenon that moves agents from the more constrained regions to the less constrained ones, cf [21].

5.2   Classes for the Mobile Robot Extension

The *DiscreteSituatedSensor* class inherits from *DiscreteSensor*. It specifies a sensor which devices are located at given angles. The signal type introduced in the beginning of the class is defined as a free type by the ::= symbol and we enumerate the possible value for this type. The different possible values are: ∅ (which means no signal), obstacle or agent (another robot). For each specific sensor one can know the signal type with *getSignalType* operation and the number of sensors activated with the *getActivatedSensor* operation.

┌─ *DiscreteSituatedSensor* ────────────────────────────────────
│ *DiscreteSensor*
│ $SignalType ::= \varnothing \mid obstacle \mid agent$
│ ┌──
│ │ $angularDistance : [0, 360]$
│ │ $numberOfSensors : \mathbb{N}$
│ ├──
│ │ $dom\ stimulus \subseteq [1, numberOfSensors]$
│ │ $angularDistance = 360/numberOfSensors$
│ └──
│
│ ┌─ *getSignalType* ────────────────────────────
│ │ $n? : \mathbb{N}$
│ │ $t! : SignalType$
│ └──
│
│ ┌─ *getActivatedSensor* ───────────────────────
│ │ $n! : \mathbb{N}$
│ ├──
│ │ $n! \leq numberOfSensors$
│ └──
└──

Eventually the *MobileRobot* class specifies a robot which behavior is based on the satisfaction altruism model. This class inherits from SAAgent. In this class we precise many things. The propagation condition of the agent is true whenever the external signal (I_{ext}) is less than zero (i.e. repulsive signal) and when there is a robot in its way. One agent perceives a hinderer when there is one agent just in front of him. An agent progresses if and only if its move is non zero. An agent is locked whenever its moving vector is zero and it can't be in regression. In order to simulate random we use a non described operation *random* which outputs a random number in the set $\{-30, -15, 0, 15, 30\}$.

┌─ *MobileRobot* ───
│ *SAAgent*
│ ┌──
│ │ $propagationCondition : \mathbb{B}$
│ ├──
│ │ $propagationCondition \Leftrightarrow (I_{ext} \leq 0)$
│ │ $\wedge\ (s.getSignalType(s.getActivatedSensor() + 180) = agent)$
│ └──
│ ┌──
│ │ $perceiveHinderer! : \mathbb{B}$
│ ├──
│ │ $perceiveHinderer! \Leftrightarrow s.getSignalType(0) = agent$
│ └──
│ ┌──
│ │ $progression : \mathbb{B}$
│ ├──
│ │ $progression \Leftrightarrow \overrightarrow{V}!_{goal} \neq \overrightarrow{0}$
│ └──
│ ┌─────────────────────────┐ ┌──────────────────
│ │ $locked : \mathbb{B}$ │ │ $regression : \mathbb{B}$
│ ├─────────────────────────┤ ├──────────────────
│ │ $locked \Leftrightarrow \overrightarrow{V}!_{goal} = \overrightarrow{0}$ │ │ $\neg\ regression$
│ └─────────────────────────┘ └──────────────────
│
└──

$$calculate\,V_f! : \mathbb{R}$$
$$calculate\,V_f! = \Sigma_{n=0}^{n=s.numberOfSensors}\, valObs(n)$$

$$valObs! : \mathbb{R}$$
$$n? : \mathbb{N}$$

$$s.getSignalType(n?) = obstacle \Rightarrow valObs(n)! = -0.75$$
$$s.getSignalType(n?) = agent \Rightarrow valObs(n)! = -0.25$$
$$s.getSignalType(n?) = \varnothing \Rightarrow valObs(n)! = 0.5$$

$$\mathrm{dom}\; progressionReward = \{altruismReaction,$$
$$individualReaction\}$$
$$\mathrm{ran}\; progressionReward = (2, 0, calculate\,V_f)$$
$$s \in DiscreteSituatedSensor$$

___calculateSlide___
$$\overrightarrow{V_{sli}} = \Sigma_{i \in \{s.getSignalType(i)=obstacle\}}((i \times angularDistance) + 90$$

___altruismReaction___
$$\overrightarrow{V}!_{goal} : Vector$$

$$\overrightarrow{V}_{slide} = calculateSlide()$$
$$\overrightarrow{V_{goal}} = \overrightarrow{V_{altruism}} + \overrightarrow{V_{slide}}$$
$$\overrightarrow{V_{altruism}} = k \times s.getMax().(s.getActivatedSensor()$$
$$\times s.angularDistance)$$

___individualReaction___
$$\overrightarrow{V}! : Vector$$

$$s.getSignalType(0) = obstacle \Rightarrow \overrightarrow{V_{goal}} = 0$$
$$s.getSignalType(0) \neq obstacle \Rightarrow \overrightarrow{V_{goal}} = random$$
$$\overrightarrow{V_{slide}} = calculateSlide()$$
$$\overrightarrow{V}! = \overrightarrow{V_{goal}} + \overrightarrow{V_{slide}}$$

___getDirection___
$$\overrightarrow{V}! : Vector$$

$$instate(Indivual) \Rightarrow \overrightarrow{V}! = individualReaction()$$
$$instate(Altruism) \Rightarrow \overrightarrow{V}! = altruismReaction()$$

The mobile robots environment is specified by the coordinate of the mobile robots and the position of obstacles. It refines the *Environment* class of the RIO framework.

___ *RobotsEnvironment* _____
Environment
Coordinate $==$ $\mathbb{R} \times \mathbb{R}$
_____
situation : *MobileRobot* $\rightarrow$ *Coordinate*
obstacles : $\mathbb{P}$ *Coordinate*
_____
$\forall\, a \in agents \bullet situation(a) \notin obstacles$
$\forall\, a, b \in agents \bullet a \neq b \Rightarrow situation(a) \neq situation(b)$
_____
$\Box(\forall\, a \in agents \bullet$
    $(x, y) = situation(a)$
    $\wedge \bigcirc(situation(a) = (x, y) + a.getDirection()))$

6   Specification Analysis

6.1   Prototyping

The prototyping is performed by using STATEMATE [10] ; an environment which allows the prototyping and the simulation of the statechart specifications. The specification analysis is based upon execution of the statecharts and can be done using two techniques. The first technique is *simulation* and the second is *animation*. In our case simulation would consist in assigning probabilities to events or actions occurrences. With this technique one can evaluate quantitative parameters of the specified system. As an example, in the satisfaction-altruism model, probabilities can be assigned to agent in order to simulate exploration of various environments.

Animation technique consists of testing the specification with predefined interaction scenarios. It enables one to test if the system behavior is consistent with requirements.

In order to evaluate our specification of the architecture we simulated the behavior of two robots evolving in a particular environment. We defined a closed narrow corridor where it is impossible for two agents to inter-cross, as showed in figure 3a. The goal of each agent is to find an exit by exploring the whole corridor. With such an environment exploration conflicts are unavoidable and lead to the emission of repulsive signals and altruistic reactions. In particular, when the agents meet around the centre they both try to push back the other, this causes a quick fall of their satisfactions. The more unsatisfied agent repulses the other to an extremity of the corridor. As the ends are closed the agents will be blocked again. The first agent to arrive at one end of the corridor will be surrounded by three walls. Thus it will be more constrained than the other agent and its satisfaction will decrease faster. The model ensures that it will then repulse the other agent and thus both will continuously explore the environment. If an exit for the corridor is artificially created the robots will take it.

The figures 3b and 3c shows an example of such a test. The x axis represents time and y axis represents discretized positions in the corridor for the 3b figure

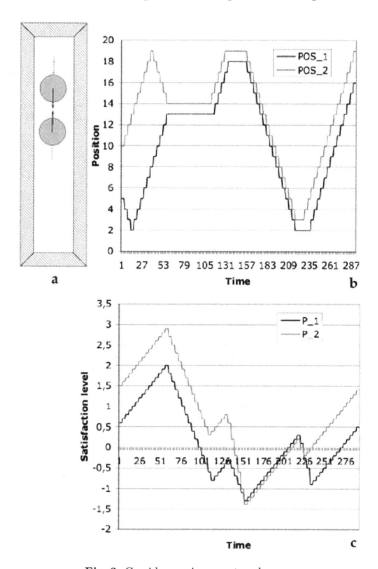

Fig. 3. Corridor environment and curves

and level of satisfaction for each robot for the 3c figure. One can see that levels of satisfaction and trajectories are correlated. Indeed, each time the two robots are locked the satisfaction levels decrease. They decrease faster when a robot is locked against a wall. As soon as the altruism test becomes true the concerned robot plays the altruist role and changes its direction (it is the case around times 109, 155 and 235). If a robot isn't locked and can explore the corridor following its initial direction its satisfaction level increases.

This animation shows an example of the execution of the specification for a specific environment (the corridor) and a specific number of agents. These

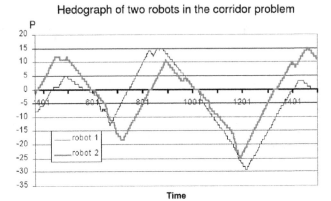

Fig. 4. Hedographs of 2 real robots

parameters can be easily modified in order to check the specification against pertinent test cases. It is important to note that the validation of the specification by simulation gives similar results as the real world experiments [16], see figure 4. This figure, called hedograph from the Greek hedos which means satisfaction, shows the satisfaction levels of two real robots.

The simulation is performed by executing the behaviour part of the obtained specifications without developing a specific simulator. The simulation tool offers an interactive simulation mode and a program controlled mode. In the latter a program written in a high level language replaces the user. One feature of this programming language is the breakpoint construct. Breakpoint stop the specification execution when a condition is verified. Possible uses of breakpoints are, for example, configuration tests with predefined interaction scenarios and output of statistics.

6.2   Verification

OZS semantics [7] is based upon transition systems as defined in [19]. It means that for each OZS specification there is an associated transition system. This transition system represents the set of possible computations the specification can produce.

With such transition systems and software tools like STeP [18] one can verify specification properties. With STeP specification properties are expressed in Linear-time Temporal Logic formulas and the verification may be done by using two techniques.

The first technique is model-checking which enables the verification of the satisfiability of a property. The STeP model-checker proves or refutes validity of LTL formulas relatively to a transition system. To establish the satisfiability of history invariant H one must actually establish that $\neg H$ is not valid. This technique is the simplest to use but is limited by the specification state space.

The second technique is semi-automatic proof. It is based on deductive method. The deductive methods of STEP verify temporal properties of systems by means of verification rules, e.g. induction and verification diagrams. Verification rules are used to reduce temporal properties of systems to first-order verification conditions. Verification diagrams provide a visual language for guiding, organising and displaying proofs. Verification diagrams allows the user to construct proofs hierarchically, starting from a high-level, intuitive proof sketch and proceeding incrementally, as necessary, through layers of greater detail. The specifier can help the proover if it can not proove a property by introducing axioms.

For our case study one has to refine the *RobotsEnvironment* class to specify the corridor example and try to verify with the STeP model-checker the satisfiability of the following informal property "When a robot is locked by another robot it's eventually be freed". This property is specified by the following LTL formula :

$$
\begin{aligned}
(\exists\, a \in\ & agents \bullet \\
& \forall\, i \in a.s.numberOfSensors \bullet \\
& a.s.getSignalType(i) = agent \\
& \vee\ a.s.getSignalType(i) = obstacle) \Rightarrow \\
\Diamond(\exists\, j \in\ & a.s.numberOfSensors \bullet \\
& a.s.getSignalType(i) = \varnothing)
\end{aligned}
$$

It means that if there exists one agent that perceives an obstacle or other agents from all its sensors (the agent is locked), eventually this agent will be freed ans thus at least one perception will be void. To be verified by a model checker the corresponding transition system should include only finite and bounded sets. All part of the specification that describe continuous or infinite types must be discretized and bounded.

7   Conclusion

In this paper we have presented an approach which allows specification, validation and verification of MAS. Moreover, we have specified a particular MAS model, the satisfaction-altruism one. This reactive-based model is useful for cooperation between situated agents (or robots). We have shown validation and verification examples for the satisfaction-altruism specification. This formalisation shows that our approach can be applied to behavior-based architectures, that were not formally analysed at the beginning. We have thus applied a reverse-engineering approach to specify formally this model. The result is composed of OZS [7] classes which specify each component of the satisfaction-altruism model. The first level of the specification specifies the kernel of the satisfaction-altruism model. The second level refines the first and specifies an extension applied to mobile robots. The advantages of our approach are first that the satisfaction-altruism model is presented in formal and non ambiguous terms and second that the specification decomposes the model in formal concepts which can be reused in specific applications. The validation phase enables specifications test with pre-defined interaction scenarios such as the corridor application. The verification phase allows the proof of logical properties. The reusability of such a specification is enhanced by the results of the validation and the verification. Indeed, all the roles and agents, validated and verified, constitute reliable components which can be used in other applications.

At this time, our approach can be improved. In particular we plan to ease the specification process by associating a methodology. A methodology must be associated to ease the specification process. A CASE tool could be helpful to support the specification. We plan to explore the verification of properties for such specifications by using semi-automatic proofs. We also plan the specification of others multi-agent models following the process described in this paper. This will constitute a library of reusable generic agent and multi-agent models a sort of design patterns for agents.

References

1. R. Arkin. *Behavior Based Robotics*. The MIT Press. 1998
2. Bergenti, F. and A. Poggi: 2000, 'Exploiting UML in the Design of Multi-Agent Systems'. In: A. Omicini, R. Tolksdorf, and F. Zambonelli (eds.): *Engineering Societies in the Agents' World*.
3. J. Chapelle, O. Simonin, and J. Ferber. How situated agents can learn to cooperate by monitoring their neighbors' satisfaction. In *15th European Conference on Artificial Intelligence*, pages 68–72, Lyon, France, 2002.
4. DeLoach, S.: 1999, 'Multiagent Systems Engineering: a Methodology and Language for Designing Agent Systems'. In: *Agent Oriented Information Systems '99*.
5. R. Duke, P. King, G. Rose, and G. Smith. The Object-Z specification language. Technical report, Software Verification Research Center, Departement of Computer Science, University of Queensland, AUSTRALIA, 1991.
6. J. Ferber and O. Gutknecht. A meta-model for the analysis and design of organizations in multi-agent systems. In Y. Demazeau, E. Durfee, and N. Jennings, editors, *ICMAS'98*, july 1998.
7. P. Gruer, V. Hilaire, and A. Koukam. Heterogeneous formal specification based on object-z and state charts: semantics and verification. *Journal of Systems and Software*, 70(1), 2004.
8. P. Gruer, V. Hilaire, A. Koukam, and K. Cetnarowicz. A formal framework for multi-agent systems analysis and design. *Expert Systems with Applications*, 23. 2002.
9. D. Harel. Statecharts: A visual formalism for complex systems. *Science of Computer Programming*, 8(3):231–274, June 1987.
10. D. Harel, H. Lachover, A. Naamad, A. Pnueli, M. Politi, R. Sherman, A. Shtull-Trauring, and M. B. Trakhtenbrot. Statemate: A working environment for the development of complex reactive systems. *IEEE Transactions on Software Engineering*, 16(4):403–414, Apr. 1990.
11. Herlea, D. E., C. M. Jonker, J. Treur, and N. J. E. Wijngaards: 1999, 'Specification of Behavioural Requirements within Compositional Multi-agent System Design'. *Lecture Notes in Computer Science* **1647**, 8–27.

12. V. Hilaire, A. Koukam, and P. Gruer. A mechanism for dynamic role playing. In *Agent Technologies, Infrastructures, Tools and Applications for E-Services*, number 2592 in Lecture Notes in Artificial Intelligence. Springer Verlag, 2002.

13. V. Hilaire, A. Koukam, P. Gruer, and J.-P. Müller. Formal specification and prototyping of multi-agent systems. In A. Omicini, R. Tolksdorf, and F. Zambonelli, editors, *Engineering Societies in the Agents' World*, number 1972 in Lecture Notes in Artificial Intelligence. Springer Verlag, 2000.

14. V. Hilaire, A. Koukam, O. Simonin, and P. Gruer. Formal specification of role dynamics in agent organizations: Applications to the satisfaction-altruism model. *Autonomous Agents and Multi-Agent Systems*, 2003. submitted.

15. Michael Luck and Mark d'Inverno. A formal framework for agency and autonomy. In Victor Lesser and Les Gasser, editors, *Proceedings of the First International Conference on Multi-Agent Systems*, pages 254–260. AAAI Press, 1995.

16. P. Lucidarme, O. Simonin, and A. Ligeois. Implementation and evaluation of a satisfaction/altruism based architecture for multi-robot systems. In *International Conference of Robotics and Automation (ICRA'2002)*, pages 1007–1012, Washington, USA, 2002.

17. Luck, M. and M. d'Inverno: 1995, 'A Formal Framework for Agency and Autonomy'. In: V. Lesser and L. Gasser (eds.): *Proceedings of the First International Conference on Multi-Agent Systems*. pp. 254–260.

18. Z. Manna, N. Bjoerner, A. Browne, and E. Chang. STeP: The Stanford Temporal Prover. *Lecture Notes in Computer Science*, 915:793–??, 1995.

19. Z. Manna and A. Pnueli. *Temporal Verification of Reactive Systems: Safety*. Springer, 1995.

20. O. Simonin and J. Ferber. Modeling self satisfaction and altruism to handle action selection and reactive cooperation. *6th International Conference On the Simulation Of Adaptive Behavior (SAB 2000 volume 2)*, pages 314–323, 2000.

21. O. Simonin, A. Liegois, and P. Rongier. An architecture for reactive cooperation of mobile distributed robots. In *DARS 4 Distributed Autonomous Robotic Systems 4*, pages 35–44, Knoxville, TN, 2000. Springer.

22. J. Odell, M. Nodine, and R. Levy. A metamodel for agents, roles and groups. In J. Odell, P. Giorgini, and J. P. Müller, editors, *The Fifth International Workshop on Agent-Oriented Software Systems*, volume in this book. Springer-Verlag, 2004.

23. E. Steegmans, D. Weyns, T. Holvoet, and Y. Berbers. Designing roles for situated agents. In J. Odell, P. Giorgini, and J. P. Müller, editors, *The Fifth International Workshop on Agent-Oriented Software Systems*, volume in this book. Springer-Verlag, 2004.

24. M. Wooldridge, N. R. Jennings, and D. Kinny. A methodology for agent-oriented analysis and design. In *Proceedings of the Third International Conference on Autonomous Agents (Agents'99)*, pages 69–76, Seattle, WA, USA, 1999. ACM Press.

An Agent Construction Model for Ubiquitous Computing Devices

Ronald Ashri and Michael Luck

Dept of Electronics and Computer Science, Southampton University,
Highfield, Southampton, SO17 1BJ, UK
ra,mml@ecs.soton.ac.uk

Abstract. One of the main challenges for the successful application of agent-based systems in mobile and embedded devices is enabling application developers to reconcile the needs of the user to the capabilities and limitations of agents in the context of environments with changing and often limited resources. In this paper we present an attempt to move towards a solution through a framework for defining and reasoning about agents in a manner that is modular and reconfigurable at run-time. Departing from the theoretical basis afforded by the SMART framework, we extend it to enable the definition of fully re-configurable component-based agent architectures. The guiding principle of this approach is an architecturally-neutral model that supports a separation between the description, behaviour and structure of an agent.

1 Introduction

The spread and rise in influence of embedded and mobile devices with limited computational power, which have found favour in many aspects of everyday life, from mobile phones to personal digital assistants (PDAs), provides a counterpoint to the tradition of desktop computing. In line with this profile, there is also an increasing demand for *integrating* the various different kinds of such devices in order to provide an environment where access to information and services is available in a seamless manner, while transcending physical location and computing platform.

Agent-based systems have a key role role to play in the effort to provide and support such integration, since agents embody several of the required characteristics for effective and robust operation in ubiquitous environments [4, 12]. A central area of concern for supporting agents operating in such heterogeneous environments, which place differing and varying demands and limitations on them, is the development of agent architectures tailored to meet both the needs of the device at hand and environment within which they are operating. We identify below three specific challenges for the development of architectures in such environments.

- The heterogeneity of operating environments and devices makes it practically impossible to adopt a single optimal design for an agent architecture. For example, a purely BDI-based approach for agents on all types of devices may simply be overly complex for a number of limited devices that do not need to deal with complicated tasks, and as such would not benefit from planning capabilities or a sophisticated

J. Odell et al. (Eds.): AOSE 2004, LNCS 3382, pp. 158–173, 2005.

representation of beliefs. Instead, we should enable developers to create solutions that are tailored to specific devices and application domains, without constraining them to specific architectural approaches.

- The necessity to have multiple types of agent architectures, while providing the required level of flexibility, also introduces new challenges since it increases the overall complexity of the system design. A multiplicity of architectures also makes it more challenging to choose the best for a specific situation.

- Finally, an agent architecture should be able to deal with the unpredictable nature of computing devices and the environments they operate in. For example, devices may stop operating due to power failure but it is important that agents are able to keep some information about their state to retrieve when the device is restarted.

In this paper, we address these issues by presenting a model for agent construction that is *conceptually grounded* and *architecturally neutral*. It is conceptually grounded by the understanding of agent systems provided through SMART [10], and it is architecturally neutral because a number of different agent architectures can be expressed through the constructs SMART offers. Through this agent construction model we advance the current state of the art for agent-oriented software engineering in three ways. Firstly, we provide an agent construction model that addresses the specific needs of agent construction on mobile devices. Secondly, through the implementation of the model we identify some specific techniques that can be used for adapting to changes in device capabilities and operating environments. Finally, as a result of this work we identify some more generalised features that can inform the construction of agents in other settings beyond ubiquitous computing.

We begin by introducing a set of *desiderata* that our agent construction model should fulfil, and then outline some of the key design decisions that guide its development as well as clarify its position within the context of application development. Subsequently, the agent construction model itself is presented followed by a discussion of its implementation for devices supporting the Java 2 Micro Edition. Finally, we conclude and compare our approach to others.

2   Design Principles

2.1   Desiderata for an Agent Construction Model

In order to address the range of concerns raised above and provide some statement of requirements for the agent construction model, we identify four desiderata. Although the set is not exhaustive, we consider it to be the minimum necessary set of requirements.

Abstract Agent Model. An agent construction model that addresses the issues raised above must be based on some understanding of how we can model agents in a manner that is independent of agent architectures. This allows the comparison of alternative architectures at this more *abstract* level, ultimately providing application developers with more informed choices *before* they proceed to provide specific implementations for the domain in question. In our case, the SMART framework provides such an abstract agent model (as discussed in Section 2.2).[1]

Architecturally Neutral. The construction model should not lead to the construction of only a limited range of agent types, but should allow the widest possible range of architectures to be defined using the same basic concepts. In order to achieve this, there are two possible avenues to explore. One option is to define a generic agent architecture and describe other architectures in terms of this generic architecture, something that Bryson et al. suggest [6]. Apart from the inherent difficulty in constructing any general, all inclusive model, the drawback of this approach is that there may be features of other architectures that cannot directly be *translated* to the generic one. The second option is to provide an architecturally-neutral model, so as to avoid this translation problem. Here, the challenge is to provide a model that is specific enough so that it actually offers something to the construction of agents, but general enough to support the development of a wide range of architectures. Through an appropriate architecturally-*neutral* model we can consider a range of architectures based on a common set of agent-related abstractions and without losing expressive capability.

Modularity. The model should allow for modular construction of agents. This is necessary both in order to meet general software engineering concerns and to delineate clearly the different aspects of an architecture. As discussed in Section 2.3, our approach calls for a separation between describing agents in terms of their *characteristics*, their *structure* and their *behaviour*. Such a fine-grained approach can lead to a better understanding of the overall functioning of the agent as well as how it can be altered, since the different aspects of the architecture are clearly identified and the relationships between them made explicit.

Run-time Reconfiguration. The reality of current computing environments is that changes are often required as the system is running. With large systems that can contain dynamic, complex dependencies between various parts, it is crucial to be able to reconfigure agents at run-time. Reconfiguration may mean providing more functionality to an agent or changing the way it behaves in order to better meet application requirements.

2.2   SMART

The agent construction model is based on SMART [10] (Structured, Modular Agent Relationships and Types), which provides the foundational agent concepts that allow us to reason about different types of agents, and the relationships between them, from through a single perspective. We chose SMART because it provides appropriate agent concepts without restricting us to a specific agent architecture. Furthermore, SMART has already been successfully used to describe several existing agent architectures and systems (e.g. [8, 9]).

We avoid here a more complete presentation of SMART and focus on just those concepts that are used for the agent construction model. In essence, SMART provides a

---

[1] The need for well-defined agent models is also advocated in [15] in this collection of papers and, indeed, use the same formalism as SMART to do so.

compositional approach to the description of agents that is based on two primitive concepts, *attributes* and *actions*. Attributes refer to describable features of the environment, while actions can change the environment by adding or removing attributes. Now, an agent is described by a set of attributes and a set of *capabilities*, where capabilities are actions an agent can perform. More importantly, an agent has *goals*, where goals are sets of attributes that represent desirable states of the environment for the agent. On top of this basic concept of an agent, SMART adds the concept of an *autonomous agent* as an agent that generates its own goals through *motivations*, which drive the generation of goals. Motivations can be preferences, desires, etc., of an autonomous agent that cause it to produce goals and execute actions in an attempt to achieve those goals.

This approach to agent description fits well with our requirement for architecture neutrality but does not sufficiently address our requirements for modularity and run-time reconfiguration. In Section 2.3 we discuss how the descriptive capabilities of SMART are enhanced to cope with these requirements.

2.3   Description, Structure and Behaviour

While SMART is suitable for *describing* agents, it lacks the necessary features for *constructing* agents. For the purposes of SMART, this was not a problem since it was intended to provide a theoretical framework that would allow the description of a number of different agent systems. However, for us it is crucial to be able to provide tools that facilitate the construction of agent architectures. Nevertheless, we do not want to *replace* the descriptive capabilities of SMART, since they offer some useful features as discussed above. Rather, we complement them with additional aspects, which are identified below.

SMART allows systems to be specified from an observer's perspective. Agents are described in terms of their attributes, goals or actions, not in terms of how they are built or how they behave. In other words, the focus is on the *what* and not the *why* or *how*. We call this a *descriptive specification*, since this essentially describes a situation without analysing its causes nor the underlying structures that sustain that situation. However, these are just the issues we need to address within a construction model. Thus, *along* with the descriptive specification, we need to have the ability to specify systems based on their structure – the individual building blocks that make up agents – as well as their behaviour. We call these other views the *structural specification* and the *behavioural specification*, respectively.

The structural specification enables the identification of the relevant building blocks or components of an agent architecture. Different sets of building blocks and different ways of connecting them can enable the instantiation of different agent types. By contrast, the behavioural specification of an agent addresses the process through which the agent arrives at such decisions as what actions to perform. These specifications, along with the descriptive specification, provide a more complete picture of the system from different perspectives. It is interesting to note that it is possible to begin from any one of these views and derive the remaining two, but the correspondence is not one to one. Several behavioural and structural specifications could satisfy a single descriptive specification, and *vice-versa*.

For example, let us consider an agent operating on a user's mobile device, whose purpose is to determine what physical devices (e.g. projector, fax machine, laser printer)

Descriptive Specification	Behavioural Specification	Structural Specification
Attributes: Agent Owner = Ronald Ashri Allowed to Use Devices = True	Step 1: Discover available devices Step 2: Discover available info services	Active Devices Discover Active Information Services Discovery
Capabilites: Search for devices Search for infromation services	Step 3: Evaluate suitability against goals Step 4: Notify user about device	Devices Evaluation Component Information Services Evaluation Component
Goals: Find laser printer Get directions to closest restaurant	Step 5: Get results from info service if one discovered	Information Services Query Component User Notification Component

Fig. 1. Distinguishing between description, structure and behaviour

and information services (e.g. local weather information, maps of the building) are available for use in a conference room and, based on the current goals of its user, identify the devices that are relevant to the user or query the information services for the required information. A *descriptive specification* of such an agent may state that the agent belongs to a user, has certain rights with regards to accessing devices and services in the conference room, the goals of printing an overview of the user's presentation and finding out where the closest restaurant is, and so forth. A *behavioural specification* may state that this agent begins operation by collecting information about available devices and services, then filters for those that are best suited to the user's goals, and decides whether to inform the user about them or interact directly with them. A *structural specification* may state that the agent has different components, each able to handle specific functionalities such as searching for Bluetooth-enabled devices, communicating with information services or directory agents, and so forth. The different aspects are illustrated in Figure 1. This separation between the different views allows us to change some aspects without necessarily impacting on the others. For example, the behaviour could be altered so that the agent reports on the first device that fits the required profile, rather than attempting to find the best one. The structural specification could also be based on a tightly integrated control loop rather than a component-based approach.

The agent construction model reflects these levels by allowing direct access to these different aspects of agents, based on a clear decoupling at the architectural level.

2.4   Component-Based Construction

In order to support the division of an architecture's different aspects as described above, and to satisfy the requirement for modularity and re-configurability, we take a component-based view of agent architectures.

Component-based software engineering is a relatively new trend in software engineering [7, 11]. Separate developments within the fields of object-oriented computing, re-usable software code, formal methods, and modeling languages have all steered towards a component-based approach [18]. Components are understood as units of composition that can be deployed independently, while a *third-party* coordinates their interactions [20]. Interaction with a component takes place through a well-defined interface, which allows the implementation of the component to vary independently of other aspects of the system.

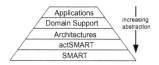

Fig. 2. From SMART+ to applications

There are three main benefits to architecture design following a component-based approach, in line with our aims. Firstly, describing an agent architecture through the composition of components promotes a clearer identification of the different functionalities and allows for their re-use in alternative contexts. Secondly, different types of components can be composed in a variety of ways to achieve the best results for the architecture at hand. Finally, by connecting the abstract agent model of SMART to component-based software engineering, we bring it much closer to practical development concerns within a paradigm that is not foreign to developers.

2.5   From SMART+ to Applications

In this section, we clarify the relationships between the agent construction model which, from now on, we will refer to as *act*SMART, the abstract agent model SMART, and the application level. These clarifications serve to indicate how the work presented here can be used within the context of the agent development process.

The relationships are illustrated in Figure 2. At the most abstract level lies SMART. Then, *act*SMART represents an extension of SMART to deal with the *construction* of agents. Architectures for agents, which can range from application-independent architectures, such as BDI, to application-specific architectures, can thus be designed using the framework provided by *act*SMART, and based on the concepts provided by SMART. We should note that application-independent architectures are not always required and may not always be advisable. For example, an agent dedicated to dealing with requests for quotes on fast-changing financial information, where performance optimisation is crucial, would benefit from an application-specific architecture tailored to that situation. Conversely, agents expected to deal with a variety of changing tasks and complex interactions with other agents, such as sophisticated negotiations, might benefit from a more generic and sophisticated deliberative architecture. One of the benefits of our approach is that while it distinguishes between the different cases, it can still consider them within the same conceptual and practical framework.

The next level is domain-specific support, which involves appropriate middleware to support agent discovery and interactions between agents in the specific distributed environments in which the applications operate, as well as other components that could supplement agent capabilities. Finally, specific applications can be built, making use of all the layers below.

3   Components

The first step towards developing our agent construction model, as discussed above, is to introduce and define *components* as the basic buildings blocks for an agent. These can be

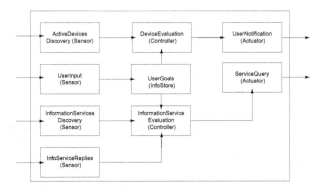

Fig. 3. Example Agent Architecture

considered as the structural representations of one or more related agent functionalities, which are considered at two different levels. At an *abstract level*, the functionality is described in generic terms, which we will present shortly. At the *implementation level*, the abstract functionality is instantiated through the actual computational mechanisms that support it. The reason for distinguishing between these different levels is so that we can use *generic* component types to specify an agent architecture at a high level of abstraction without making direct reference to the detailed behaviour of each component. This allows us to move between the different levels while retaining a good understanding of the overall architecture, and identifying which specific components best suit each of the generic functionalities.

Generic Component Types. From here on, we set out the terms that can be used to describe components at an *abstract* level. We begin by dividing components into four generic types, each one representing a class of functionality for the agent.

We use the example architecture illustrated in Figure 3 to explain each generic component type. The diagram presents an architecture for an agent, based on the example discussed in Section 2.3.[2] The domain specific functionality of components is as follows. Information about available devices and information services is collected by the *ActiveDevicesDiscovery* and *InformationServicesDiscovery* components. The user provides information through the *UserInput* component, which defines the goals of the user. These goals are stored in the *UserGoals* component. Based on these goals, the *DeviceEvaluation* and the *InformationServiceEvaluation* components choose which of the devices and services are relevant to the user. Information services are queried through the *ServiceQuery* component and replies are received by the *InfoServiceReplies* component. Finally, the user is notified about relevant devices and replies from information services through the *UserNotification* component.

The *generic* functionality of the components can be divided into information collection (sensors), information storage (infostores), decision-making (controllers) and finally those directly able to effect change in the environment (actuators). These four

---

[2] Note that while this architecture is sufficient for illustrating the agent construction model and how it can benefit agent design we do not claim that it is a complete design for such an agent.

generic types of components, described in more detail below, can be used to describe a wide range of agent architectures and fit particularly well with the context of ubiquitous devices, where there is clear distinction between the external environment of the device and the agent itself.

- *Controllers* are the main decision-making components in an agent. They analyse information, reach decisions as to what action an agent should perform, and delegate those actions to other components.
- *Sensors* are able to sense environmental attributes, such as signals from the user or messages received from other agents. They provide the means through which the agent gains information from the environment.
- *Actuators* cause changes in environmental attributes by performing actions.
- *Infostores* are components whose main task is that of storing information. Such information could be anything from the beliefs of an agent about the world, to plans, to simply a history of the actions an agent has performed or a representation of its current relationships.

Component Statements. The *internal* operation and structuring of components, irrespective of their type, is divided into a functionally-specific part and a generic part. In this subsection, we describe the generic operation that is common to all components. In addition, we describe the types of information that components can exchange and how that information is processed by a component.

Each component accepts a predefined set of inputs and produces a predefined set of outputs. A component generates an output either as a direct response to an input from another component, a signal from the environment or an internal event. For example, a sensor component attached to a thermometer may produce an output every five minutes (based on an internal clock), or when the temperature exceeds a certain level (an external signal), or when requested from another component (as a response to the other component).

In *act*SMART, inputs and outputs share a common structure; they are *statements*, which have a *type* and a *body*. The body carries the main information (e.g., an update from a sensor), while the type indicates how the information in the main body should be treated. We make use of three types of statements, described below.

- INFORM-type statements are used when one component simply passes information to another component. In order for one component to inform another of something, it must be able to produce the INFORM-type statement as an output and the other must be able to accept it as an input.
- REQUEST-type statements are used when one component requires a reply from another component. In this case, the receiving component processes the request and produces an INFORM statement that is sent to the requesting component. The mechanisms through which statements are transmitted from one component to another are introduced in Section 4.
- EXECUTE-type statements are used to instruct a component to execute a specific action. Typically, controller components send such statements to actuators so that changes can be effected in the environment.

```
while active and not executing do
        listen for statements

        if statements received then
                store statements

        if call to execute then
                retrieve stored statements
        while stored statements not empty do
                if INFORM then
                        update relevant attributes
                if REQUEST then
                        retrieve relevant attributes
                        create INFORM statement
                        push statement to outbound stack
                if EXECUTE then
                        push statement to execution stack

        pop statements from execution stack and perform actions

        send statements to other components
```

Fig. 4. Component Lifecycle

The information within a statement's body is, in its most general form, described through *attributes*, as per the definitions given in Section 2.2. Attributes can be divided along the lines of *architecture-specific* attributes and *domain-specific* attributes. Architecture-specific attributes are attributes that are only relevant within the internal scope of an agent architecture. For example, a BDI-based architecture could define attributes such as *plans*, *beliefs*, *intentions* and so forth.[3] Architecture-specific attributes can be considered as defining the *internal* environment of an agent. Domain-specific attributes define features that are relevant to the environment within which the agent is operating. So, in the example above, these attributes may include features such as *device name*, *location*, and so forth. Generic agent architectures, such as BDI-based ones, typically make use of both types of attributes, including domain specific attributes *within* the architecture-specific attributes. Thus a *plan* may prescribe an action to contact a service, as identified by its *service name*. The components of an AgentSpeak(L) architecture, for example, could then manipulate *plans* and *beliefs*, and have some generic way of manipulating the *domain-specific* attributes. However, a developer may also choose to develop an agent that has no architecture-specific attributes, creating components that can directly manipulate domain-specific attributes.

Component Operation. An outline of the component operation is shown in Figure 4. Components begin their operation in an inactive state, but once activated (by the shell that is described in Section 4, perform any relevant initialisation procedures and wait for receipt of statements or for the command to execute by the shell. When a statement is received, it is stored within the component until the component enters its component execution phase. At this point, all statements received by a component are processed. The processing of statements may result in the component performing a set of actions or firing statements itself. This process stops when the component is de-activated.

The reason that components store statements instead of dealing with them immediately is that components can be made to react immediately after each statement is

---

[3] This approach was followed by d'Inverno and Luck when formalising AgentSpeak(L) [9].

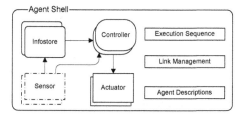

Fig. 5. Agent shell

received through external control, as we discuss in the next section. In other words, the behaviour of a component within the context of the entire architecture (i.e., when it acts or sends messages) depends on an external controller.

At any given time, the state of a component, in terms of the information to be manipulated, is given by the set of statements that have not yet been processed, the set of statements in the execution stack, the set of statements in the outbound stack, and any attributes that the component manipulates. Depending on the specific implementation of a component, it may be possible to interrogate components for their individual states. We discuss this issue further in Section 5.

With components, we are able to differentiate between the different tasks an agent architecture needs to perform, from a structural perspective. In contrast, the composition of components and the control of the flow of information between them provides the behavioural specification. In the next section we see how this is managed.

4   Shell

As discussed in Section 2.4, the basic principle of a component-based approach is that components should be independent of each other and the coordination between them should be handled by a third-party. The design of the components presented above achieves independence by defining the interface of the components so that interaction is reduced to the exchange of statements, with no consideration as to where a statement arrives from. The third-party coordination is achieved by placing components within a *shell*, which acts as the *third party* that manages the sequence in which components execute and the flow of information between components. This management takes place by defining *links* between components and the *execution sequence* of components. The basic aspects of a shell are illustrated in Figure 5. We use different representations for the different types of components in order to aid the illustration of agent architectures. *Sensors* are dashed rectangles, *infostores* are rounded corner rectangles, *actuators* are continuous line rectangles, and *controllers* are accented rounded corner rectangles. Components are placed within a shell, links are created between components to allow the flow of statements, and an execution sequence is defined. In addition, the shell can be used to maintain *descriptions* of agents in terms of attributes, capabilities and goals. We consider each of these aspects in more detail below.

Links. Information flows through *links* that the shell establishes between components. Each link contains *paths* from a *statement-producing* component to a *statement-recei-*

ving component. Each component that produces statements has a link associated to it that defines the components that should receive those statements. Links also ensure that, in the case of a REQUEST statement, the reply is sent to the component that produced the request. Thus, links manage paths, which are one-to-one relationships between components. They are usually unidirectional, except in the case of a REQUEST statement, for which an INFORM may be returned in the opposite direction.

The shell then uses the information within links to coordinate the flow of statements between components. Ultimately, coordination depends on the choices that a developer makes, since it requires knowledge of each component and how they can be composed.

By decoupling the handling of statements between components from the components themselves, we gain considerable flexibility. We can manage the composition of components and the flow of information without the components themselves needing to be aware of each other. It is the architecture developer's task to ensure that the appropriate links are in place. At the same time, we have flexibility in altering links, and it becomes easier to introduce new components. Furthermore, basic transformations can be performed on a statement from one component to the other to ensure compatibility if the output of one component does not exactly match the required input for another. For example, if a sensor component provides information from a thermometer based on the Celsius scale, while a controller that uses that information makes use of the Fahrenheit scale, the link can be programmed to perform the necessary transformation. These features satisfy our requirement for facilitating the reconfiguration of architectures.

Execution Sequence. Apart from the management of the flow of information, we also need to consider the execution of components for a complete view of agent behaviour. This is defined via an *execution sequence* that is managed by the shell. Execution of a component includes the processing of statements received, the dispatch of statements and the performance of any other actions that are required. The execution sequence is an essential part of most agent architectures and, by placing the responsibility of managing the sequence within the shell, we can easily reconfigure it at any point during the operation of the agent. For many architectures this may be purely sequential, but there are cases in which concurrent execution of components is desired (e.g., the DECAF architecture is based on a fully concurrent execution of *all* components [13]). In general, the issue of supporting complex execution sequence constructs, such as conditional paths and loops, is considered to be an issue that goes beyond the scope of this research, and there is a wealth of existing research that can be accessed to address this need. For example, recent developments within the field of Semantic Web Services provide a process model language for describing the operation of a web service [1]. Nonetheless, through our proposed mechanisms, we facilitate the necessary separation of concerns to enable the integration of such work within the scope of agent architecture development. In Section 5, where we present an implementation of *act*SMART, we only implement a sequential execution sequence, which is sufficient for our current purposes.

Agent Description. The description of the agent as a whole is maintained by the shell, which can store attributes that describe the agent owner, its location, user preferences, etc. The level of detail covered by this description is mostly an application-specific issue, and this information can either be provided directly to the shell by the developer, or collected from the various components. The shell could query a component that is able to provide information about current location, for example, and add that to the profile of the whole agent. Likewise, it may keep a record of the current goal an agent is trying to satisfy, or the plan it is pursuing. The capabilities collecting and providing attributes describing the agent within the shell may be particularly useful in a situation in which a developer wants to export a view of the agent for debugging purposes, or when some information needs to be advertised, such as the agent's capabilities.

Agent Design. With the main aspects of the agent construction model in place, we now briefly describe the agent design process. Agent design begins with an empty shell. We could envisage implementations of shells being provided by environment owners, which would ensure compatibility with their environment, while allowing the agent developer relative freedom as to the structure and behaviour of the agent within the confines of the shell. Then, based on the purpose of the agent, the necessary components for sensing, acting, decision-making (controllers) and information storage can be identified. If such components already exist, the main task of the developer is to decide on the desired behaviour, in terms of execution sequence and flow of information, and whether any of the outputs of components need to be transformed in order to be aligned with the input needs of other components.

The components are then loaded into the shell, and links, as well as an execution sequence, can be defined. With the execution sequence in place, the operational cycle of the agent can begin. Agent operation can be suspended or stopped by stopping the execution sequence. This operational cycle can be modified by altering the execution sequence, and modifying links between components.

5   Implemenation of *act*SMART

In order to evaluate the viability of the agent construction model, we have developed an implementation of the ideas described above in Java. The resulting toolkit consists of a core set of applications programming interfaces (APIs) that represent the basic code required for defining a shell, components and links between components. This core has been programmed solely using classes supported within the Mobile Information Device Profile (MIDP) of the Java 2 Micro Edition [14]. As such, the core ideas can be used by wide range of devices, from workstations to limited capability mobile phones.

There are two extensions to the core, one for more powerful devices such as desktop and laptop computers and one for mobile devices, respectively. The extension for powerful devices provides enhancements to the core, such as a graphical user interface for building entities and run-time loading of components, that are not possible for limited capability devices. Furthermore, in order to speed up the development process, we can define the required components, attributes, links and execution sequence within an XML file and use that to create an agent in the desktop environment. The extension for mobile devices provides functionality that is specific to mobile devices such as permanent record stores and user interfaces for mobile devices. In both cases, we can manage the information flow between components at run-time as well as change the execution sequence within the limits of the types of execution sequence that we currently support.

The user interfaces provided with *act*SMART, for both the mobile and desktop devices, allow direct access to all the relevant information on the state and operation of an agent, as well as the capability to manipulate each agent as a whole or as individual components. As such, they can serve as the basis for effective debugging tool for agents as well as a means to manipulate and change agent configurations during run-time.

5.1   Implementing an Architecture

In order to illustrate some of the benefits of this approach for mobile devices we have implemented the architecture and scenario described in Section 3 for a MIDP 2.0 compliant device using the J2ME Wireless Toolkit, which provides an environment that can simulate various mobile devices and the operation of MIDP applications within them. The discovery of available services and devices is simulated, with the mobile device using the APIs provided by MIDP 2.0 (Generic Connection Framework) for network communication and communicating via TCP/IP with independent processes that provide the relevant information. We avoid here detailed descriptions of the exact statements exchanged between components, due to a lack of space, and focus on some of the specific implementation issues for mobile devices.

Adapting to Changes in the Environment. Pervasive environments present a constantly changing set of devices and services to interact with as well as modes of interactions. For example, a device may be able to communicate with other devices through a variety of low-level protocols such as 802.11b wireless, Bluetooth or even SMS messages as well as higher level agent language communication protocols. By isolating the functionality required for these different types to dedicated sensor components we can dynamically choose which to use at runtime based on device capabilities. For example, upon initialisation, a shell can determine if a device supports Bluetooth communication and accordingly activate and link the Bluetooth-enabled sensor component. Similarly, a device can determine that a certain protocol, although supported by the device, is not supported by anything else in the environment, and by consequence unlink and deactivate the component, thus minimising the load the agent places on the device.

Suspending Operation. A useful feature of *act*SMART is the easy access it provides to the state of individual components and the agent as a whole. This allows us to *suspend* the operation of an agent either through a user command or when the device is interrupted (e.g. by a phone call). The MIDP application management model supports the persistent storage of the relevant information on a device, thus enabling operation to resume from where it left off. This feature can also be used to periodically save data in order to be able to recover operation if the device unexpectedly switches off.

Modifying the Architecture

Finally, through the mechanisms provided by Java mobile device technologies and, in particular, *over-the-air* provisioning of MIDP [14], applications we can take advantage of the flexibility afforded by *act*SMART to replace existing architectures with modified versions that can support more functionality. For example, in Figure 6 the basic architecture is extended to support interaction with other user devices that can provide profiles

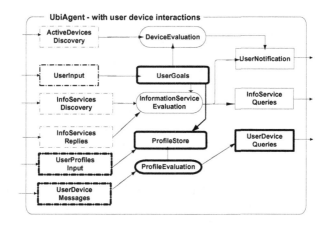

Fig. 6. Extended Ubiquitous Agent Design

of their owners. The bold components are the additional or modified components over the existing architecture. They allow the user to input another goal, which is handled by the new components to store, evaluate and send profiles to other devices.

5.2   Discussion

The implementation of the architecture in *act*SMART has provided useful experience as to the suitability of the model for agent construction in a ubiquitous computing environment setting. Although the implementation of interactions with other sources are based on a simulation of the environment, the APIs used are those directly supported by the majority of high-end mobile phone devices.

The fine-grained control over every aspect of the agent aids in testing and debugging, since components can be tested individually and they can be tested in *conjunction* with other components without requiring an instantiation of the entire architecture. Moreover, the state of each component, and the agent as a whole, is clearly defined, and changes to individual components and to the overall architecture are easy to achieve.

6   Conclusions

A component-based approach to agent design is, of course, not unique. The majority of current agent toolkits (e.g. [21, 16, 3, 19]) support some sort of component-based approach. However, they do not explicitly support the definition of a *range* of architectures. A notable exception is JADE [3], which provides limited support for agent architectures and does not constrain the developer to a specific one. However, at the same time, it does not aid the developer by providing a conceptually grounded construction model, such as *act*SMART. We note that the generic nature of JADE could allow for the use of *act*SMART in *conjuction* with it, enabling developers to take advantage of both a dedicated agent construction model, and the extensive infrastructural support provided by JADE.

Methodologies for agent development have also introduced similar notions. The most relevant example is the DESIRE design method [5], where compositional design is an integral part of the methodological approach proposed. Components are seen as encapsulating processes and composition of components is, therefore, a composition of processes. Our approach is complementary to DESIRE since it can be seen as *restricting* many of the concepts already supported within DESIRE. It is a more *lightweight* construction that is more specific in defining the types of individual components and the ways that they can communicate. As a result, it deals well with the issues related to ubiquitous computing devices and makes implementation more straightforward since *act*SMART maps directly to implementation. We are able to describe very simple architectures, such as just a reactive agent[4], to more complex architectures[5] , while retaining a clear separation between an abstract specification level and practical implementation.

The approach offers several real contributions to the state-of-the-art, as follows: it addresses development concerns directly by providing clear links between conceptual models and implementation; it builds on existing theoretical work while adopting the most valuable practical developments; and it tackles some of the implementation concerns of mobile devices, supported by a sound foundational approach that is easily realisable in practice.

References

1. A. Ankolenkar, M. Burstein, J. R. Hobbs, O. Lassila, D. L. Martin, S. A. M. Drew McDermott, S. Narayanan, M. Paolucci, T. R. Payne, and K. Sycara. DAML-S: Web Service Description for the Semantic Web. In I. F. Cruz, S. Decker, J. Euzenat, and D. L. McGuinness, editors, *The First Semantic Web Working Symposium*, pages 411–430. Stanford University, California, 2001.
2. R. Ashri, I. Rahwan, and M. Luck. Architectures for Negotiating Agents. In V. Marik, J. Muller, and M. Pechoucek, editors, *Mutli-Agent Systems and Applications III*, volume 2691 of *LNAI*, pages 136–146. Springer, 2003.
3. F. Bellifemine, A. Poggi, and G. Rimassa. Developing Multi-agent Systems with JADE. In C. Castelfranchi and Y. Lespérance, editors, *Intelligent Agents VII. Agent Theories Architectures and Languages*, volume 1986 of *LNCS*, pages 89–103. Springer, 2001.
4. F. Bergenti and A. Poggi. Ubiquitous Information Agents. *International Journal of Cooperative Information Systems*, 11(3–4):231–244, 2002.
5. F. T. Brazier, C. Jonker, and J. Treur. Principles of Component-Based Design of Intelligent Agents. *Data and Knowledge Engineering*, 41:1–28, 2002.
6. J. Bryson and L. A. Stein. Architectures and Idioms: Making Progress in Agent Design. In C. Castelfranchi and Y. Lespérance, editors, *Intelligent Agents VII. Agent Theories Architectures and Languages*, volume 1986, pages 73–88. Springer, 2001.
7. J. Cheesman and J. Daniels. *UML Components: A Simple Process for Specifying COmponent-Based Software*. Addison-Wesley, 2000.
8. M. d'Inverno, D. Kinny, M. Luck, and M. Wooldridge. A Formal Specification of dMARS. In M. P. Singh, A. S. Rao, and M. Wooldridge, editors, *Intelligent Agenrs IV: Proceedings of the Fourth International Workshop on Agent Theories, Architectures and Languages*, volume 1365 of *LNCS*, pages 155–176. Springer, 1996.

---

[4] In our case a reactive architecture would consist of just sensors linked directly to actuators.

[5] We have used the same approach to describe complex negotiating agent architectures [2].

9. M. d'Inverno and M. Luck. Engineering AgentSpeak(L): A Formal Computational Model. *Journal of Logic and Computation*, 8(3):233–260, 1998.

10. M. d'Inverno and M. Luck. *Understanding Agent Systems*. Springer, 2nd edition, 2004.

11. D. D'Souza and A. Wills. *Objects Components and Frameowrks with UML*. Addison-Wesley, 1998.

12. T. Finin, A. Joshi, L. kagal, O. V. Patsimor, S. Avancha, V. Korolev, H. Chen, F. Perich, and R. S. Cost. Intelligent Agents for Mobile and Embedded Devices. *International Journal of Cooperative Information Systems*, 11(3–4):205–230, 2002.

13. J. Graham and K. Decker. Towards a Distributed Environment-Centered Agent Framework. In N. Jennings and Y. Lesperance, editors, *Intelligent Agents VI Agent Theories, Architectures, and Languages*, volume 1757 of *LNCS*. Springer, 1999.

14. J. . E. Group. Mobile Information Device Profile for the Java 2 Micro Edition - Version 2.0. Technical report, Java Community Press, 2002.

15. V. Hilaire, O. Simonin, A. Koukam, and J. Ferber. A Formal Approach to Design and Reuse Agent and Multiagent Models. In P. Giorgini, J. P. Muller, and J. Odell, editors, *Agent-Oriented Software Engineering V*. Springer, 2004.

16. H. Nwana, D. Ndumu, L. Lee, and J. Collis. ZEUS: A Tool-Kit for Building Distributed Multi-Agent Systems. *Applied Artifical Intelligence*, 13(1):129–186, 1999.

17. J. Spivey. *The Z Notation*. Prentice Hall, 2nd edition, 1992.

18. I. Srnkovic, B. Hnich, T. Jonsson, and Z. Kiziltan. Specification, Implementation and Deployment of Components. *Communications of the ACM*, 45(10):35–40, 2002.

19. V. Subrahmanian, P. Bonatti, J. Dix, T. Eiter, S. Kraus, F. Ozcan, and R. Ross. *Heterogeneous Agent Systems*. MIT Press, 2000.

20. C. Szyperski. *Component Software: Beyond Object-Oriented Programming*. Addison-Wesley, 1998.

21. T. Wagner and B. Horling. The Struggle for Reuse and Domain Independence: Research with TAEMS, TDTC and JAF. In T. Wagner and O. Rana, editors, *Infrastructure for Agents, MAS and scalable MAS, Workshop in Autonomous Agents 2001*, pages 17–23, 2001.

A Framework for Patterns in Gaia: A Case-Study with Organisations

Jorge Gonzalez-Palacios and Michael Luck

School of Electronics and Computer Science,
University of Southampton, Southampton, SO17 1BJ, UK
{jlgp02r, mml}@ecs.soton.ac.uk

Abstract. The agent-oriented approach has been successfully applied to the solution of complex problems in dynamic open environments. However, to extend its use to mainstream computing and industrial environments, appropriate software tools are needed. Arguably, software methodologies form the most important type of these software tools. Although several agent-oriented methodologies have been proposed to date, none of them is mature enough to be used in industrial environments. In particular, they typically don't include catalogues of patterns that are necessary for addressing issues of reuse and speed of development. Two possible approaches to overcome such weaknesses in current agent-oriented methodologies are: to propose new methodologies, or to enhance existing ones. In this paper, the latter approach is taken, offering an enhancement of the Gaia methodology to include a catalogue, specifically concerned with a set of organisational patterns. Each of these patterns contains the description of a structure that can be used to model the organisation of agents in specific applications. The use of these patterns helps to reduce development time and promotes reusability of design models.

1   Introduction

The agent-oriented paradigm views a software system as composed of autonomous, pro-active entities that interact using a high level of discourse to achieve overall goals. Research and experimental work in the agent community have shown that this approach is suitable for modelling complex dynamic problems. However, to encourage its use in mainstream computing, some means of engineering agent-based applications is needed. Software methodologies provide one way to engineer such applications in an efficient, repeatable, robust and controllable fashion.

As is indicated in the previous paragraph, interaction plays a relevant role in any multi-agent system. For that reason, the particular focus of our work is on the use of *organisations*, which are important because they provide suitable abstractions to describe, analyse and design the interactions between agents operating in a multi-agent system; thus, organisations may serve as a first-class abstraction to model applications. In the organisational approach, each agent plays one or more roles that interact according to predefined protocols. However, an organisation is more than just a set of interactive roles, so that when modelling an organisation, some means of capturing its essential properties is needed (*organisational abstractions*).

Although many agent-oriented methodologies have been proposed, none is mature enough to be used in industrial and commercial environments [17]. To overcome this, new

J. Odell et al. (Eds.): AOSE 2004, LNCS 3382, pp. 174–188, 2005.

methodologies are being proposed, but there are two disadvantages. First, increasing the number of available methodologies may cause undesirable effects, such as difficulty in reaching standards, and confusion in selecting a methodology for a specific problem [19]. These effects are particularly undesirable in industrial environments; for instance, adopting a technology in which standards have not been reached is a highly risky decision. Second, there is a tendency to bypass the reuse of work contained in current methodologies. Although they are not mature enough, recent evaluations ([4, 19]) show that some contain valuable contributions. Thus, we focus our research on enhancing current work rather than creating yet another methodology.

Among all the current methodologies, those that encourage the use of organisational abstractions are of special interest, since some evidence suggests that they are potentially suitable for building open systems in complex dynamic environments [22, 15]. One of the first methodologies to incorporate organisational abstractions was that presented in [23] (hereafter called Gaia Extended with Organisational Abstractions, or simply GaiaExOA), which is an evolving extension of the Gaia methodology [20]. In particular, GaiaExOA offers the following valuable features.

- It is easy to understand even by non-specialists, since the process is straightforward and the modelling language simple.
- It is also architecture-independent so that no commitment is made to a specific agent architecture, allowing different architectures to be used in the development process.
- Equally important, GaiaExOA is very well known, being one of the most cited (and consequently used) methodologies, and is suitable for extensions and enhancements. This is already indicated by the various different extensions that have been built around Gaia itself [21, 11].

However, GaiaExOA also requires further work. For example, it lacks a catalogue of patterns to support the development of applications and, in particular, it lacks *organisational patterns*, the importance of which is highlighted in [23], but no such set exists. In this paper, we fill this gap by presenting a framework in which organisational patterns may be developed. We also present an example of such a pattern (but lack of space prohibits other cases). Since the advantages of using patterns are multiple (they reduce development time, promote reusability, act as communication facilitators, and serve as reference and documentation), a valuable enhancement has been achieved.

The rest of the document is organised as follows: Section 2 presents a review of the GaiaExOA methodology with the aim of providing the reader with the context in which the patterns will be used. In Section 3 the exact purpose and scope of the patterns is established. The way patterns are described is important for a fast and appropriate selection; thus in Section 4 we justify the layout used. Due to space limitations, we present only one pattern, and this is done in Section 5. Section 6 contains a review of related work. Finally, Section 7 presents our conclusions.

2 Methodological Context

With the aim of providing the reader with the context in which the patterns will be used, a summary of the GaiaExOA methodology is presented in this section (for a more detailed description see [23] and [20]).

Table 1. Roles in GaiaExOA

name
description
protocols
activities
responsibilities
liveness properties
safety properties
permissions

2.1 Organisations in GaiaExOA

As suggested earlier, GaiaExOA is based on the organisational metaphor, which implies that a multi-agent system is seen as a set of agents playing *roles* and *interacting* to achieve individual or societal goals. In turn, these interactions give rise to the composition of *organisations*. In this section, we first describe how the components of roles and interactions are characterised in GaiaExOA, and then outline the mechanism used to describe what constitutes an organisation.

First, we consider the various components. Roles are characterised by a set of features defining their nature and activity as shown in Table 1. The *name* identifies the role and reflects its main intent; the *description* provides a brief textual description of the role; the *protocols* describe the interactions with other roles; the *activities* detail those computations that the role performs without interacting with other roles; the *responsibilities* express the functionality of the role (divided into two parts: *liveness properties* and *safety properties*, which relate to states of affairs that a role must bring about, and the conditions whose compliance the role must ensure, respectively); and the *permissions* identify both the resources that the role needs in order to fulfil its responsibilities, and its rights of access to use them. The characterisation of a role is depicted graphically by means of a *role schema*, an example of which is shown in Figure 4.

Interactions are characterised by means of *protocol definitions*, which comprise the following features: a *purpose* that provides a brief textual description of the interaction; a list of *initiators* that enumerates the roles that start the interaction (usually a single element); a list of *responders* that enumerates the roles involved in the interaction, apart from the initiators; a list of *inputs* and *outputs* that provides the information required or produced during the interaction; and a brief textual *description* that outlines the processing performed by the initiators during the interaction. This characterisation is represented graphically using a diagram like that shown in Figure 1.

Organisations are characterised using two concepts: *organisational rules* and *organisational structures*. The former are constraints imposed on the components of the organisation; that is, roles and protocols. In other words, organisational rules express relationships and constraints between roles, between protocols and between protocols and roles. For example, in an electronic commerce application, an organisational rule might state that an agent cannot play the roles of seller and buyer in the same transaction. To specify organisational rules, first-order temporal logic is used in GaiaExOA [23],

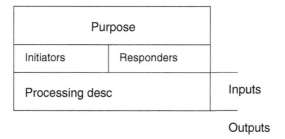

Fig. 1. Protocols in GaiaExOA

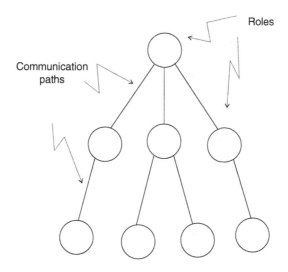

Fig. 2. Topology representation

together with the temporal connectives. The following formula makes use of this logic to express the rule cited above.

$$\neg\Diamond\,[plays(a, seller) \wedge plays(a, buyer)]$$

Organisational structures encompass two aspects: *topology* and *control regime*. The topology of an organisation is formed of all the communication paths between the member roles, and it is commonly depicted using a diagram in which roles are represented by nodes, and communication paths are represented by arcs between nodes (see Figure 2). The control regime refers to the power relationship between the member roles. Common control regimes are peer-to-peer (when no role is subordinated to another) and master-slave (when the existence of one role is justified only in terms of supporting another role).

2.2   Phases of Development

Although GaiaExOA is one of the best known and most used methodologies, it is limited in terms of its applicability to the full cycle of development, primarily addressing the

Table 2. Services in GaiaExOA

name	name of the service
inputs	information needed
outputs	information produced
pre-conditions	constraints
post-conditions	effects

analysis and upper-design phases, leaving the rest (e.g. detailed design and implementation) largely unconsidered. A brief description of each of its phases follows.

The analysis phase deals with collecting the features needed to model the system, and consists of the following three steps. First, the overall goals of the organisation and its expected global behaviour are identified. Second, based on this information, the basic skills the organisation must accomplish and the interactions needed to achieve them are recognised. Then, a preliminary set of roles is derived from the basic skills. The set of the corresponding role schemata is called the *preliminary roles model*. In addition, the interactions are used to define a preliminary set of protocols. The corresponding set of protocol definitions is called the *preliminary interactions model*. During this step it is important to keep the roles and interactions independent of any specific organisational structure. Finally, the organisational rules of the system are collected.

The design phase deals with building a specification of the system and consists of five steps. To begin with, the organisational structure of the system is determined. This structure might not resemble the physical structure in which the system is immersed, since additional considerations must be taken into account, like efficiency. Secondly, the roles and interactions models are completed. This activity includes the incorporation of new roles and interactions that may have resulted from the application of the previous step, and it is suggested that structure-dependent aspects be separated from those independent of the structure. Thirdly, *organisational patterns* are exploited with the aim of designing the organisational structure and the final interactions model (see Section 3 for details). Next, a decision is made about which roles will be played by which agents at runtime. This decision must consider factors such like coupling, coherence and efficiency. Finally, a list with the *services* (or coherent blocks of activity in which an agent is engaged) of all the roles in the system is produced. A service is a coherent block of activity in which an agent is engaged. Services are derived from the functionality of the roles played by the agents, and their description is shown in Table 2.

3   Organisational Patterns: Purpose

The use of the patterns is highlighted in Section 2.2 of the design phase of the methodology. It is observed that before selecting a pattern, the developer has already completed the roles and interactions models and has also identified the organisational rules and defined the organisational structure (topology and control regime). The developer chooses the pattern that best matches the structure that he or she has defined. Since the organisational structure has already been decided, we believe that the organisational pattern must provide at least the following additional value to the developer, all of them oriented towards facilitating the development process.

- A more formal description.
  For example, the developer may sketch the structure using an informal diagram, while the pattern must describe the structure in a more formal way. A more formal description is helpful to reduce ambiguity.
- Description of each role in the structure.
  Each pattern must include the schemata of the participating roles, including the characteristics related to the structure, so that the developer can focus his or her attention on application-specific features.
- Suggestions about their use.
  These suggestions would provide general advice on matters related to implementation. An appropriate level of detail is needed here for avoiding technology dependence.
- Description of the situations in which the pattern's use is appropriate.
  This should include a list of known situations in which the pattern or a closely related one has been used.
- A detailed description of the structure.
  This would be more detailed than a developer normally would achieve at this stage of the design, such as a list of organisational rules corresponding to the management of the organisation. Another example is the inclusion of extensions or variations of the pattern in which greater efficiency is achieved but perhaps the structure is less intuitive. This would let the developer focus on domain specific details rather than general design matters.

After selecting the right pattern, the developer must be ready to complete the final roles and interactions models. GaiaExOA goes as far as this in modelling the system, but a complete methodology should continue towards implementation.

It should be noted that the main question when selecting one of these patterns is what organisational structure best models the characteristics of the system-to-be. As pointed out in [23], such a structure must not only appropriately describe the characteristics of the system but must also take into account issues like efficiency and flexibility. According to Fox [6], when designing a distributed system, one must consider two issues: task decomposition and selection of a control regime. In GaiaExOA, a preliminary task decomposition is achieved during the analysis phase, but the decision of the definitive *topology* is postponed until design. For that reason the selected pattern must provide the topology and the control regime for the organisation.

A first attempt to create a set of patterns may be to take all possible combinations of known topologies and control regimes. This, of course, would lead to an unmanageable number of patterns. Another approach is to consider only those combinations that are potentially useful, either based on experience, or by analogy to other areas in which organisational structures have been applied. We assume that a small number of organisational structures would suit a broad range of applications.

4   The Description of the Patterns

The importance of a comprehensive structured description for the patterns is twofold. First, it must facilitate the selection of the most appropriate pattern for a specific application. Second, it must be meaningful and helpful when patterns are used as part of a methodology. Some layouts have previously been proposed to describe software patterns (e.g., [8]), and in particular agent patterns (e.g., [5, 14]). In [5] the following sections are suggested as mandatory in any layout: *name, context, problem, forces* and *solution*. Apart from these, *rationale* and *known uses* are also included, specifically for the description of patterns for agent coordination. The layout employed in [14] to describe a catalogue of agent patterns is also divided into two parts: one common to all patterns, and one specific to each of the categories presented in it. The common part includes: name, *alias*, problem, forces, *entities, dynamics, dependencies, example, implementation, known uses, consequences*, and *see also* (a description of the meaning of these components is presented below).

It should be noted, however, that there is no common agreement about what constitutes a good pattern description. For instance, there are different opinions about whether a unique description is appropriate to encompass a variety of patterns. On the one hand, doing this could result in a superficial description. On the other hand, different descriptions make it difficult to compare patterns when selecting one for a specific application. In the agent-oriented approach, it is even less clear what a good pattern description is, mainly because of the immaturity and diversity of agent-oriented methodologies. Rather than engage in that debate, we adopt a very pragmatic approach and opt for a simple description that complies with the Context-Problem-Solution notion (CPS)[2]. According to CPS, the essence of a pattern relies on the relationship between the problem, the situations in which it commonly occurs, and its solution. Thus, every pattern description must include these three elements.

The layout proposed in this document is divided into two parts. It includes a general part, similar to those found in other pattern descriptions; and a particular part, which is specific to organisational patterns. Since the purpose of the latter part is to describe an organisation, we consider the following sections to be necessary: *roles, structure, dynamics* and *rules*. The sections of the pattern layout, together with a brief explanation, are presented next.

- Name: short descriptive name for the pattern.
- Alias: other names for the pattern.
- Context: a description of the situation in which the pattern applies. Note that the context is a general description and thus is not sufficient to determine if the pattern is applicable. To this end, the context is complemented with the *forces* (see below).
- Problem: the problem solved by the pattern.
- Forces: description of factors that influence the decision as to when to apply the pattern in a *context*. Forces push or pull the problem towards different solutions or indicate possible trade-offs [5]. We have identified the following forces in organisational patterns.
  - Coordination efficiency: organisation structure strongly influences efficiency of coordination in terms of information shared and number of messages interchanged.

- Coupling: the degree of interdependence between the *roles*. Although coupling is inherent in all the structures, it varies in degree. A structure with high coupling imposes strong constraints on joining the system.
- Subordination relationships: some structures impose specific control regimes on their roles, which may not be appropriate for some applications.
- Topology complexity: simple topologies exhibit low coordination overhead but require powerful *roles* in terms of resources and task processing.

- Solution: a description of the solution.
- Restrictions: scope of the pattern.
- Consequences: side-effects of the use of the pattern.
- Implementation: short advice on how to implement the pattern.
- Based on: the references that served as a basis for the pattern.
- Roles: the participating *roles* and their characteristics. When appropriate, the roles in the pattern are described using role schemata. Since these patterns are intended for the development of open systems, a certain characterisation of roles is needed. For example, in a hierarchy, the manager role is more critical than those of subordinates in terms of integrity of the organisation. Thus, a simple characterisation would be: highly critical and less critical. Regarding their complexity, roles may be qualified as basic or potentially decomposable.
- Structure: the topology and the control regime between roles. As stated above, an organisational structure is defined by the topology and control regime of the organisation. Although the structure of an organisation is easily understood by means of a diagram, a formalism is needed to express it for purposes of manipulation, validation and comparison, particularly if tools are developed to support the design process (although this is out of the scope of this paper). In [23] the importance of such a formalism is recognised but the choice of it is left for future work. Here, we propose a simple formalism inspired by the ontology in [7], based on first-order predicate logic, and using the following predicates:

  - $hasInteraction(r, s)$: There exists an interaction protocol that involves role r and role s.
  - $subordinated(r, s)$: The role r is subordinated to the role s.

- Dynamics: the way the roles interact to solve the problem. The interactions between the roles are described using protocol definitions (see Section 2).
- Rules: Constraints to be respected in the organisation independent of the application domain. There are two types: those that spread over all the protocols and roles, and those that express relations between roles, protocols, or between roles and protocols. The formalism used to express the rules is the one proposed in [23] (see Subsection 2.1), together with the following predicates:

  - $plays(a, r)$: agent a performs role r.
  - $initiates(r, p)$: role r begins protocol p.
  - $participates(r, p)$: role r participates in the execution of protocol p.

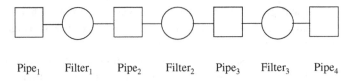

Pipe₁   Filter₁   Pipe₂   Filter₂   Pipe₃   Filter₃   Pipe₄

Fig. 3. Pipeline topology

5   The Pipeline Pattern

After the trivial case in which a structure contains only one role, the group is the simplest type of organisation. One characteristic of this type of structure is that the control regime is peer-to-peer; that is, no role is subordinated to another. According to the complexity of the topology, two patterns can be easily devised: pipeline and network. The former has a simple linear topology while the latter has a topology in which every role is connected to every other role. Below, the pipeline organisational pattern is described (see Figure 3).

– Name: Pipeline.
– Alias: Flat.
– Context: according to the GaiaExOA process, before selecting a pattern the developer has already completed the roles and the interactions models, and has also compiled the organisational rules and defined the organisational structure (topology and control regime). After selecting the appropriate pattern, the developer must be ready to complete the final roles and interactions models.
– Problem: to find the organisational structure that best describes the system under development. In GaiaExOA, the processes of the organisation are provided by the roles model, so what is missing is to define the topology and the control regime of the organisation. On the other hand, some characteristics of the problem have been identified. First, the overall goals are achieved by a strong collaboration among the participating roles. Second, such a collaboration can be seen as a processing line in which each role performs a transformation on a given information and delivers it to the next member of the line.
– Forces:
  • Coordination efficiency: low.
  • Coupling: low.
  • Subordination relationships: none.
  • Topology complexity: very simple.
– Solution: this structure has been extensively used in mainstream software engineering to design applications in which the overall processing can be decomposed into independent sequential tasks. The tasks are performed by *filters*, which are the processing components. Each filter is connected to the next by means of a *pipe*, which transfers data from the filter to its successor. Usually, the data are uniform and the tasks apply some sort of transformation on them, such as addition, modification or reduction of information. Although several descriptions exist for this style [2, 16, 10], the pattern presented here is suitable for the agent paradigm and has been adapted to be useful within the methodological context of GaiaExOA. In particular,

the components have been modelled as roles and agents, and their interactions as organisations.

- Restrictions: first, the overall task must be decomposable into independent sequential tasks. Second, the flow of information is restricted to be linear, sequential and only in one direction (no loops or feedback). Third, the processing speed is determined by the slowest filter, although the use of buffers in pipelines can alleviate this restriction to some extent. Finally, to avoid bandwidth and storage problems, the data transferred from stage to stage must be small.
- Consequences: the mechanism of coordination provided is rather simple and is not suitable for operations such as error management. This structure is flexible, since filters can be replaced or bypassed and new filters can be added easily.
- Implementation: the overall task of the system has to be decomposed into independent sequential tasks, with each assigned to one filter. The pipelines may be immersed in the communication layer.
- Roles: filters are obvious candidates to become roles. In addition, we decided to model pipes also as roles since this highlights their existence within the structure. (The decision of joining a filter and a pipe in a single agent can be postponed to the detailed design phase. Alternatively, pipes could have been modelled as resources, but GaiaExOA does not provide an explicit environment model.) However, it should be noted that filters are *active* entities while pipes are *passive* ones. Filters are allowed to be organisations themselves, but pipes are assumed to be primitive entities. For

Role Schema:	$Filter_i$
Description:	Performs the process corresponding to stage i on the input data
Protocols and Activities:	<u>ProcessData</u>$_i$, GetInput, SupplyOutput
Permissions:	changes supplied *Data*
Responsibilities:	
Liveness:	$Filter_i =$ (GetInput.<u>ProcessData</u>$_i$.SupplyOutput)^w
Safety:	•true

Fig. 4. The Filter role

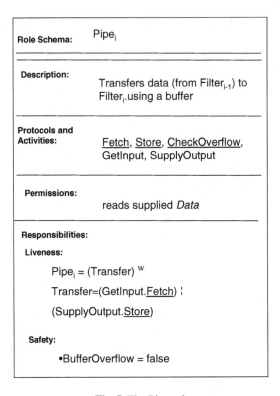

Fig. 5. The Pipe role

simplicity of the pattern, we decided not to include the roles of data source (the component which supplies data to the first pipe) and the data sink (the component to which the data to the last pipe is supplied). Figures 4 and 5 show templates of role schemata for the filter and pipe roles respectively.

– Structure: let us denote with N the number of filters in the structure and with $Filter_i$ and $Pipe_j$ the filters and pipes ($1 \leq i \leq N$ and $1 \leq j \leq N+1$) respectively (note that the number of pipes is $N+1$). Figure 3 depicts a pipeline for the case $N = 3$. The structure is described by the following constraints:

Each role has interaction only with its neighbours:

$$\forall i : hasInteraction(Filter_i, p) \Rightarrow$$
$$(p = Pipe_i \lor p = Pipe_{i+1})$$

$$\forall i : hasInteraction(Pipe_i, f) \Rightarrow$$
$$(f = Filter_{i-1} \lor f = Filter_i)$$

There are no subordinate relations between the roles:

$$\forall s, t : \neg subordinated(s, t)$$

– Dynamics: as shown in Figures 4 and 5, the protocols involved in the coordination of the organisation are $GetInput$ and $SupplyOutput$. Their descriptions are shown in Figure 6 a) and b) respectively. The typical operation of the structure at stage i is the following. First, the filter requests the pipe to its left for the next data using the $GetInput$ protocol (the filter confirms the correct reception of the data). Next, the filter processes the data. Then, the filter requests the pipe to its right to store the processed data using the $SupplyOutput$ protocol.

a)

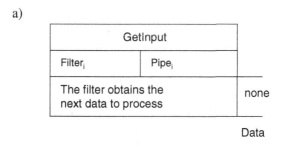

b)

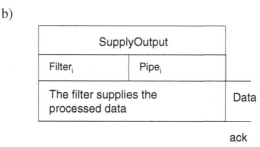

Fig. 6. Pipeline Protocols

– Organisational rules:
All the roles are played by at least one agent:

$$\forall i : \exists a \mid plays(a, Filter_i)$$

$$\forall j : \exists a \mid plays(a, Pipe_j)$$

All the roles are played by at most one agent:

$$\forall i : plays(a, Filter_i) \wedge \\ plays(b, Filter_i) \Rightarrow (a = b)$$

$$\forall j : plays(a, Pipe_j) \wedge \\ plays(b, Pipe_j) \Rightarrow (a = b)$$

6   Related Work

The patterns presented here are intended to be used during the methodological process outlined by Zambonelli et al. [23], in which the importance of a set of organisational patterns is stated but no such set is presented.

Patterns are extensively used to facilitate the development of software systems; in the agent-oriented approach they have been employed to design multiple aspects of an application. Some examples of agent-based methodologies that include the use of patterns in their processes are Tropos, Kendall's methodology and PASSI, considered below. Kolp et al. present a set of patterns in [13] as part of the Tropos methodology, which uses patterns (called *styles*) to describe the general architecture of a system under construction. Although there are similarities with our work, we include organisational rules and classify structures based on topology and control regime (or task decomposition).

Kendall [12] also includes a catalogue of patterns as a part of a technique to analyse and design agent-based systems. The patterns in that catalogue are more general than those presented here, since they include not only interactions but also the roles themselves (it should be noted that the concept of *role* there comes from role theory and is not identical to the concept used here). Since there is no reference to organisational abstractions, however, that work cannot be directly used in the GaiaExOA methodology, but perhaps the structure of those patterns may be used as a base to populate the set of patterns proposed here.

Cossentino et al. present in [3] the design of a particular type of agent pattern immersed in the PASSI methodology. They define a pattern as consisting of a model and an implementation. The model includes two parts: structure and behaviour. Structural patterns are classified into: action patterns, which represent the functionality of the system; behaviour patterns, which can be viewed as a collection of actions; component patterns, which encompass the structure of an agent and its tasks; and service patterns, which describe the collaboration between two or more agents. Implementations are available for two agent platforms, namely, JADE and FIPA-OS. As can be noted from this brief description, the concept of organisation is not explicitly addressed in their work.

Other patterns in the agent literature do not use a specific methodology. For instance, Aridor and Lange [1] present a catalogue that covers different aspects of an application: *travelling*, *task* and *interaction* but these are appropriate only for mobile-agent systems, and are *object-based* rather than role-based. Lind [14] proposed a structure of a pattern catalogue in which the work presented here may fit in their *Society* section, but it is not always clear how to apply the general-purpose patterns within a specific methodology. This is also true for [5], in which Deugo et al. present a set of coordination patterns that are not embedded in a methodology process, so usage is not clear. In fact, there is no separation of coordination patterns, task delegation patterns and matching patterns. A similar set of patterns is presented by Hayden et al. [9] but this focuses on defining how a goal assigned to a particular agent is fulfilled by interacting with other agents.

Finally, Silva and Delgado [18] present an agent pattern that provides distribution, security and persistence transparency. This does not suit our purposes because it focuses on access to a single agent rather than considering a society of them.

7   Conclusions

Although several agent-oriented methodologies have been proposed recently, none of them is mature enough to develop commercial and industrial applications. One step towards achieving mature methodologies is to enhance current methodologies with the inclusion of software engineering best practices, and one such best practice is the use of patterns in key parts of the design process. In this paper, we have presented a framework in which organisational patterns may be developed to model the organisational structure of software applications. Also included is an example of such a pattern (but lack of space prohibits other cases). No framework or set of patterns like these have been proposed before.

We argue that the development presented here is useful for the following reasons. First, it completes Gaia, which is one of the most used methodologies, and the exploitation of organisational patterns is an integral part of its process. Second, it increases the accessibility of the methodology, since the inclusion of patterns makes the methodology easier to use, especially by non-expert users. Third, it helps to reduce development time since developers may reuse the models to avoid building their applications from scratch. Finally, it provides a basis on which further patterns can be developed and improvements can be discussed.

It should be noted that although some patterns are very simple in concept, like the one presented in this document, their usefulness is twofold: they explicitly state the structure a system must conform to; and they serve as a basis for designing complex applications, since most real applications can be described by a composition of several simpler structures. Though this is a first step, it is an important one if the move to industrial-strength design and development is to be successful.

References

1. Y. Aridor and D. Lange. Agent design patterns: Elements of agent application design. In *Autonomous Agents (Agents'98)*. ACM Press, 1998.
2. F. Buschmann, R. Meunier, H. Rohnert, P. Sommerlad, and M. Stal. *Pattern-Oriented Software Architecture*. Wiley, 1996.
3. M. Cossentino, P. Burrafato, S. Lombardo, and L. Sabatucci. Introducing pattern reuse in the design of multi-agent systems, 2002.
4. K. Hoa Dam and M. Winikoff. Comparing agent-oriented methodologies. In *The Second International Joint Conference on Autonomous Agents and Multiagent Systems (AAMAS03)*, 2003.
5. D. Deugo, M. Weiss, and E. Kendall. *Coordination of Internet Agents: Models, Technologies and Applications*, chapter Reusable Patterns for Agent Coordination. Springer, 2001.
6. M. Fox. An organizational view of distributed systems. *IEEE Transactions on Systems, Man, and Cybernetics*, 11(1):70–80, 1981.
7. M. Fox, M. Barbuceanu, M. Gruninger, and J. Lin. *Simulating Organizations*, chapter An Organizational Ontology for Enterprise Modeling. AAAI Press/The MIT Press, 1998.
8. E. Gamma, R. Helm, R. Johnson, and J. Vlissides. *Design Patterns: Elements of Reusable Object-Oriented Software*. Addison-Wesley, 1995.
9. S. Hayden, C. Carrick, and Q. Yang. Architectural design patterns for multiagent coordination. In *International Conference on Agent Systems '99 (Agents'99)*, 1999.

10. G. Hohpe and B. Woolf. *Enterprise Integration Patterns*. Addison-Wesley, 2003.
11. T. Juan, A. Pearce, and L. Sterling. Roadmap: Extending the gaia methodology for complex open systems. In *AAMAS '02*. ACM, 2002.
12. E. Kendall. Role models: Patterns of agent system analysis and design. *BT Technology Journal*, 17(4):46–57, 1999.
13. M. Kolp, J. Castro, and J. Mylopoulos. A social organization perspective on software architectures. In *First Int. Workshop From Software Requirements to Architectures*, 2001.
14. J. Lind. Patterns in agent-oriented software engineering. In Fausto Giunchiglia, James Odell, and Gerhard Weiss, editors, *Agent-Oriented Software Engineering III*, volume 2585 of *Lecture Notes in Computer Science*. Springer, 2003.
15. X. Mao and E. Yu. Organizational and social concepts in agent-oriented software engineering. In *this volume*, 2004.
16. M. Shaw and D. Garlan. *Software Architecture: Perspectives on an Emerging Discipline*. Prentice Hall, 1996.
17. O. Shehory and A. Sturm. Evaluation of modelling techniques for agent-based systems. In J.P. Muller, Elisabeth Andre, Sandip Sen, and Claude Frasson, editors, *Proceedings of the Fifth International Conference on Autonomous Agents*, pages 624–631. ACM Press, 2001.
18. A. Silva and J. Delgado. The agent pattern for mobile agent systems. In *3rd European Conference on Pattern Languages of Programming and Computing, EuroPLoP'98*, 1998.
19. A. Sturm and O. Shehory. A framework for evaluating agent-oriented methodologies. In *The Second International Joint Conference on Autonomous Agents and Multiagent Systems*, 2003.
20. M. Wooldridge, N. Jennings, and D. Kinny. The Gaia methodology for agent-oriented analysis and design. *Autonomous Agents and Multi-Agent Systems*, 3(3):285–312, 2000.
21. F. Zambonelli, N. Jennings, A. Omicini, and M. Wooldridge. *Coordination of Internet Agents: Models, Technologies and Applications*, chapter Agent-Oriented Software Engineering for Internet Applications. Springer, 2001.
22. F. Zambonelli, N. Jennings, and M. Wooldridge. Organisational abstractions for the analysis and design of multi-agent systems. In *First International Workshop on Agent-Oriented Software Engineering*, pages 127–141, 2000.
23. F. Zambonelli, N. Jennings, and M. Wooldridge. Organisational rules as an abstraction for the analysis and design of multi-agent systems. *International Journal of Software Engineering and Knowledge Engineering*, 11(3):303–328, 2001.

Enacting and Deacting Roles in Agent Programming

Mehdi Dastani, M. Birna van Riemsdijk, Joris Hulstijn,
Frank Dignum, and John-Jules Ch. Meyer

Institute of Information and Computing Sciences,
Utrecht University, P.O.Box 80.089, 3508 TB Utrecht,The Netherlands
Tel: +31 - 30 - 253 3599
{mehdi, birna, jorish, dignum, jj}@cs.uu.nl

Abstract. In the paper we study the dynamics of roles played by agents in multiagent systems. We capture role dynamics in terms of four operations performed by agents: 'enactment', 'deactment', 'activate', and 'deactivate'. The use of these operations is motivated, in particular for open systems. A formal semantics for these operations is provided. This formalization is aimed at serving as a basis for implementation of role dynamics in an agent programming language such as 3APL.

1 Introduction

Several methodologies for the development of multiagent systems have been proposed to date [1, 8, 10, 14, 18]. Increasingly, these methodologies are based on organizational structures and normative concepts as cornerstones of the multiagent systems. In these methodologies, the specification and the design of the organizational structure involves two key concepts: *agent roles* and *agent types*. The basic idea is as follows. The analysis of an application results in the specification of an organizational structure, defined in terms of roles and their interactions. Subsequently, at the design phase, sets of roles are translated into agent types which constitute the system architecture. Finally, the designed system will be implemented. We recognize that there is no consensus on the exact definition of agent roles and agent types. In the next section we will discuss some of the causes for the apparent difficulty to give a precise definition of roles that would cover all its uses.

An important issue in developing multiagent systems and in particular open multiagent systems, in which agents may enter and leave, is the need to account for the dynamics of roles at all phases of the development methodology. The role in which agents enter the system may determine the course of actions they can undertake within the system and which other roles they may or may not switch to. E.g. an agent playing a buyer role at an auction has different rights than the seller or the auctioneer at the same auction. The dynamics of roles has been recently studied [4, 13]. In [13], role dynamics is studied informally at the specification level. The most important operations are *classify* and *declassify*,

J. Odell et al. (Eds.): AOSE 2004, LNCS 3382, pp. 189–204, 2005.

which means that an agent starts and finishes to occupy a role, and *activate* and *suspend*, which means that an agent starts executing actions belonging to the role and suspends the execution of the actions. Our approach is based on similar intuitions, and therefore uses very similar operations: *enact* and *deact*[1], and *activate* and *deactivate*. In our view, enacting a role means internalizing the specification of the role, while activating a role means reasoning with the (internalized) specification of the role.

Our approach to role dynamics differs from (or complements) the approach proposed in [13] as we consider role dynamics also at the implementation level. For the implementation level, we have to explain how roles are internalized, which means that we need to assume a certain agent architecture. For this purpose, we consider cognitive agents whose behaviors are determined by reasoning (deliberating) with their mental attitudes. As we aim to describe role dynamics at the implementation level, we have to define this dynamics formally. We do this by providing the formal semantics of the operations concerning role dynamics. Based on the formal semantics for these operations, we propose programming constructs with which these can be implemented. Based on these observations we want to address the following issues.

1. Which concepts play a crucial role in each of the development stages (analysis, design and implementation) of multiagent methodologies for defining roles?
2. How can we in general specify concepts such as agent role, agent type, and role dynamics?
3. In particular, how can we extend a dedicated agent-oriented programming language with programming constructs to implement role dynamics?

To address these issues, we discuss in section 2 our views on the development of multiagent systems, and on the use of agent roles, agent types and role dynamics in specification and design. In section 3 we present a small example of an auction house to illustrate the concepts. In section 4 we present an abstract view on agent roles, agent types, and role dynamics, and relate it to an implementation in the dedicated agent-oriented programming language 3APL [6, 12].

2   Roles and Agent Types in Multiagent Methodologies

Complex system applications are analyzed by multiagent development methodologies in terms of groups, roles, agents, and their relations [10, 1, 8, 14, 18]. Although everyone has an intuitive idea about what constitutes a role, the way roles are defined and used within multiagent systems differs widely. For example, roles may be used to analyze access demands for information systems, as is done in role-based access control models (RBAC) [15], or they may be used to model aspects of stake holders in a virtual museum [2]. Different usage of a concept,

---

[1] Although 'deact' is not an English word, we think it will convey the meaning we have in mind.

means that different demands are made. However, in all approaches it seems that roles are used to identify some task, behavior, responsibility or function that should be performed within the multiagent system. Typically, roles have a descriptive and prescriptive aspect. A role describes the expected behavior and properties of an agent. For example, an agent in the buyer role is expected to want to buy something. Based on such expectations, other agents can reason about ways to interact with agents in the role. A role also prescribes the procedures and rules in an organization. In an auction, for example, one should first register as a buyer, before being allowed to bid.

We consider an agent role as a set of normative behavior rules, a set of expected objectives and a specification of the information that is expected to be available to agents playing that role. Moreover, we consider an agent type as a set of agent roles with certain constraints and assume that an agent of a certain type decides itself to enact or deact a role. We also assume that agents can have multiple enacted roles simultaneously and that an agent can enact the same role multiple times. In our approach only *one* role can be *active* at each moment in time; all other enacted roles are deactive. This is because in our view a (cognitive) agent has one single reasoning process, also called the agent's deliberation, that determines the behavior of the agent based on the enacted (internalized) roles. One single reasoning process cannot be based on two or more enacted roles at the same time. Which role should be reasoned with at each moment in time is thought to be the agent's decision.

In this paper we focus on the use of roles as a guideline for the specification, design and implementation of multiagent systems. With respect to the specification and design, we have a similar view as, for example, the Gaia methodology [18]. The details on our view on multiagent methodology can be found in [5]. The main focus of our proposed methodology is based on the distinction between closed and open multiagent systems. Our methodology aims at developing open systems in which role dynamics is an important issue. The consideration of open multiagent systems thus forms the main motivation of this work.

2.1   Open and Closed Systems

In a *closed system*, agents can be implemented to fulfill a fixed set of roles. In this setup it makes sense to design agent types as a set of roles. Not much additional structure is needed. If for example objectives from two roles could conflict, this would be a reason to alter the design and change the agent types in such a way that conflicts are avoided. So, the tasks each agent will perform are completely determined by the roles it plays. Roles themselves have no existence outside the agents in the implemented system anymore. By contrast, in an *open system* [7] agents can enter and leave such that roles have existence outside the agents in the implemented multiagent systems. In this setting, agents are not completely defined by the roles they play. Part of their behavior is determined by their own wishes and objectives, which are set and motivated from outside the multiagent system. This has a number of consequences. Roles specify the permitted and expected behavior of an agent for as long as it will be part of the system.

First, roles can be described differently in the two situations. In a closed system, roles can be described in terms of fixed tasks, or fixed motivational attitudes such as responsibilities. Although a system specification in terms of norms and roles can still be useful as a development guideline, norms and roles are not necessary at the implementation level. In an open system, the norms and roles become unavoidable at the implementation level. For example, in situations where agents cannot be trusted, the role description must provide a kind of API for the agent, to function within the multiagent system. In ISLANDER [9] this idea is made concrete by implementing roles exactly as API's through which visiting agents have to interact with other agents in the system. In more liberal systems, in which agent behavior is allowed to deviate from the expected, one could define a role in terms of norms or potential goals, together with sanctions. In this case it remains a decision of the agent how far it will comply to the norm.

Second, for closed systems, role dynamics may still be a useful development guideline to specify multiagent systems. Roles may for example be associated with certain phases in a procedure. Role dynamics can then be used to specify the progress through the procedure. But again, such notions are not necessary for the implementation of such multiagent systems. For open systems, having a proper implementation model of what it means to enact or deact a role, becomes unavoidable. Not only the order in which roles are played, but also possible conflicts and constraints need to be maintained.

Finally, in the social sciences, whether or not an agent is currently enacting a role is regarded as a *social fact* [16]. While the decision to enact/deact a role is the initiative of the agent itself, the success of performing the enactment/deactment operation is determined by the whole community. E.g. an agent entering an auction will be enlisted as a customer: the first action an agent has to perform is the enactment of the customer role. Even more important is that agents cannot decide to deact a role at any moment. For example, an agent cannot deact the customer role and leave the auction, without paying for the items it buys. So the success of a deactment action depends at least partly on external factors. Enacting and deacting are joint actions, performed by system and agent together. Although we believe that these social aspects are important, for simplicity however, we do not consider it in this paper and assume that a role change operation is always allowed. Instead, we will focus on the internal aspects of an agent enacting or deacting a role.

3   Example: Multiagent Specification and Design

In this section we present an example to illustrate the dynamics of roles and agent types in multi-agent systems. The way the example is handled is based on ideas from Islander [9] and work on skeleton programming [17]. Consider a software agent A who participates in an English auction.

1. Suppose A wants to buy a contemporary dinner table at the auction. To acquire the money, she first needs to sell her antique dinner table.

2. *A* enters the registration phase (scene) of the auction house in the role of a customer. *A*'s name, address and bank account number are registered.
3. *A* can now enter the auction phase (scene) and take up the role of the seller. The antique dinner table is then registered and a reserve price is set.
4. *A* can also enter the auction phase (scene) and take up the buyer role. When the auction lot on the contemporary dinner table starts, *A* carries out her strategy of increasing her bid until she either acquires the contemporary dinner table or reaches her personal maximum price.
5. After the auction phase, *A* can set down its seller and buyers roles, enters the payment phase (scene), and take up its customer role to settle her business. She gets a receipt for the money made by the antique table and pays for the contemporary dinner table if it has succeeded to buy it.

To analyze cases such as these, it makes sense to distinguish various *scenes*. A scene defines a social context that delimits the applicability of roles. As indicated in Figure 1, the auctioning institution of our example can be analyzed as consisting of three scenes: the registration scene, the auction scene, and the payment scene. In the registration scene, agents can enact the customer role in order to register their names, address, bank account, and other relevant information. In the auction scene, an agent can enact the seller role to register its item to be sold and set a reservation price, the buyer role to bid and buy its desired item, or the auctioneer role which controls the lots and bids. Note that the agents in the auction scene can still enact their customer role, but only in the deactivated mode. In the auction scenario, only one role (buyer, seller, or auctioneer) can be activated at the same time. Finally, agents can put down their buyer and seller roles and enter the payment scene by activating their customer role again to settle their business.

Scenes are interconnected by transitions that indicate under what conditions an agent is allowed to migrate to another scene [9, 17]. For example, in the auction scene, agents should enact the buyer, the seller, or the auctioneer role in order to enter the auction scenario. These transitions are meant to specify which activities can take place in which order. An agent can enact different roles simultaneously and this implies that an agent can be active in different scenes simultaneously. For example, in the auctioning institution, an agent can enact the customer role to enter the registration scenario (get the identity $customer_1$).

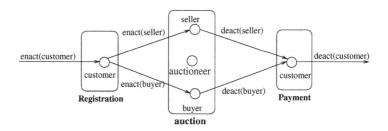

Fig. 1. Transitions between scenes

After registration, it can enact the buyer role and enter the auction scenario (get the identity $buyer_1$). At this moment, the agent can activate the customer role and enter the registration scenario once again.

A role can be specified in terms of the information that becomes available to agents when they enact the role, the objectives or responsibilities that the enacting agent should achieve or satisfy, and normative rules which can for example be used to handle these objectives.

4   Formalizing Role Enactment and Role Activation

4.1   Preliminaries

In section 2, we have explained the notions of agent roles and agent types in multiagent specification and design. In this section, we formalize these concepts and describe the notions of enacting, deacting, activating, and deactivating of roles by an agent. In the following, we assume a first order language L and a set of basic actions A based on which we define the belief language L_B, the goal language L_G, and the plan language L_P.

- $L_B = \beta ::= \mathbf{B}\phi \mid \neg\beta \mid \beta \wedge \beta'$ for $\phi \in L$.
- $L_G = \kappa ::= \mathbf{G}\phi \mid \neg\kappa \mid \kappa \wedge \kappa'$ for $\phi \in L$.
- $L_P = \pi ::= \alpha \mid \beta? \mid \pi; \pi' \mid \pi + \pi' \mid \pi\|\pi' \mid \pi^*$ for $\alpha \in A,\ \beta \in L_B$

Intuitively, $\mathbf{B}\phi$ should be read as "believes ϕ", $\mathbf{G}\phi$ as "has objective ϕ", $\beta?$ as "test if β", $\pi; \pi'$ as "first do π then do π'", $\pi + \pi'$ as "choose either π or π'", $\pi\|\pi'$ as "do π and π' simultaneously", and π^* as "repeat doing π". The formal semantics of these languages are not presented in this paper since it is not relevant for the purpose of this paper.

Moreover, we assume various types of rules which can be used for various purposes. For example, as we will see in the context of role specifications, these rules can be used to specify different types of norms and obligations, and in the context of agent specifications, they can be used to specify the dynamics of mental attitudes of agents such as modification or planning of objectives. For the purpose of this paper, we assume three different types of rules as specified below. The interpretation of these rules will be given when we define agent role and agent specification. Moreover, we do not claim that these types of rules are exhaustive, but believe that they make sense for the purpose of enacting and deacting of roles by agents. The three types of rules are represented by the following three sets PS (called plan selection rules), GR (called goal revision rules), and PR (called plan revision rules):

- $PS = \{\kappa \wedge \beta \Rightarrow \pi \mid \kappa \in L_G, \beta \in L_B, \pi \in L_P\}$
- $GR = \{\kappa \wedge \beta \Rightarrow \kappa' \mid \kappa, \kappa' \in L_G, \beta \in L_B\}$
- $PR = \{\pi \wedge \beta \Rightarrow \pi' \mid \pi, \pi' \in L_P, \beta \in L_B\}$

In the following, we assume that roles are abstract entities which can be instantiated whenever they are enacted. Therefore, we use $Rname$ to denote the set of names for role instantiations including a special name e for the passive role. We also use *Rules* to indicate the set of all triples of subsets of PS, GR, and PR, i.e. $Rules = 2^{PS} \times 2^{GR} \times 2^{PR}$.

4.2   Agent Roles and Agent Types

In this approach, we assume that a role determines the information that the enacting agent should have, the objectives that it should achieve, and the norms and obligations it has to fulfill [4]. For the buyer role, the information that the enacting agent should have, includes, for example the code of the item at the auction and the starting price if it has the information of the item, i.e.
$\mathbf{B}(item(name, attr) \rightarrow code(name, CodeOf(attr)) \land price(name, PriceOf(attr)))$
where $CodeOf$ and $PriceOf$ are assumed to be functions that map item attributes to the code and the starting price of the item, respectively.

In this paper, we consider agent's objectives as the states that the agent *wants* to achieve. For example, the buyer role may have the goal to buy an item which can be represented as $\mathbf{G}(wantedItem(name))$. Agent norms and obligations can be considered as *states* that should be achieved (e.g. an item should be paid if it is bought), but they can also be considered as *actions* that should be performed (e.g. a buyer should register). Moreover, we consider that the norms and obligations are context-dependent and therefore conditional in nature [11]. Norms and obligations are thus represented as being conditionalized on the states. For example, the norm to ask for the information about the item that the enacting agent wants to buy can be represented by a PS rule such as $\mathbf{G}(wantedItem(name)) \Rightarrow Ask(itemInf, name)$. Note that an answer to the *Ask* action can cause a belief update such that $\mathbf{B}(item(name, attr))$ becomes derivable from the belief base. Note also that from this update and the information above, the enacting agent may derive the code and the starting price of the agent. Moreover, an obligation to pay for a bought item can be represented by a GR rule as follows: $\mathbf{B}(bought(item)) \Rightarrow \mathbf{G}(pay(item))$.

Definition 1. *(Role) A role is a tuple $\langle \sigma_i, \gamma_i, \omega_i \rangle$, typically denoted by r, where $\sigma_i \in L_B$ specifies the information that an agent receives when enacting this role, $\gamma_i \in L_G$ specifies the objectives to be achieved by the agent that enacts this role, and $\omega_i \in Rules$ be a triple consisting of rules representing conditional norms and obligations.*

We assume that the objectives γ_i in the above definitions are achievement goals. Maintenance goals can be defined in terms of normative rules of the form $\neg \kappa \land \top \Rightarrow \kappa$ which means that goals κ should be adopted whenever κ is not the case. A role can be incoherent in the sense that it may be specified in terms of inconsistent beliefs and goals. Also, normative rules that are ascribed to a role may suggest the adoption of inconsistent objectives. One may therefore introduce coherence conditions to exclude these cases.

Definition 2. *(Role coherency) Let $\omega_i = (\omega^{PS}, \omega^{GR}, \omega^{PR}) \in Rules$. A role $r = \langle \sigma_i, \gamma_i, \omega_i \rangle$ is coherent, denoted as $coherent(r)$, iff:*

1. $\sigma_i \not\models \bot$: *consistent beliefs*
2. $\gamma_i \not\models \bot$: *consistent objectives*
3. $\sigma_i \not\models \gamma_i$ *if* $\top \not\models \gamma_i$: *non-trivial objectives are not achieved*
4. $(\bigwedge_{(\kappa \wedge \beta \Rightarrow \kappa') \in \omega^{GR}} \kappa') \not\models \bot$: *potential objectives are mutually consistent*
5. $\forall (\kappa \wedge \beta \Rightarrow \kappa') \in \omega^{GR} : \kappa' \wedge \gamma_i \not\models \bot$: *potential objectives are consistent with role's objectives*

Note that clause 4 in this definition is very strong in that it requires that all potential objectives should be mutually consistent. This requirement can be dropped resulting in a less restricted notion of coherence.

Roles can be mutually inconsistent since they may have contradictory information and objectives. Below, we define the notion of role consistency.

Definition 3. *(Role consistency) Two roles* $r = \langle \sigma_1, \gamma_1, \omega_1 \rangle$ *and* $r' = \langle \sigma_2, \gamma_2, \omega_2 \rangle$ *are consistent, denoted as* $consistent(r, r')$, *iff their 'combined role' is coherent, i.e.*

$$consistent(r, r') \Leftrightarrow coherent(\langle \sigma_1 \wedge \sigma_2, \gamma_1 \wedge \gamma_2, \omega_1 \oplus \omega_2 \rangle)$$

where $(R_1, \ldots, R_n) \oplus (R'_1, \ldots, R'_n) = (R_1 \cup R'_1, \ldots, R_n \cup R'_n)$.

Proposition 1. *An agent role* r *is coherent iff it is consistent with itself, i.e.*

$$coherent(r) \Leftrightarrow consistent(r, r)$$

An agent can enact different roles during its execution (one actively at a time) and enacting a role influences its mental attitudes. As explained in section 2, the type of the agent determines the roles that the agent can enact. Therefore, we require that the roles that an agent can enact should be mutually consistent since these roles influence the agent's mental attitudes.

Definition 4. *(Agent Type) Let* $\mathcal{R}$ *be the set of agent roles. An agent type* t *with respect to* $\mathcal{R}$ *is a consistent subset of agent roles, i.e.* $t \subseteq \mathcal{R}$ *such that* $\forall r, r' \in t : consistent(r, r')$.

Proposition 2. *All agent roles from an agent type* $t \subseteq \mathcal{R}$ *are coherent, i.e.*

$$\forall r \in t : coherent(r)$$

4.3   Role Enacting and Role Deacting Agents

In this paper, we assume that role enacting agents have their own mental attitudes consisting of beliefs, goals, plans, and rules that may specify their conditional mental attitudes as well as how to modify their mental attitudes. In addition, a role enacting agent is assumed to enact a set of roles among which only one of them is active at each moment in time; all other enacted roles are inactive. The reason for assuming one active role at each moment of time is explained in section 2. Therefore, role enacting agents have distinct objectives and rules associated to the active role it is enacting, and sets of distinct objectives and rules adopted from enacted but inactive roles. The roles enacted by an agent are instantiations of the roles specified in t. This can be compared to objects which are instantiations of classes. It is therefore possible that one role from t is enacted and instantiated several times. We call an agent with its own mental attitudes, an active role instantiation, a set of inactive role instantiations, and a type, a *role enacting agent*.

Definition 5. *(role enacting agent: rea) Let $\gamma_a \in L_G$, $\gamma_r \in L_G \times Rname$, and $\gamma \subseteq L_G \times Rname$. Let $\Pi_a \subseteq L_P \times L_G$ and $\Pi_r \in 2^{L_P \times L_G} \times Rname$, $\Pi_s \subseteq 2^{L_P \times L_G} \times Rname$. Let $\omega_a \in Rules$, $\omega_r \in Rules \times Rname$, $\omega \subseteq Rules \times Rname$, and $e \in Rname$ be a special role instantiation name for passive role. Then, a role enacting agent is a tuple $\langle \sigma, \Gamma, \Pi, \Omega, t \rangle$, where:*

- *$\sigma \in L_B$ specifies rea's beliefs*
- *$\Gamma = (\gamma_a, \gamma_r, \gamma)$ specifies rea's objectives*
- *$\Pi = (\Pi_a, \Pi_r, \Pi_s)$ specifies rea's plans*
- *$\Omega = (\omega_a, \omega_r, \omega)$ specifies rea's rules*
- *$t \subseteq \mathcal{R}$ s.t. $\forall r \in t : consistent(\langle \sigma, \gamma_a, \omega_a \rangle, r)$ specifies rea's type.*

A passive-role enacting agent (p-rea) is defined as a rea where $\Gamma = (\gamma_a, (\top, e), \gamma)$, $\Pi = (\Pi_a, (\emptyset, e), \Pi_s)$, and $\Omega = (\omega_a, ((\emptyset, \emptyset, \emptyset), e), \omega)$.

In the above definition, γ_a and ω_a specify the agent's own objective and rules, respectively. Moreover, γ_r and ω_r specify respectively the objective and rules associated to the active role that the agent enacts, and γ and ω are sets of objectives and sets of rules of the enacted roles which are not active, respectively. Finally, Π_a specifies agent's own plans, Π_r specifies the plans that are generated by the active role, and Π_s specifies the plans of enacted but inactive roles. Note that an objective is associated with each plan to indicate the (initial) purpose of that plan. Also, a role instantiation name is associated with the objectives in γ_r and γ, to the plans in Π_r and Π_s, and with the sets of rules in ω_r and ω. Finally, note that the last clause ensures that agent roles are consistent with the mental attitudes of the agent. As for roles, one can also define coherency for rea's.

Definition 6. *(coherent rea) Let $r_0, r_1, \ldots, r_n \in Rname$, $\gamma_0, \gamma_1, \ldots, \gamma_n \in L_G$, and $\omega_0, \omega_1, \ldots, \omega_n \in Rules$ for $n \geq 0$. The rea $\langle \sigma, (\gamma_a, \gamma_r, \gamma), \Pi, (\omega_a, \omega_r, \omega), t \rangle$ is coherent iff its belief is consistent and it consists of corresponding objective/rules pairs from the enacted (active and inactive) roles each with a unique role instantiation name, i.e. iff the following conditions hold:*

1. *$\sigma \not\models \bot$*
2. *$\gamma_r = (\gamma_0, r_0)$ & $\omega_r = (\omega_0, r_0)$*
3. *$\gamma = \{(\gamma_1, r_1), \ldots, (\gamma_n, r_n)\}$ & $\omega = \{(\omega_1, r_1), \ldots, (\omega_n, r_n)\}$ & $r_i \neq r_j$ for $1 \leq i \neq j \leq n$*

Note that we use r_i, r_j as typical denotations for role instantiation names, and r, r' as typical denotations to role specifications. The first clause states that the belief base of a rea should be consistent, the second states that objectives and rules of the active role should be from one and the same role instantiation, the third states that there should be a bijection between objectives and rules of inactive roles, and the last clause states that the role instantiation names used in a rea should be unique. Note that the notion of coherence can be made stronger by demanding that the agent's own objective does not conflict with the objectives of the enacted (active and inactive) roles, i.e. by adding the following condition: $\gamma_a \wedge \gamma_i \not\models \perp$ for $0 \leq i \leq n$. Note that a passive-role enacting agent (p-rea) is a coherent rea.

In our view, enacting a role by an agent means that the agent adopts the role (i.e. it adopts the information, objectives, and rules that are associated with the role) and uses a name to refer to the instantiation of this role. Enacting a role can be specified by a function that maps rea's, roles, and role instantiation names to rea's. This function is defined on rea's in general, rather than on coherent rea's. In proposition 3 below, we relate this function and the notion of coherent rea's.

Definition 7. *(Role enacting function) Let S be the set of rea's, $\langle \sigma, \Gamma, \Pi, \Omega, t \rangle \in S$, $\mathcal{R}$ be the set of roles, $\langle \sigma_i, \gamma_i, \omega_i \rangle \in \mathcal{R}$, and $r_i \in Rname$ be a role instantiation name. The role enacting function $\mathcal{F}_{enact} : S \times \mathcal{R} \times Rname \to S$ is defined as follows:*

$$\mathcal{F}_{enact}(\langle \sigma, \Gamma, \Pi, \Omega, t \rangle , \langle \sigma_i, \gamma_i, \omega_i \rangle , r_i) = \langle \sigma \wedge \sigma_i, \Gamma', \Pi, \Omega', t \rangle$$

where $\Gamma = (\gamma_a, \gamma_r, \gamma)$ and $\Gamma' = (\gamma_a, \gamma_r, \gamma \cup \{(\gamma_i, r_i)\})$,
$\Omega = (\omega_a, \omega_r, \omega)$ and $\Omega' = (\omega_a, \omega_r, \omega \cup \{(\omega_i, r_i)\})$.

An agent may decide to deact a role which means that the agent stops enacting the role. In our view, the agent that deacts a role will remove the objective and plans adopted by enacting the role. Note that the plans can be generated during the enactment of the role.

Definition 8. *(Role deacting function) Let S be the set of rea's, $\langle \sigma, \Gamma, \Pi, \Omega, t \rangle \in S$, and $r_i \in Rname$ be a role instantiation name. The role deacting function $\mathcal{F}_{deact} : S \times Rname \to S$ is defined as follows:*

$$\mathcal{F}_{deact}(\langle \sigma, \Gamma, \Pi, \Omega, t \rangle , r_i) = \langle \sigma, \Gamma', \Pi', \Omega', t \rangle$$

where $\Gamma = (\gamma_a, \gamma_r, \gamma \cup \{(\gamma_i, r_i)\})$ and $\Gamma' = (\gamma_a, \gamma_r, \gamma)$,
$\Pi = (\Pi_a, \Pi_r, \Pi_s \cup \{(X, r_i)\})$ and $\Pi' = (\Pi_a, \Pi_r, \Pi_s)$,
$\Omega = (\omega_a, \omega_r, \omega \cup \{(\omega_i, r_i)\})$ and $\Omega' = (\omega_a, \omega_r, \omega)$.

In the following, we say that a role instantiation name r_i does (or does not) occur in a rea $s = \langle \sigma, (\gamma_a, \gamma_r, \gamma), \Pi, (\omega_a, \omega_r, \omega), t \rangle$ if r_i does (or does not) occur in the pair γ_r and ω_r and does (or does not) occur in the pairs contained in γ and ω.

Proposition 3. *Let $s = \langle \sigma, \Gamma, \Pi, \Omega, t \rangle$ be a coherent rea, $r \in t$, and $r_i \in Rname$. Then, the rea $\mathcal{F}_{enact}(s, r, r_i)$ is coherent if r_i does not occur in s, and the rea $\mathcal{F}_{deact}(s, r_i)$ is coherent.*

Note that the deacting function can only deact an inactive role. Note also that for some $s = \langle \sigma, \Gamma, \Pi, \Omega, t \rangle$, $r \in t$ and $r_i \in Rname$ the following hold:

$$\mathcal{F}_{deact}(\mathcal{F}_{enact}(s, r, r_i), r_i) \neq s \quad \text{and} \quad \mathcal{F}_{enact}(\mathcal{F}_{deact}(s, r_i), r, r_i) \neq s$$

For example, consider $s = \langle p, (\gamma_a, \gamma_r, \gamma), \Pi, (\omega_a, \omega_r, \omega), t \rangle$, $\langle q, \gamma_i, \omega_i \rangle$ be a role, and $r_i \in Rname$ which does not occur in s. Then,
$\mathcal{F}_{enact}(s, \langle q, \gamma_i, \omega_i \rangle, r_i) = \langle p \wedge q, (\gamma_a, \gamma_r, \gamma \cup \{(\gamma_i, r_i)\}), \Pi, (\omega_a, \omega_r, \omega \cup \{(\omega_i, r_i)\}), t \rangle$
and $\mathcal{F}_{deact}(\mathcal{F}_{enact}(s, \langle q, \gamma_i, \omega_i \rangle, r_i), r_i) = \langle p \wedge q, (\gamma_a, \gamma_r, \gamma), \Pi, (\omega_a, \omega_r, \omega), t \rangle \neq s$.

However, starting with a role enacting agent whose belief base entails the belief base of a role, then enacting followed by deacting of the role by the same agent gives the identity function.

Proposition 4. *Let rea s' be of the form $\mathcal{F}_{deact}(\mathcal{F}_{enact}(s, r, r_i), r_i)$ and rea s'' be of the form $\mathcal{F}_{enact}(\mathcal{F}_{deact}(s, r_i), r, r_i)$, for the role $r \in t$ and $r_i \in Rname$. Then,*

$$\mathcal{F}_{deact}(\mathcal{F}_{enact}(s', r, r_i), r_i) = s' \quad \text{and} \quad \mathcal{F}_{enact}(\mathcal{F}_{deact}(s'', r_i), r, r_i) = s''$$

4.4   Activating and Deactivating Roles

In our view, enacting a role does not imply activating the role. However, since enacting a role updates the belief base of the rea, the enacted role will indirectly influence the behavior of the role enacting agent. In order to direct the role enacting agent to achieve the role's objectives, the enacted role should be activated. In fact, activating a role is selecting and processing it. For this reason, we introduce two new functions for *activating* and *deactivating* agent roles. The role activating function maps passive-role enacting agents to role enacting agents. The objectives, plans, and rules of the enacted role become active entities and will affect the behavior of the role enacting agent.

Definition 9. *(Role activating function) Let $\mathcal{S}$ be the set of rea's, $\mathcal{S}^e$ be the set of passive-role enacting agents, $\langle \sigma, \Gamma, \Pi, \Omega, t \rangle \in \mathcal{S}^e$, $\mathcal{R}$ be the set of roles, $\langle \sigma_j, \gamma_j, \omega_j \rangle \in \mathcal{R}$, and $r_i \in Rname$. The role activating function $\mathcal{F}_{activate} : \mathcal{S}^e \times \mathcal{R} \times Rname \to \mathcal{S}$ is defined as follows:*

$$\mathcal{F}_{activate}(\langle \sigma, \Gamma, \Pi, \Omega, t \rangle \, , \, \langle \sigma_j, \gamma_j, \omega_j \rangle \, , \, r_i) = \langle \sigma \wedge \sigma_j, \Gamma', \Pi', \Omega', t \rangle$$

where
$\Gamma = (\gamma_a, (\top, e), \gamma \cup \{(\gamma_i, r_i)\})$ *and* $\Gamma' = (\gamma_a, (\gamma_i, r_i), \gamma)$,
$(\Pi = (\Pi_a, (\emptyset, e), \Pi_s)$ *and* $\forall X \subseteq L_P \times L_G$ $(X, r_i) \notin \Pi_s$ *and* $\Pi' = \Pi)$ *or*
$(\Pi = (\Pi_a, (\emptyset, e), \Pi_s \cup \{(X, r_i)\})$ *and* $\Pi' = (\Pi_a, (X, r_i), \Pi_s))$,
$\Omega = (\omega_a, ((\emptyset, \emptyset, \emptyset), e), \omega \cup \{(X, r_i)\})$ *and* $\Omega' = (\omega_a, (X, r_i), \omega)$.

Note that the second argument of the role activating function is a role specification while we only use the information component of the role specification, i.e. σ_j. Alternatively, we can specify the role activating function without agent specification as argument, but then we have to modify the rea specification to represent the information associated to the inactive roles. The second condition in the above definition is relevant when an enacted role is activated for the first time. Note that the roles do not contain plans in their specifications and enacting them do not add any plan to a rea. The plans related to a role can be generated only by activating the role. The third condition guarantees that the plans of an already activated role, which have been stored by their deactivation (see definition 10 for deactivation of roles), are activated again.

The role deactivating function, to the contrary, t maps role enacting agents to passive-role enacting agents. In fact, the activated enacting role may consist of objectives that are not achieved and plans that are not executed. These entities are saved and can be activated once again.

Definition 10. *(Role deactivating function) Let $\mathcal{S}$ be the set of rea's, $\langle \sigma, \Gamma, \Pi, \Omega, t \rangle \in \mathcal{S}$, $\mathcal{S}^e$ be the set of passive-role enacting agents, and $r_i \in Rname$. The role deactivating function $\mathcal{F}_{deactivate} : \mathcal{S} \times Rname \to \mathcal{S}^e$ is defined as follows:*

$$\mathcal{F}_{deactivate}(\langle \sigma, \Gamma, \Pi, \Omega, t \rangle , r_i) = \langle \sigma, \Gamma', \Pi', \Omega', t \rangle$$

where
$\Gamma = (\gamma_a, (\gamma_i, r_i), \gamma)$ *and* $\Gamma' = (\gamma_a, (\top, e), \gamma \cup \{(\gamma_i, r_i)\})$,
$\Pi = (\Pi_a, (X, r_i), \Pi_s)$ *and* $\Pi' = (\Pi_a, (\emptyset, e), \Pi_s \cup \{(X, r_i)\})$,
$\Omega = (\omega_a, (X, r_i), \omega\})$ *and* $\Omega' = (\omega_a, ((\emptyset, \emptyset, \emptyset), e), \omega \cup \{(X, r_i)\})$.

Proposition 5. *Let $s = \langle \sigma, \Gamma, \Pi, \Omega, t \rangle$ be a passive-role enacting rea (p-rea), $r \in t$, and $r_i \in Rname$ occurs in s. Then, the rea's $\mathcal{F}_{activate}(s, r, r_i)$ and $\mathcal{F}_{deactivate}(s, r_i)$ are coherent.*

A role enacting agent can be activated and deactivated. Note that there exists a rea $s = \langle \sigma, \Gamma, \Pi, \Omega, t \rangle$ and $s^e = \langle \sigma', \Gamma', \Pi', \Omega', t' \rangle$ in which $r_i, r_i' \in Rname$ occurs, respectively, such that the following hold:

$$\mathcal{F}_{activate}(\mathcal{F}_{deactivate}(s, r_i), r, r_i) \neq s \quad \text{for } r \in t$$

$$\mathcal{F}_{deactivate}(\mathcal{F}_{activate}(s^e, r', r_i'), r_i') \neq s^e \quad \text{for } r' \in t'$$

In general, the behavior of the recursive applications of activating and deactivating functions is characterized by the following proposition.

Proposition 6. *Let the rea s be of the form $\mathcal{F}_{activate}(s^e, r, r_i)$ where $s = \langle \sigma, \Gamma, \Pi, \Omega, t \rangle$, $r \in t$, and $r_i \in Rname$, then*

$$\mathcal{F}_{activate}(\mathcal{F}_{deactivate}(s, r_i), r, r_i) = s$$

The enacting agent can enact the role in various ways. For example, the agent may prefer to achieve the objectives adopted from the role before aiming to achieve its own objective, or otherwise it may prefer to achieve its own objective first. The exact way to enact a role should be determined either beforehand or during the execution of the agent.

5   Implementation of Roles

Like other programming languages, an agent programming language should provide data structures to specify the (initial) state, and a set of programming constructs to specify how the states should evolve. In the case of programming languages for cognitive agents the data structures consist of mental attitudes such as beliefs, goals, and plans, and the specification of their dynamics is captured by the modification rules. The programming constructs consist of a set of basic operations, which are defined on mental attitude and the rules, and a set of operators to compose complex programming constructs in terms of basic operations. The program that specifies the operations on these entities is usually called the deliberation program, deliberation cycle, or decision making mechanism of agents [3].

In general, there are two ways to implement the enactment and deactment of roles by cognitive agents. The first approach is to introduce two special actions that can be invoked in the agent's plan and which, when executed, realize the enactment and deactment of roles. In this approach, the agent will enact and deact a role according to its plans that are conditionalized for example by its beliefs or goals. For example, an agent *buyer* may have the plan if $\mathbf{B}(\texttt{registered(me)})$ then $\texttt{enact}(r_{\texttt{buyer}}, \texttt{buyer}_1)$ which, when executed, updates the *buyer* according to the instantiation of the role $r_{\texttt{buyer}}$ (denoted by $\texttt{buyer}_1$) if he believes that he is already registered. Also, one may specify the goals and rules, which specify a role in such a way that the agent will execute the deact action when the objectives of the agent are achieved. For example, in our auction example, the role $r_{\texttt{buyer}}$ (instantiated and denoted by the role name $\texttt{buyer}_1$) may contain a rule $\mathbf{B}\,\texttt{bought(item)} \Rightarrow \texttt{deact(buyer}_1)$. This rule indicates that whenever the role enacting agent believes that it bought the item, then he should deact the buyer role $\texttt{buyer}_1$.

The second approach is to introduce two basic programming (deliberation) operations which, when executed, result in enacting or deacting of agent roles. These and other operations such as selecting goals and plans, executing plans, or applying modifications rules constitute the agent's deliberation program. For example, a deliberation program can consist of selecting and enacting a role (in this case based on goal $\mathbf{G}(buy(item))$) before starting an iteration in which a goal of the agent is selected and planned and the plan executed. In this iteration, the rules may also be selected and applied to modify the goals and plans of the agent. Let $\texttt{enact}(r_{\texttt{buyer}}, \texttt{buyer}_1)$ and $\texttt{deact(buyer}_1)$ be deliberation operations for enacting and deacting the instantiation of the role buyer, respectively. Then, the following illustrates a deliberation program in which the agent first selects which role to enact, then enact the role, and finally deact it.

```
1- If G(buy(item)) then
2- BEGIN
3-     enact(r_buyer, buyer_1); activate(r_buyer, buyer_1);
4-     While goalbase ≠ ⊤ do Select_goal(G); Plan(G,P); Execute(P) od;
5-     deactivate(buyer_1); deact(buyer_1)
6- END
```

In both approaches, the enactment and deactment of roles result in a modification of the role enacting agent as specified in definitions 7 and 8. According to these definitions, enacting a role results in adoptions of beliefs, goals, and rules, and deacting it results in removal of goals, plans, and rules. The choice for one of these two approaches will be based on a pragmatic consideration and is a methodological issue [5]. For example, one should consider if role modification is a part of the agent's mental attitudes or is it an issue of an agent decision making process.

5.1   Semantics of Enact and Deact Operations

The semantics of programming languages can be specified in terms of updates (or transitions) of states (agent specification) based on programming operations. For example, we have provided in [6] the operational semantics of 3APL, which is a programming language for cognitive agents. In this section, we assume an arbitrary cognitive agent programming language for which operational semantics is defined. We sketch how the semantics of this language can be modified as the result of extending the language with enact and deact operations. In particular, we explain which parts of the existing semantics should be modified, and how the semantics of the enact and deact operations should be defined.

In section 4, we have defined an agent specification in such a way to allow agents to have an explicit representation of the role they enact. In particular, we have defined the agent's goal base and rule bases as tuples to have a distinguished representations of the objectives and rules of the agent itself and the objectives and rules that specify the active and inactive roles. The fact that the goal base and the rule base are tuples raises the question how to verify whether a goal is derivable from the goal base and how to select a rule from the rule base. Given $\langle \gamma_a, \gamma_r, \gamma \rangle$ as the goal base of a role enacting agent and κ a goal, the first question can be answered by verifying if the goal is derivable from the conjunction of the goal bases, i.e. $\gamma_a \wedge \gamma' \models \kappa$. Given $\langle \omega_a, \omega_r, \omega \rangle$ as the rule base of the role enacting agent (with active role r_i), a rule can be selected from the set $\omega_a \cup \omega'$. We assume that rules will be selected from the set of rules based on orderings defined on ω_a and ω', and based on a selection criterion. An example of selection criteria is the attitude of the role enacting agent, e.g. social (first select from ω' before selecting from ω_a), or selfish (first select from ω_a before selecting from ω').

In the following, we specify the update of agent states based on the enacting and deacting operations. The provided updates can be used to define transitions if the semantics of the programming language is an operational semantics. In the following, we use the semantic function $Sem(\alpha, s) = s'$ to indicate that the state s' is the result of updating the state s through operation α.

Definition 11. *Let $\mathcal{S}$ be the set of role enacting agents, $s = \langle \sigma, \Gamma, \Pi, \Omega, t \rangle \in \mathcal{S}$, $\mathcal{R}$ be the set of roles, $r \in \mathcal{R}$, $r_i \in Rname$, and $\omega' \in Rules$. Let $\mathcal{F}_{enact}, \mathcal{F}_{deact}$, $\mathcal{F}_{activate}$, and $\mathcal{F}_{deactivate}$ as defined in definitions 7, 8, 9, and 10, respectively. The semantics of the operations $OP = \{$ enact(r, r_i), deact(r_i), activate$($ $r, r_i)$, deactivate$(r_i)\}$, is captured by the function $Sem : OP \times \mathcal{S} \to \mathcal{S}$, defined as follows:*

$$Sem(\texttt{enact}(r, r_i), s) = \mathcal{F}_{enact}(s, r, r_i) \qquad for \ \ r \in t$$
$$Sem(\texttt{deact}(r_i), s) = \mathcal{F}_{deact}(s, r_i) \qquad for \ \ \Omega = (\omega_a, \omega_r, \omega) \ \& \ (\omega', r_i) \in \omega$$
$$Sem(\texttt{activate}(r, r_i), s) = \mathcal{F}_{activate}(s, r, r_i) \ for \ \ \Omega = (\omega_a, \omega_r, \omega) \ \& \ (\omega', r_i) \in \omega$$
$$Sem(\texttt{deactivate}(r_i), s) = \mathcal{F}_{deactivate}(s, r_i) \ for \ \ \Gamma = \langle \gamma_a, (\gamma', r_i), \gamma \rangle$$
$$and \ \Omega = \langle \omega_a, (\omega', r_i), \omega \rangle$$

Based on this semantics for the proposed programming instructions and assuming that other programming instructions maintain the coherence of rea's, then we can formulate the following safety proposition.

Proposition 7. *(safety) Let s be a coherent rea and P be an agent program consisting of a set of programming instructions among which those related to enacting and activating roles as suggested in definition 11. Let the following conditions hold:*

- *each instruction* deact(r_i) *is preceded by an instruction* enact(r, r_i) *between which r_i is used uniquely*
- *each instruction* deactivate(r_i) *is preceded by only one instruction* activate(r, r_i) *between which r_i is used uniquely, and no* activate(r, r_i) *is preceded by another* activate(r', r_j)
- *all other programming instructions maintain coherence of rea's*

Then, if the program P is executed on rea s, the resulted rea after the execution of P is coherent.

6   Future Research and Concluding Remarks

In this paper we have argued for the importance of enactment/deactment of roles by agents in multiagent programming, in particular when dealing with open systems where the match between the agents in the system and the roles to be played is not fixed but changing dynamically. Since we furthermore believe that an agent can only be actively engaged in one role at a time, we have also proposed an activate/deactivate mechanism for roles. We have provided a formal semantics of the enactment and deactment as well as the activate and deactivate operations. Since this formalization is conceptually based on the notion of cognitive agents (and employs concepts used in the semantics of an agent language such as 3APL in particular), we claim that the implementation of the proposed mechanism by agent-oriented programming languages is straightforward.

References

1. P. Bresciani, P. Giorgini, F. Giunchiglia, J. Mylopoulos, and A. Perini. TROPOS: An agent-oriented software development methodology. *Journal of Autonomous Agents and Multi-Agent Systems*, to appear.
2. J. Castro, M. Kolp, and J. Mylopoulos. Towards requirements-driven information systems engineering: the TROPOS project. *Information Systems*, 27:365–389, 2002.

3. M. Dastani, F. de Boer, F. Dignum, and J.-J. Meyer. Programming agent deliberation. In *Second International Joint Conference on Autonomous Agents and Multi-Agent Systems (AAMAS'03)*. 2003.

4. M. Dastani, V. Dignum, and F. Dignum. Role-assignment in open agent societies. In *Second International Joint Conference on Autonomous Agents and Multi-Agent Systems (AAMAS'03)*. 2003.

5. M. Dastani, J. Hulstijn, F. Dignum, and J.-J. Meyer. Issues in multiagent system development. In *Proceedings of The Third Conference on Autonomous Agents and Multi-agent Systems (AAMAS'04)*. New York, USA, 2004.

6. M. Dastani, M. B. van Riemsdijk, F. Dignum, and J.-J. Meyer. A programming language for cognitive agents: Goal directed 3APL. In M. Dastani, J. Dix, A. E. Fallah-Seghrouchni, and D. Kinny, editors, *Proceedings of the First Workshop on Programming Multiagent Systems: Languages, frameworks, techniques, and tools (ProMAS03)*. 2003.

7. P. Davidsson. Categories of artificial societies. In A. Omicini, P. Petta, and R. Tolksdorf, editors, *Engineering Societies in the Agent World II*, LNAI 2203. Springer Verlag, Berln, 2001.

8. V. Dignum. *A Model for Organizational Interaction, based onAgents, founded in Logic*. PhD thesis, University of Utrecht, 2003.

9. M. Esteva, D. de la Cruz, and C. Sierra. ISLANDER: an electronic institutions editor. In *First Interantional Joint Conference on Autonoumous Agents and Multiagent Systems (AAMAS'02)*, pages 1045 – 1052. ACM Press, 2002.

10. J. Ferber, O. Gutknecht, and F. Michel. From agents to organizations: An organizational view of multi-agent systems. In P. Giorgini, J. P. Müller, and J. Odell, editors, *Agent-Oriented Software Engineering IV, 4th International Workshop, AOSE 2003, Melbourne, Australia, July 15, 2003, Revised Papers*, LNCS, pages 214–230. Springer Verlag, 2003.

11. B. Hansson. An analysis of some deontic logics. *Nous*, 3:373–398, 1969.

12. K. Hindriks, F. de Boer, W. van der Hoek, and J.-J. Meyer. Agent programming in 3APL. *Autonomous Agents and Multi-Agent Systems*, 2(4):357–401, 1999.

13. J. Odell, H. V. D. Parunak, S. Brueckner, and J. Sauter. Temporal aspects of dynamic role assignment. In P. Giorgini, J. P. Müller, and J. Odell, editors, *Agent-Oriented Software Engineering IV, 4th International Workshop, AOSE 2003, Melbourne, Australia, July 15, 2003, Revised Papers*, LNCS, pages 201–213. Springer Verlag, 2003.

14. A. Omicini. SODA: Societies and infrastructures in the analysis and design of agent-based systems. In *AOSE*, pages 185–193, 2000.

15. R. S. Sandhu, E. J. Coyne, H. L. Feinstein, and C. E. Youman. Role-based access control models. *IEEE Computer*, 29(2), 1996.

16. J. Searle. *The Construction of Social Reality*. The Free Press, New York, 1995.

17. W. W. Vasconcelos, J. Sabater, C. Sierra, and J. Querol. Skeleton-based agent development for electronic institutions. In *First Interantional Joint Conference on Autonoumous Agents and Multiagent Systems (AAMAS'02)*, pages 696–703. ACM Press, 2002.

18. M. Wooldridge, N. R. Jennings, and D. Kinny. The gaia methodology for agent-oriented analysis and design. *Autonomous Agents and Multi-Agent Systems*, 3(3):285–312, 2000.

A Platform for Agent Behavior Design and Multi Agent Orchestration*

G.B. Laleci, Y. Kabak, A. Dogac, I. Cingil, S. Kirbas, A. Yildiz, S. Sinir, O. Ozdikis, and O. Ozturk

Software Research and Development Center & Dept. of Computer Eng.,
Middle East Technical University (METU)
06531 Ankara Türkiye +90 312 2105598
asuman@srdc.metu.edu.tr

Abstract. Agents show considerable promise as a new paradigm for software development. However for wider adoption and deployment of agent technology, powerful design and development tools are needed. Such tools should empower software developers to cater agent solutions more efficiently and at a lower cost for their customers with rapidly changing requirements and differing application specifications.

In this paper, an agent orchestration platform that allows the developers to design a complete agent-based scenario through graphical user interfaces is presented. The scenario produced by the platform is a rule based system in contrast to the existing systems where agents are coded through a programming language. In this way, the platform provides a higher level of abstraction to agent development making it easier to adapt to rapidly changing user requirements or differing software specifications. The system is highly transportable and interoperable.

The platform helps to design a multi-agent system either from scratch, or by adapting existing distributed systems to multi agent systems. It contains tools that handle the agent system design both at the macro level, that is, defining the interaction between agents and at the micro level which deals with internal design of agents.

Agent behaviour is modeled as a workflow of basic agent behaviour building blocks (such as receiving a message, invoking an application, making a decision or sending a message) by considering the data and control dependencies among them, and a graphical user interface is provided to construct agent behaviours. The platform allows agent templates to be constructed from previously defined behaviours. Finally through a Scenario Design Tool, a multi-agent system is designed by specifying associations among agents. The scenario is stored in a knowledge base by using the Agent Behaviour Representation Language (ABRL) which is developed for this purpose. Finally to be able to demonstrate the execution of the system on a concrete agent platform, we mapped the ABRL rules to JESS and executed the system on JADE.

---

* This work is supported by the European Commission's IST Programme, under the contract IST-2000-31050 Agent Academy.

J. Odell et al. (Eds.): AOSE 2004, LNCS 3382, pp. 205–220, 2005.

1   Introduction

In the recent years agent technology has found many interesting applications in e-commerce, decision support systems and Internet applications. An increasing number of computer systems are being viewed in terms of autonomous agents [12]. They have proven particularly useful in business and production scenarios where they have facilitated the buying and selling of goods and services in electronic marketplaces, handling workflows, helping with personalization by managing user profiles or by tackling production planning. As the benefits of using agent societies in such applications become clear so does the need for developing high-level agent system building tools and frameworks.

Agent based approaches enable the development of increasingly powerful and complex distributed systems, since they provide a natural way to define high level of abstractions. The problems can be decomposed in terms of autonomous agents that can engage in flexible, high level interactions [12, 19]. However the design and development of multi-agent-systems are not straight forward and these issues are among the main research areas in multi-agent systems [9]. There are considerable amount of work on designing a multi-agent system at a macro level, i.e., defining the interactions between the agents; however it is still cumbersome to design and develop multi-agent systems at a micro-level which deals with internal details of agents.

The aim of the work described in this paper is to abstract the application development from the detailed agent coding, and thus enabling the user to construct a multi-agent system by making use of her existing applications and by providing her an extensive and powerful design platform.

The orchestration platform we have developed allows users to define agent behaviour types, agent types (containing possibly more than one behaviour) and multi-agent scenarios through graphical user interfaces avoiding the coding effort. The scenario produced by the platform is a rule based system in contrast to the existing systems where agents are coded through a programming language. Thus the platform provides a higher level abstraction to agent development. The behaviours of the agents can easily be modified by changing the rules. The formalism developed within the scope of this work to represent the behaviours in a rule based system can be used in any agent platform to execute the multi-agent scenario, since there are rule based languages that can be used with most of the programming languages (For example CLIPS [4] language can be embedded within languages such as C, Java, FORTRAN and ADA). In this way, the system becomes highly transportable and interoperable, empowering the software developers to cater agent solutions more efficiently.

There are three main tools in the platform both for macro-level (societal) and for micro-level (agent internals) design. The *Behaviour Type Design Tool* helps to design agent behaviour templates which are then used by the *Agent Type Design Tool* for building agent types, which in return are exploited by the *Scenario Design Tool* to create application specific multi-agent scenarios.

The *Behaviour Type Design Tool* allows users to define the behaviours of an agent as a workflow template of basic agent operations such as sending a message, receiving a message, performing an action, or making a decision. There are also "if" and "while" blocks to control the flow of operations an agent performs. The existing applications can be inserted in the behaviours as activity blocks, so the platform provides an easy way for adapting existing distributed systems to multi-agent systems.

The platform enables the user to define the ontologies of the messages between the agents through an Ontology Design Tool.

Once the behaviour templates are designed through the *Behaviour Type Design Tool*, the *Agent Type Design Tool* helps the user to design an agent type by including the desired behaviour templates. Notice that these two graphical tools help with the micro level design. To assist the user with the design of agent societies, that is, for macro level design, *Scenario Design Tool* is used. This tool helps to select the necessary agent types (or new agents can also be built at this level with the *Agent Type Design Tool*) and to define the associations among agents. The scenario specific agent information is also given at this time with the proper interfaces provided, and then, the scenario is initialized. Once the scenario is initialized, it is converted into Agent Behaviour Representation Language (ABRL) developed for this purpose and the multi-agent system becomes ready for operation.

There are four more tools in the platform called the *Consistency Checker Tool*, the *Ontology Design Tool*, the *Physical Asset Design Tool* and the *Monitoring Tool*. *Consistency Checker Tool* basically checks the consistency of the design in terms of the sent and received messages, i.e., if an agent A is sending a message to an agent B, then B should have the necessary mechanisms in place to receive this message. The *Ontology Design Tool* helps to design the ontologies and the *Physical Asset Design Tool* assists the users in designing external sources for the input variables of the behaviours. The *Monitoring Tool* provides a graphical interface for tracing the running agents.

The platform has some additional functionalities, such as monitoring the running agents, adding new behaviours to certain agent instances, killing some of their behaviours, killing some of the agents, or changing the parameters of the scenario.

To be able to demonstrate the execution of the system in a concrete agent platform, we mapped the ABRL rules to JESS [13] and executed the system on JADE [11]. The paper is organized as follows: Section 2 summarizes the related work. Section 3 is devoted to the description of the Agent Orchestration Platform developed. In Section 3.1, the *Behaviour Type Design Tool* is described and in Section 3.2 the *Agent Type Design Tool* is presented. These two tools address the micro level agent design. Section 3.3 explains the macro level multi-agent system design, that is the *Scenario Design Tool*. Section 3.4 presents the *Agent Behaviour Representation Language* and a brief example is provided in Section 3.5 to clarify the concepts. Section 3.6 describes the initialization of a multi-agent scenario in the orchestration platform. Finally Section 4 concludes the paper.

2   Related Work

Considering the increasing need for developing high-level agent system building tools, there has been a considerable amount of research on agent oriented software design, most of which are mainly based on Object Oriented analysis and design methods. Several methodologies are defined to specify the macro-level (agent society and organization structure) design of multi-agent systems [20]. These methodologies enable developers to go systematically from a statement of requirements to a design that is sufficiently detailed to be implemented directly.

There are two well known methodologies that provide a top-down and iterative approach towards modeling and developing agent-based systems, namely, Gaia [19], and MaSE [7]. They basically define the roles in a scenario, the responsibilities of these roles, and the interactions between them. These methodologies have been used in some applications, such as ZEUS [22] which uses Gaia and agent tool [7] which uses MaSE. However these methodologies and their applications mostly concentrate on the macro level agent design; their aim is not micro design. For example in ZEUS, the user has to define the functionality of the agents by writing Java codes with the given API.

In parallel with these methodologies, UML is started to be used extensively for modelling agents. AML [5], is a semi-formal visual modelling language, specified as an extension to UML 2.0. It is used for specifying, modelling and documenting systems that incorporate concepts drawn from MAS theory. Similarly inn [10], Agent UML Interaction diagrams for representing agent interaction protocols based on UML 2.0 Interaction diagrams is being presented.

As indicated in [1,18], there is still a gap between Agent-Oriented design and implementation. In this paper we provide one more level of abstraction with the platform developed; a user is able to define the whole functionality of the behaviour via a GUI, and can make use of her existing applications through an API without the need to modify them.

COLLAGEN (COLLaborative AGENt) [17] is a Java middleware developed at MERL to make it easier to implement collaborative interface agents. Its aim is to develop a system that mediates the interaction between a software interface agent and a user. COLLAGEN provides a generic implementation of discourse interpretation, plan recognition, and plan generation algorithms, all of which take a given task model as data. Users can map the tasks with user interfaces, for generating "collaborative interface agents". Our approach's main focus is not developing interface agents, alternatively the platform presented in this paper aims to model and develop the interactions between agents through a GUI for creating Multi Agent System.

A similar tool to our platform is PASSI. PASSI [6](a Process for Agent Societies Specification and Implementation) is a step-by-step requirement-to-code methodology for designing and developing multi-agent societies integrating design models and concepts from both OO software engineering and artificial intelligence approaches using UML notation. It also provides graphical tools for designing agent behavior and agent interactions. On top of PASSI, in our tool, it is possible to integrate existing java applications into agent behavior. Additionally our platform can create agents with decision making capability by integrating "inference engines" executing well known data mining techniques.

3   Agent Orchestration Platform

As shown in Figure 1, there are three interacting tools, namely, the *Behaviour Type Design Tool* (BTDT), the *Agent Type Design Tool* (ATDT) and the *Scenario Design Tool* (SDT) in the agent orchestration platform developed. In this section, the details of these tools are presented.

3.1   Behaviour Type Design Tool (BTDT)

Behaviours of an agent specify its role in a scenario. We note that basic operations that an agent may perform include:

- An agent may receive input from the outside world. This could be data from sensors or messages from other agents.
- After evaluating the messages and/or some application data, an agent may take a decision, perhaps by invoking an inference engine.
- An agent may need to invoke existing applications. In doing this, the received messages and/or some application specific data may be used as input parameters to the invoked applications.
- An agent may decide to send messages to other agents.

An agent behaviour can be modeled as a workflow of these behaviour building blocks since there are data and control flow dependencies among them. In this

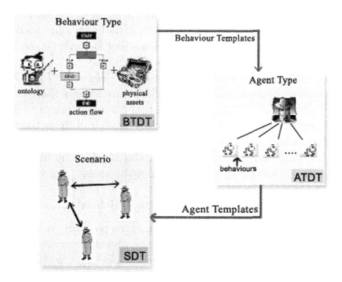

Fig. 1. The Components of the Agent Orchestration Platform

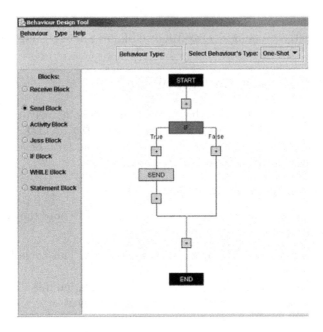

Fig. 2. Behaviour Type Design Tool

way, it becomes possible to construct an agent behaviour as a workflow through a GUI by using these basic behaviour blocks. Note that behaviour blocks other than the ones specified above can also be defined.

A design tool needs the power to express the control statements like "if" or "while" to organize the flow among blocks an agent needs to execute. Furthermore an agent may be continuously executing its behaviours (called "Cyclic Behavior" in JADE terminology), or once ("One-Shot Behavior"), and such control statements should also be provided by a design tool.

With these observations, we have developed the *Behaviour Type Design Tool* (BTDT) as shown in Figure 2 as a workflow design tool where there is a node for each possible generic action of an agent. The tool allows the users to select basic behaviour building blocks, drag them onto the canvas and draw the transitions among them. After a block is placed on the canvas, the user specifies the required semantics of the block. For example, for a "send block", the block name, the performative such as "inform" or "request", and the ontology of the message are specified.

The tool allows the following functionality to be defined through these nodes:

Receive Block: Receive block models the task of receiving a message by an agent. Note that the users may wish to filter the messages received by an agent by specifying some constraints. For example, a user may wish to define the ontology, the performative, or the sender of the message expected. The GUI tool provides a construct that enables the user to define all kinds of filters on messages. Since only the generic behaviour template is designed at this stage, the sender of the message is not specified here (This is specified through *Scenario Design Tool* while designing a specific scenario). While specifying the ontology of the message the user is provided with an Ontology Design Tool, and Protégé [15] is used for this purpose. Here the user defines the ontology of the message, then the ontology is saved as an Resource Description Framework (RDF) [16] file. The platform parses the RDF files, constructs and compiles the ontology classes to be used by the agents.

In order to provide data flow and sharing among the different building blocks of an agent, a "Global Variable Pool" is defined, which holds the variables that are produced and consumed as a result of the execution of the behaviour blocks. "Global Variable Pool" may contain the following types of variables:

- The variables extracted from a message received: The output of a receive block is a message in a specific ontology, and is stored in the "Global Variable Pool". In doing this, all the fields of the message are extracted and are stored in a collection of variables by conforming to the class/subclass hierarchy of the given ontology.
- The variables produced by an activity: The collection of variables that are produced as a result of the execution of activity blocks.
- The variables produced as a result of executing a rule engine: The collection of variables that are produced from an Inference Engine block.

Through global variable pool it becomes possible to handle agent interaction as 'conversation level', i.e. evaluating message in the context of a sequence of messages, since the results of the received messages can be further processed by other blocks, and necessary action can be taken.

Activity block: To be able to construct a multi-agent-system for an existing distributed system, the platform enables the user to invoke predefined applications, by involving them as activity blocks in the agent behaviour workflow. The tool gives the ability to the user to specify a predefined application, choose one of its methods and specify the input variables of that method. Variables from the "Global Variable Pool" can be assigned to the input variables of the methods, and/or the user can provide some external sources to be used to provide values to the input variables. These external sources are termed as "Physical Assets". The platform provides a tool also to define and manipulate the physical assets as shown in Figure 3. There are three kinds of physical assets:

- Simple variables: The user can assign a simple value to a variable. A simple variable is composed of the name of the variable, its type and its value.
- URLs (Uniform Resource Locators): The user can state that the value that is to be mapped to the variable should be extracted from an XML file. After getting the URL of the XML file, the tool presents the user the nodes of the XML file as a Document Object Model (DOM) hierarchy through the use of an XML parser (Xerces parser [21] is used in the implementation). When the user selects one of the nodes, an XPath expression is created by the tool to access the related node by simply constructing the path to the root of the XML file.

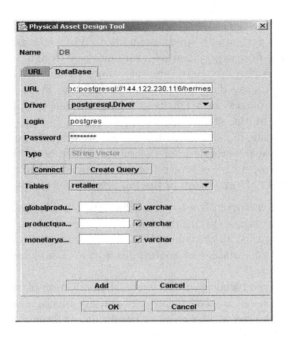

Fig. 3. Physical Asset Design Tool

- Databases: The value of the variable can also be extracted from a database
  by providing the proper coordinates, that is, the database name, its URL,
  and the necessary login id and password. The tool helps the user to visualize the tables and their related rows. When the user selects the row she
  wants to extract, the query to obtain that information from the database is
  formulated.

Note that to realize this functionality, traditional database techniques are used
such as connecting to databases through their JDBC interfaces, querying the data
dictionary to obtain the table names and their fields, querying the database for the
content and displaying these results graphically. Although these technologies are
mainstream and does not constitute the innovative aspects of our work; facilitating the job of the designer in this way is valuable. As a future work, ontology files
in OWL (Web Ontology Language) will be presented to the user and it will be
possible to extract tuples as physical assets through OWL-QL queries.

With the *Behaviour Type Design Tool*, only the types of behaviours (i.e.,
templates) are designed, hence providing the names and types of the physical
assets are sufficient. These physical assets are assigned to actual specific values
through the *Scenario Design Tool* at the initialization phase. For example, with
BTDT, we may design a behaviour that consists of a receive block and an activity
block which will access a database. The specific type of agent that will send the
expected message to this receive node and the specific database to be accessed
are only known in the scenario design time and hence specified through *Scenario
Design Tool*.

It is clear at this point that the tools of the platform share information. For example the physical assets designed through *Behaviour Type Design Tool* are later initialized through the *Scenario Design Tool*. We chose to store the shared information, such as the physical assets, as XML files to facilitate information sharing among the different tools of the platform.

Note that the output of an application may be used to set the global variables, which may be the input to other applications.

Send Block: Defining send blocks is similar to defining receive blocks. The user needs to define the performative of the message, the ontology of the message, and the content language of the message. To fill the content of the message, the ontology of the message is presented to the user pictorially as a hierarchy, where the user assigns each node a value, by either choosing a variable from the global variable pool, or by defining new physical assets with the help of *Physical Asset Design Tool*. The receiver of the message and the contents of the physical assets are defined in the *Scenario Design Tool*, since these values are specific to a given scenario.

Inference Engine: An agent may want to execute an inference engine to decide on what to do at certain point in the flow of its behaviour, i.e., it may have some predefined rules, and according to the facts it gathers, it may execute these set of rules against the newly obtained facts. These rules may be predefined, or they can be dynamically obtained according to the changing aspects of its environment.

After the user finishes the design of a new behaviour type, it is saved as an XML file which includes the parameters of the blocks, and the order of execution of these blocks. Again, XML is chosen as the intermediary format to facilitate information sharing among different tools of the platform. This XML definition is used in the *Scenario Design Tool* to visualize the flow of execution, where the scenario specific values are provided such as the missing values for physical assets, or the receiver and sender of the messages.

3.2   Agent Type Design Tool (ATDT)

After having defined the behaviours, the next step is to define the agent types. *Agent Type Design Tool* helps user to give a name and assign behaviour types to an agent type from the existing behaviour types that have been designed previously through the Behaviour Type Design Tool. These are saved again in an XML file to be used in the Scenario Design Tool. New agent types can be constructed either from scratch or by modifying the existing agent types. "Agent Types" are aggregations and specializations of agent behaviors for specific applications and can be thought as to role models in agent systems.

3.3   Scenario Design Tool (SDT)

After having designed the necessary behaviour types and agent templates, the user is now ready to design her multi-agent scenario. Through a GUI, she first adds the agents' types necessary in her scenario to the panel. She selects the agents from the predefined agent types, or she can build a new agent type, with the help of Agent Type Design Tool. Then she edits each of the agents to make these agent types specialized to the scenario. From a graphical user interface she visualizes the agents and their behaviour types, she can edit each of these behaviours to instantiate specific behaviour instances to the agent, i.e., she assigns the senders and receivers of the messages selecting from the agents defined in that scenario. Finally, she configures the predefined physical assets to map them to specific values for this scenario. Once the initialization of the scenario is completed it is converted to the ABRL rules and stored in a knowledge base.

3.4   Agent Behaviour Representation Language (ABRL)

We represented the behaviours in the scenario through a rule based system specifically designed for this purpose, called Agent Behaviour Representation Language (ABRL), which is composed of rules, facts and functions. Representing the whole scenario in this way in a rule-based system makes it highly interoperable.

Note that in a rule based system, there is no way to specify an order of execution implicitly. A rule is like an "if-then" statement in a procedural language, but it is not used in a procedural way. While "if-then" statements are executed at a specific time and in a specific order, according to how they are written in the source code, rules are executed whenever their "if" parts (their left-hand-sides) are satisfied.

On the other hand, there could be "execution dependencies" among the behaviour blocks in an agent behaviour. Assume that an agent is expecting a message from another agent, and after having received this message, the agent is expected to invoke a predefined activity, say A, by using a field in this message as an input parameter. Clearly there is an execution dependency over here; the activity block can only be executed after the expected message is received. In other words, we need to introduce a mechanism to enforce an execution sequence among the rules.

Execution dependency issues has been addressed previously in the literature within the context of workflow systems and a formalism has been developed [14, 3] to specify inter-task dependencies as constraints on the occurrence and temporal order of events.

In the following we provide an intuitive explanation for the mechanism we have developed for enforcing an execution order in an agent behaviour. The formal treatment of the subject for workflow systems is given in [8].

We associate a "guard expression" with each behaviour block to manage the control flow in an agent behaviour through the rule-based system. For the example given above, the "start guard" of activity A is a condition expression stating that the previous receive block has to be executed before this block can start.

We represent the behaviour blocks in Agent Behaviour Representation Language (ABRL) as follows:

- Represent each block as a rule and a fact pair,
- Put the necessary guard expressions in the left-hand-side of the rules to enforce the required execution order,
- Represent global variables and physical assets as facts to satisfy the information passing constraints among blocks,
- Use some auxiliary functions to implement the required actions in a specific agent platform, whenever the rules are fired.

In order to model the behaviour blocks and their execution order through a rule-based system, we define fact templates for representing the semantics of the blocks and the rules and the guard expressions to describe the execution order as explained in the following.

The fact templates are given in the Figure 4. These facts include all the necessary attributes to define each block. For example the "ReceiveBlock" fact includes the name of the block, the sender of the message, its ontology and performative. The facts are asserted while the behaviours are initialized through ABRL.

To describe the set of actions that will be performed when a block is encountered, an ABRL rule is defined. The general template of a rule is given in Figure 5. On the left-hand-side of a rule, there is a fact and a guard expression. The fact informs the rule that "there is a block with the specified attributes pending to be executed in the flow of the behaviour", and the guard expression informs the rule about "the preconditions of that block to be fulfilled so that the block can be executed".

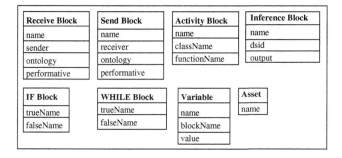

Fig. 4. The Fact Templates

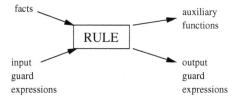

Fig. 5. The Rule Template

When a rule finds the related fact, and the asserted guard expression, the rule is fired. When a rule is fired, the necessary actions are executed. To represent these set of actions, one auxiliary function per block is defined. There are four auxiliary functions one for each of the send, receive, inference engine, and action blocks. When a block is successfully handled, the guard expression of the block that follows is asserted. This in return fires the next rule in the sequence.

As explained in section 3.1 blocks have two kind of information sources: global variables and physical assets. Global variables are used to pass information among blocks and physical asset represent external information sources as shown in Figure 4. These are the inputs and outputs of the blocks. The "blockName" in Figure 4 of "Variable" specifies the block that outputs this global variable. Since Physical Assets are stored as XML files, and their values are extracted by parsing the XML files, there is no "value" slot in their template.

3.5   An Example

In this section, we provide an example to clarify the concepts introduced. Consider the example flow given in Figure 2. In this example, an agent behaviour template is defined as follows: first, the agent is expected to receive a message. Then it executes an "if" block, and depending on the "if condition", it either invokes an application within a "while" block or it activates an inference engine to take a decision. When one of these branches terminates successfully, it sends a message to another agent.

The behaviour design given in Figure 2 can be described through a "behaviour" tree as shown in Figure 6 to visualize the execution dependencies.

The nodes of this tree correspond to the blocks in the design tool and the top level "Behaviour" node implies that the child blocks will be executed sequentially (as default). By considering the execution dependencies in this tree (Figure 6) the guard expressions and their associated conditions can automatically be obtained.

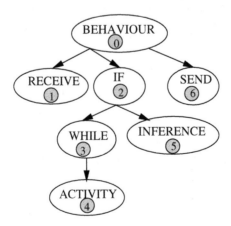

Fig. 6. The Process Tree

Table 1. Guards of the blocks of the example behaviour

Task Number	Start Guard	Start Condition	Terminate Guard	Fail Guard	Terminate Cond.	Fail Cond.
0	TRUE		6 terminates	1, 2, 6 fails		
1	O starts	receive fact asserted	TRUE	TRUE	msg. received	msg. could not be received
2	1 terminates	if fact asserted, cond. var. available	3 or 5 terminates	3 or 5 fails		
3	2 evaluates to TRUE	while facts asserted, iteration var. available	TRUE 4 fails	4 fails	while cond. is false	
4	While Condition is TRUE	activity fact asserted, input var. available	TRUE	TRUE	activity terminates successfully	activity fails
5	2 evaluates to TRUE	jess fact asserted, input var. available	TRUE	TRUE	inference eng. terminates successfully	inference eng. fails
6	2 terminates	send fact asserted, msg. content ready	TRUE	TRUE	msg. sent	msg. could not be sent

For example, which branch of the "if" block will be executed depends on the "guard expression" to be inserted by the "if" block, and this information, that is, the result of "if" condition is only available at run time. Table 1 gives an informal description of the guard expressions and conditions generated for this example. Note that if there are more than one block to be executed in parallel, more than one rule will fire at the same time.

For each block a rule is designed using these guard expressions. For example, for the "receive block" in Figure 2, the start guard is the start of the behaviour, and its start condition is satisfied when the "receive fact" is asserted. The "receive fact" is prepared according to the templates given in Figure 4, and it includes all the necessary attributes for defining the semantics of this block. By using these information, the following rule is generated for the "receive block":

```
(Rule receiveBlockRule
    (receiveBlock (name ?n) (sender ?s) (ontology ?o)
    (performative ?p))
    (startGuard BehaviourStarted)
    ⇒
    (receiveBlockFunction ?s ?o ?p)
    (assert (startGuard (?n finished)))
)
```

On the left-hand-side of the rule, there are the "receive fact" and the "start-Guard" of the "receive block". When the behaviour design is completed, all the facts of the blocks in the behaviour are asserted into the knowledge base, and the "BehaviourStarted" guard is asserted to initialize the first block in the flow of the behaviour. So the "receiveBlockRule" finds its left-hand-side conditions satisfied and it fires. When it fires, the auxiliary function "receiveBlockFunction" is called with the necessary parameters, that is, the sender, the ontology, and the performative of the message expected. This function executes the specific actions which, in this case, is to receive the expected message from the sender. When the message is received, its content is asserted into the "Global Variable Pool" using the template given in Figure 4. Finally, to indicate that the "receive block" has successfully terminated, the "start guard" of the block that follows (i.e. the "if block") is asserted. Hence the "if block" fires and the execution continues in this way. When the last block (i.e. the "send block") in the flow of the behaviour successfully terminates, the guard that terminates the execution of the behaviour is asserted. Note that if the behaviour is "cyclic", the start guard that initiates the behaviour is asserted once again.

3.6   Initialization

When configuration of all agents in a scenario are completed, it is necessary to initialize them in a multi-agent scenario. At this point, a concrete agent platform is needed and we have chosen the JADE platform to run the agents.

The platform has a default agent called as "Agent Factory" (AF) which initializes each agent in the scenario as a JADE agent with the following default behaviours: The first behaviour is called "Behaviour Initialization Behaviour", which listens to "Agent Factory" for new Behaviour Messages. AF agent sends new behaviour messages to the newly created agents to inform them about their behaviours. With this message, the agent receives the content of its behaviours, its ontologies, physical assets, and decision structures (used by the inference engine). The agent first initializes its ontologies by parsing the received RDF ontology file and it constructs JADE Ontology classes. It uses these ontology classes while receiving and sending messages. Then it parses the Physical Asset files and initializes its physical asset collection. The agent retracts the rules from a specified database (if this is specified at the design phase); converts the rules into JESS rules, and initializes its Decision Structures collections accordingly. After all of the parameters necessary for its behaviour to execute (i.e. ontologies, physical assets, decision structures) are in place, the agent behaviour is initialized. Then, a JESS engine is instantiated; the ABRL representation of the behaviours are asserted to the engine, and the behaviour starts to execute which completes the agent initialization.

The platform also provides a monitoring tool, where the user can monitor the existing agents, their behaviours, ontologies, physical assets, and decision structures in a scenario. With the help of this tool, the user can also visualize the messages exchanged by the agents. Having a view of the scenario from this tool, the user may want to add new behaviours to an agent, kill one of its behaviours. The AF agent sends the messages to the agent, which in turn handles the necessary actions. The user may also want to change the values of some physical assets; the platform provides a tool for this functionality. Again the AF agent sends the necessary update messages to the agent, this time, with the help of its second default behaviour, "UpdateListeningBehaviour", so that it updates its physical asset collection accordingly. This behaviour also handles the Decision Structure update messages.

4   Conclusions

For wider deployment and exploitation of agent technology, it is important to provide software companies with powerful agent design tools to help them develop solutions for their customers effectively. There are agent development frameworks that aim to ease this process by providing APIs, but the developer still has to define the behaviour of the agents by writing code in a programming language.

In this paper, we present an orchestration platform that allows the developers to design a complete agent-based scenario through graphical user interfaces. To address the micro level design of an agent community, agent behaviours are modelled as workflow processes and designed accordingly. The multi-agent scenario produced by the platform is stored as a rule based system which makes it easy to accommodate the changing requirements of user scenarios. The formalism developed within the scope of this work to represent the behaviours in a rule based system can be used in any agent platform to execute the multi-agent scenario, since there are rule based languages that can be used with most of the programming languages.

Guard expressions are used to enforce an execution sequence in a rule-based system. Traditional database and file processing techniques are integrated into the system to facilitate the design for the developers. The platform also provides macro level design capabilities such as defining the ontologies of the agents, their roles in the system, and their interactions in a systematical way.

The aim of the tool is to design a multi-agent system either from scratch, or by adapting existing distributed systems to multi agent systems. Given a multi-agent scenario and existing applications, the orchestration tool helps to create the necessary agents, handles all the interactions between the agents, and outputs a multi-agent system that is ready to be executed on an agent platform.

Note that although any agent platform can execute the multi-agent scenario presented as a rule based system, to be able to demonstrate the execution of the system on a concrete agent platform, we mapped the ABRL rules to JESS and executed the system on JADE. The developed tool has been extensively tested and evaluated through the pilot application scenarios of the Agent Academy Project. One of these case studies is presented at [2]. One of the limitations of the current version of the tool is that it is not possible to design agents interacting with the user through a GUI. This limitation will be handled in the future versions. Finally the tool is available at "https://sourceforge.net/projects/agentacademy".

References

1. M. Amor, L. Fuentes, A. Vallecillo, "Bridging the Gap Between Agent-Oriented Design and Implementtaion". in. Proc. of AOSE 2004, July, 2004, NewYork, USA.
2. I. N. Athanasiadis, P. A. Mitkas, G. B. Laleci, Y. Kabak, "Embedding data-driven decision strategies on software agents: The case of a Multi-Agent System for Monitoring Air-Quality Indexes", in 10th International Conference on Concurrent Engineering (CE-2003),Workshop on intelligent agents and data mining:research and applications, Maderia, Portugal (2003)
3. P.A. Attie, M.P. Singh, A. Sheth, and M. Rusinkiewicz, "Specifying and enforcing intertask dependencies", in Proc. of 19th Intl. Conf. on Very Large Data Bases, September 1993.

4. C Language Integrated Production System (CLIPS), http://www.ghg.net/clips/ CLIPS.html

5. R. Cervenka, I. Trencansky, M. Calisti, D. Greenwood, "AML: Agent Modleing Language Toward Industry-Grade Agent-Based Modeling". in. Proc. of AOSE 2004, July, 2004, NewYork, USA.

6. M. Cossentino, C. Potts, "A CASE tool supported methodology for the design of multi-agent systems". Proc. of the 2002 International Conference on Software Engineering Research and Practice (SERP'02). Las Vegas, NV, USA, June 2002

7. S. A, DeLoach, M. Wood (2000), "Developing Multiagent Systems with agentTool", in Proc. of Intelligent Agents: Agent Theories, Architectues, and Languages - 7th International Workshop, ATAL-2000, Boston, MA, USA.

8. Dogac, A., Gokkoca, E., Arpinar, S., Koksal, P., Cingil, I., Arpinar, B., Tatbul, N., Karagoz, P., Halici, U., Altinel, M., "Design and Implementation of a Distributed Workflow Management System: METUFlow", In *Workflow Management Systems and Interoperability*, Dogac, A., Kalinichenko, L., Ozsu, T., Sheth, A., (Edtrs.), Springer-Verlag NATO ASI Series, 1998.

9. M. Esteva, D. de la Cruz, C. Sierra, "ISLANDER: an electronic institutions editor", in Proc. of AAMAS02, July, 2002, Bologna,Italy.

10. M. P. Huget, J. Odell, "Representing Agent Interaction Protocols with Agent UML". in. Proc. of AOSE 2004, July, 2004, NewYork, USA.

11. Java Agent Development Framework, http://sharon .cselt.it/projects/jade/

12. N.R. Jennings (2000), "On agent-based software engineering", 117 (2) 277-296. Artificial Intelligence

13. Jess, The Expert System Shell for the Java Platform, http:// herzberg.ca.sandia.gov/jess

14. J. Klein, "Advanced rule driven transaction management", in Proc. of 36th IEEE Computer Society Intl. Conf. CompCon Spring 1991, San Francisco, CA, March 1991.

15. The Protege Project, http://protege.stanford.edu /index.html

16. Resource Description Framework (RDF), http:// www.w3.org/RDF/

17. C. Rich and C. L. Sidner. COLLAGEN: A collaboration manager for software interface agents. User Modeling and User-Adapted Interaction, 8(3-4):315350, 1998.

18. J. Sudeikat, L. Braubach, A. Pokahr, W. Lamesdorf, "Evaluation of Agent-Oriented Software /Methodologies - Examination of the Gap Between Modeling and Platform in. Proc. of AOSE 2004, July, 2004, NewYork, USA.

19. M. Wooldridge, N. R. Jennings, and D. Kinny, "The Gaia Methodology for Agent-Oriented Analysis and Design", Journal of Autonomous Agents and Multi-Agent Systems 3 (3), 2000.

20. M. Wooldridge, N. R. Jennings, and D. Kinny, "A Methodology for Agent-Oriented Analysis and Design", Proc. 3rd Int Conference on Autonomous Agents (Agents-99), 1999.

21. Xerces Java Parse, http://xml.apache.org/xerces2-j /index.html

22. ZEUS, http://www.labs.bt.com/projects/agents/zeus

A Formal Reuse-Based Approach
for Interactively Designing Organizations

Catholijn Jonker, Jan Treur, and Pınar Yolum

Vrije Universiteit Amsterdam, Department of Artificial Intelligence,
De Boelelaan 1081a, NL-1081 HV Amsterdam, The Netherlands
{jonker, treur, pyolum}@few.vu.nl

Abstract. Multiagent organizations provide a powerful way for developing multiagent systems. This paper presents a methodology for designing organizations based on formal specification of requirements for organizational behavior and requirements refinement related to organizational structure. The approach allows parts of an organization to be designed in parallel and later be put together to satisfy the broader requirements of the organization. Using this approach, organizational building blocks can be formally specified, appropriately indexed and stored in an organization design library. The library structure is supported by software tools and allows designers with varying levels of expertise to benefit from it by accommodating queries at different abstraction levels and by providing support for query reformulation.

1   Introduction

Organizations are an important metaphor for developing multiagent systems. Organizations provide a template of rules for agents to follow to accomplish large-scale tasks [3]. When designed modularly, organizations make it possible to divide a large-scale task among small groups of practice and coherently put together the individual outputs of the groups to accomplish the large-scale tasks of interest. More specifically, by appropriately carrying out individual tasks and communicating as needed, organizations provide a way to solve broader tasks.

This paper deals with the problem of designing organizations. An example organization design process may start by formally specifying requirements for the overall organization behavior. The requirements express the dynamic properties that should hold if appropriate organizational building blocks, such as groups and roles and their interactions, are combined in an appropriate manner. In addition, there could be requirements on the structure of the desired organization that need to be fulfilled by the organization design. Given these requirements on overall organization (and, perhaps, some additional requirements), organizational structure and organizational behavior are designed and formally specified so that the organizational requirements are fulfilled. However, designing the individual groups from scratch is labor-intensive, requiring expertise and domain knowledge.

We argue that once designed and formally specified, parts of an organization can be reused by other organizations. We propose a methodology for designing organizations based on reusing formal specifications of existing organizational components.

J. Odell et al. (Eds.): AOSE 2004, LNCS 3382, pp. 221–237, 2005.
© Springer-Verlag Berlin Heidelberg 2005

The methodology indexes organizational components based on abstract identifiers that capture their functionality (what it does) and additional metadata that provide information on the workings of the component (how it does). An organization designer can interactively search a library of components to find a component that fits her needs and possibly tailor it to her needs. Since the components are indexed with identifiers in different contextual dimensions, a designer can find the same component by formulating a query in a variety of ways. Further, the system is interactive in that it can exploit the library structure to suggest variations on the query in order to help designers reformulate their queries more precisely.

The rest of this paper is organized as follows. Section 2 gives a technical background on the AGR methodology, which is used as a basis for the developed approach and the formal languages for specifying organizations and ontologies. Section 3 discusses our approach for designing organizations by refining requirements. Section 4 introduces the reuse methodology and discusses different indexing techniques for groups. Section 5 presents a methodology for classifying organizations based on multi-dimensional taxonomies. Section 6 discusses the relevant literature.

2   Technical Background

This section presents some of the technical preliminaries.

2.1   Agent/Group/Role Methodology

We start with the Agent/Group/Role (AGR) approach for modeling organizations [5]. This approach specifies a structure for an organization based on a definition of groups, roles and their relationships. An organization as a whole is composed of a number of *groups*. A group structure identifies the *roles* and the *transfers* between roles needed for interactions: the possible communication lines.

A group is a unit of communications. Two roles can communicate to each other if and only if they are in the same group. The *inter-group role interactions* (abbreviated as *group interactions*) between roles of different groups specify the connectivity of groups within an organization. *Agents* are allocated to roles; they realize the organization. However, the aim of an organization model is to abstract from specific agent allocations. Therefore instead of particular agents, roles are used as abstract entities, defining properties agents should have when they are to function in a given role within an organization.

Consider a negotiation group as a running example.

Example 1. A buyer and a seller need to agree on a price for an item. The seller proposes a price. The buyer can either accept or propose a different price. The seller can then accept or propose a new price. The process repeats itself until either the buyer or the seller accepts a proposed price.

The AGR approach to organization modeling has been extended to incorporate dynamic properties for the organization behavior [7].

Role Dynamic Properties: Role dynamic properties specify how the inout of a role affects the output of that role. The input includes incoming communication from other roles as well as observations about the external world. The output includes outgoing communication as well as actions to be performed in the external world. The external world is considered as the environment of the organization that interacts with the organization by providing observational input to roles and which can be changed by actions in the output of roles. In general, the inputs and output of role properties capture public facts rather than private facts that are internal to an agent. Hence, a role dynamic property is observable.

Transfer Dynamic Properties: A transfer property relates output of the source role to input of the destination role. Typically, such a property expresses that a communicated information is indeed transferred from source to destination, and, for example, transfer is brought about within certain time duration. The parameters of the transfer property denote the roles that use this transfer. Intuitively, these roles should be uniquely identified.

Group Dynamic Properties: Group dynamic properties relate input or output of roles within a group.

Example 2. A group property of the negotiation group explained before could be:

If   at some point in time the Seller proposes a price,
then   at some later time point the Buyer will receive an agreed, final price.

A special case of a group property is an *intragroup role interaction* property (RI) relating the outputs of two roles within a group. A role interaction property in this context always refers to roles in the same group.

Group Interaction Dynamic Properties: Group interaction properties specify how input of a source role in one group affects output of a destination role in another group. The same agent plays the two roles involved in a group interaction.

Organization Dynamic Properties: Organization dynamic properties relate to input or output of roles within the organization. A typical (informal) example of such a property is: 'if within the organization, role A promises to deliver a product, then role B will deliver this product'.

Table 1 provides an overview of these combinations. Group interaction properties can be considered a specific type of organization property. Similarly, role interaction and transfer properties can be considered a specific type of group properties. Note that with respect to simulation, the above dynamics definition can contain elements that are redundant: a smaller subset of dynamical properties can form an executable specification of the dynamics of an AGR organization. For example, on the basis of the roles, transfer properties, and group interactions, the organization can be simulated. The group dynamic properties, including the role interaction properties, and the organization properties should emerge in the execution, and testing for them can validate the model.

Table 1. Types of dynamic properties for an AGR organization model

Property type	Notation	Relating	
Organization	OP	Input or Output of	roles in O
Group interaction	GI	Role r1 Input in G1	Role r2 Output in G2
Group	GP	Input or Output of	roles in G
Role interaction	RI	Role r1 Output in G	Role r2 Output in G
Transfer	TP	Role r1 Output in G	Role r2 Input in G
Role	RP	Role r Input [Role r Internal]	Role r Output

2.2   A Formal Specification Language for Organization Structure

In this paper we use a subset of the formal language developed for specifying the structure and behavior for AGR-models of organizations; cf. [7]. This language is used to specify the properties explained in Section 2.1.

Table 2. Sorts of the language

Sort	Description
ROLE	Sort for a role within an organization.
AGENT	Sort for an agent that can be allocated to a certain role.
GROUP	Sort for a group within an organization.
GROUP_INTERACTION	Sort for a connection between two roles in different groups
TRANSFER	Sort for a connection between two roles within one group.
CONNECTION	An element of TRANSFER or GROUP_INTERACTION
DYNPROP	Sort for names of dynamic properties
DYNPROPEXP	Sort for possible TTL expressions (see Section 2.4)

Table 2 gives an overview of the possible sorts to specify the elements of an organization. From a structural perspective, some of these sorts relate to the each other through the predicates of Table 3. These predicates specify the groups in the organizations, the roles in the groups, the agents allocated to these roles, and the communication between two roles.

Table 3. Predicates for specifying the structure of an organization

Predicate	Description
exists_role: ROLE	A role exists within an organization.
exists_group: GROUP	A group exists within the organization
role_belongs_to_group: ROLE * GROUP	A role is part of a group.
intra_group_connection: ROLE * ROLE * GROUP * TRANSFER	A role is connected to another role (directed) within a certain group by means of a transfer connection. The source and destination roles are allowed to be equivalent.

The predicate in Table 4 is used to define (a relevant part of the) behavior of the organization through dynamic properties. These properties essentially specify the role, group, and organization properties as well as the interaction properties between groups. Modeling the behavior of an organization makes use of dynamic properties expressed in terms of the Temporal Trace Language TTL. The different types of properties are defined in Table 3.

Table 4. Predicates for specifying the behavior of an organization

has_expression: DYNPROP * DYNPROPEXP	A specific dynamic property has an expression.

2.3   A Formal Language for Ontologies

In addition to the language described above we developed a language to formally specify ontologies for the input and output states of roles. The language is based on first-order many-sorted logic; e.g., [10].

Definition 1. A signature Σ is a four tuple $<S, C, F, P>$ such that, **S** is a set of sorts, **C** is a set of constants, which have sorts defined in **S**, **F** is a set of functions with possibly varying arity and whose domain and range elements have sorts defined in **S**, and **R** is a set of relations with possibly varying arity and whose domain elements have sorts defined in **S**.

Table 1 provides the constructs of the language. Here, we describe them briefly. The ontology can refer to many sorts. Let $s_1...s_n$ denote sorts and $o_1...o_n$ denote ontologies. The sorts of the ontology are those for which the is_a_sort_in(s_1, o_1) predicate holds. Let $r_1...r_n$ denote relations and $f_1...f_n$ denote functions. The relations in the ontology are shown with is_a_relation(n, r_1, o_1), where n denotes the arity of relation r_1. Similarly, the functions in the ontology are shown with is_a_relation(n, f_1, o_1), where n denotes the arity of function f_1. For each relation in the ontology, dom_of(n, s_1, r_1) specifies the domain sorts for each of the n parameters in the relation. Similarly, for each function in the ontology, dom_of(n, f_1, r_1) gives the domain sort for all n parameters for the function. For the functions, we also define the predicate range_of(f_1, r_1), which gives the range sort for the function. These predicates allow us to formally specify an ontology in the form of signatures. Given such a signature, one can also define well-formed formulae as follows.

Table 5. Basic elements of a language for signatures

PREDICATE	DESCRIPTION
is_a_sort_in:SORT * ONTOLOGY	SORT exists in ONTOLOGY
is_a_relation_in:INTEGER*RELATION*ONTOLOGY	RELATION exists in ONTOLOGY with arity n
is_a_function_in:INTEGER*FUNCTION* ONTOLOGY	FUNCTION exists in ONTOLOGY with arity n
Dom_of: INTEGER*SORT * RELATION	Domain of RELATION is in SORT
Dom_of: INTEGER*SORT * FUNCTION	Domain of FUNCTION is in SORT
Range_of: SORT * FUNCTION	Range of FUNCTION is in SORT

Definition 2. Let $\Sigma = <S, C, F, P>$ be a signature and **V** a set of variables with sorts defined in **S**. The set of well-formed formulae over Σ, WFF(Σ) are generated the as usual.

2.4   A Formal Specification Language for Organization Behavior

To formally specify dynamic properties characterising organization behavior, an expressive language is needed. In this paper for most of the properties both informal or semi-formal and formal representations are given. The formal representations in the sort DYNPROPEXP (see Section 2.2) are based on the Temporal Trace Language (TTL; cf. [7]), which is briefly defined as follows.

A *state ontology* is a specification (in order-sorted logic) of a vocabulary, i.e., a signature. A state for ontology Ont is an assignment of truth-values {true, false} to the set At(Ont) of ground atoms expressed in terms of Ont. The *set of all possible states* for state ontology Ont is denoted by STATES(Ont). The set of *state properties* STATPROP(Ont) for state ontology Ont is the set of all propositions over ground atoms from At(Ont). A fixed *time frame* T is assumed which is linearly ordered. A *trace* or *trajectory* $\mathcal{T}$ over a state ontology Ont and time frame T is a mapping $\mathcal{T}$: T → STATES(Ont), i.e., a sequence of states $\mathcal{T}_t$ (t ∈ T) in STATES(Ont). The set of all traces over state ontology Ont is denoted by TRACES(Ont). Depending on the application, the time frame T may be dense (e.g., the real numbers), or discrete (e.g., the set of integers or natural numbers or a finite initial segment of the natural numbers), or any other form, as long as it has a linear ordering. The set of *dynamic properties* DYNPROPEXP(Σ) is the set of temporal statements that can be formulated with respect to traces based on the state ontology Ont in the following manner: For an organization or part thereof, Ont is the union of all input, output and internal state ontologies of the roles in the organization (part). Given a trace $\mathcal{T}$ over state ontology Ont, the input state of a role at time point t is denoted by state($\mathcal{T}$, t, input(r)); analogously, state($\mathcal{T}$, t, output(r)), and state($\mathcal{T}$, t, internal(r)) denote the output state and internal state of the role.

These states can be related to state properties via the formally defined satisfaction relation |=, comparable to the Holds-predicate in the Situation Calculus: state($\mathcal{T}$, t, output(r)) |= p denotes that state property p holds in trace $\mathcal{T}$ at time t in the output state of the organization. Based on these statements, dynamic properties can be formulated in a formal manner in a sorted first-order predicate logic with sorts T for time points, Trace for traces and F for state formulae, using quantifiers over time and the usual first-order logical connectives such as ¬, ∧, ∨, ⇒, ∀, ∃.

3   Designing Organizations by Requirements Refinement

Consider an organization design problem for which the requirements of the overall behavior are given in the form of dynamic properties. In other words, the organization designed for this problem should at least satisfy these given properties. One approach for designing such an organization is a top-down approach. The design process starts from these global organization properties. The properties are then refined into a set of smaller properties that can be satisfied by parts of the organization. Hence, the design problem is reduced to designing correct groups that can satisfy some properties and establishing effective communications between these groups. That is, dynamic properties for the groups and their interactions give the dynamics properties for the organization.

Example 3. Consider an organization where a Buyer chooses an item and then the Buyer and Seller agree on a price. This organization can be designed by first obtaining (designing from scratch or reusing) two groups as follows. The first group will communicate in a certain way that will allow the Buyer to choose an item. The second group's functions as described in Example 1. When these groups are linked correctly (by a group interaction) then the overall requirements of the organization are satisfied.

An important aspect of this approach is its formality. The informal group property of Example 2, where a Buyer and a Seller negotiate the price of a commodity, can be formalized as follows. In this and the following examples, a communication ontology is used. The `communication_from_to` predicate is used to describe the roles that communicate, the type of the communicative act, and the content of the act. An alternative would be to to use the content of the communicative act by itself to denote the states. Further, the communication ontology could be replaced by other ontologies, for example with a service ontology.

Example 4. Let `communication_from_to(Role1, Role2, inform, de-sired_price_for(a))` denote that `Role1` is informing `Role2` that it is interested in agreeing on a price for item `a` and `communication_from_to(Role1, Role2, inform, agreed_price_for(p, a))` denote that `Role1` is informing `Role2` that it is agreeing to the price `p` for item `a`. Then the following TTL formulation of a group property means that if the Buyer and the Seller roles inform each other on a desire to agree on a price, then at a later time they will agree on a price.

$\forall t$ [state(γ, t, output(Buyer)) $\models$ communication_from_to(Buyer, Seller, inform, desired_price_for(a))
&
state(γ, t, output(Seller)) $\models$ communication_from_to(Seller, Buyer, inform, desired_price_for(a))
$\Rightarrow$
$\exists t' \geq t \, \exists p$
state(γ, t', input(Buyer)) $\models$ communication_from_to(Seller, Buyer, inform, agreed_price_for(p, a)) &
state(γ, t', input(Seller)) $\models$ communication_from_to(Buyer, Seller, inform, agreed_price_for(p, a))]

The refinement scheme shows that to fulfill the overall dynamic properties, dynamic properties of certain groups and group interactions together imply the organization behavior requirements. The process to determine the requirements for parts of the organization and groups is called *requirements refinement*. It provides new, refined requirements for the behavior of groups and group interaction. It is possible to arrive at requirements of groups in one step, but it is also possible to first refine requirements for the behavior of the organization as a whole to the requirements on the behavior of parts of the organization, before further refinement is made to obtain dynamic properties for groups. Notice that the groups are not given at forehand, but this requirements refinement process just determines which types of groups (i.e., with which properties) are chosen as part of the organization being designed. Similarly, the required dynamic properties of groups can be refined to dynamic properties of certain roles and transfers, such that the dynamics properties for the roles and the transfers between the roles give the dynamic properties for the group of which they are part of.

This provides the roles to be used, requirements on the behavior of these roles and transfer between them, which together imply the requirements on the behavior of the group. Again it is possible to first refine requirements on the behavior of a group to requirements of the behavior of parts of the group, before further refinement to required role behavior is made.

An overview of the inter-level relationships between these dynamic properties at different aggregation levels is depicted as an AND-tree in Figure 1. In summary, from the design perspective, a top-down refinement approach can be followed. That is, the requirements on overall organizational behavior can be first refined to requirements on behavior of groups and group interaction, and then the requirements on behavior of groups can be refined to requirements on roles and transfers. This design perspective may suggest that designing organizations always has to be done from scratch. However,

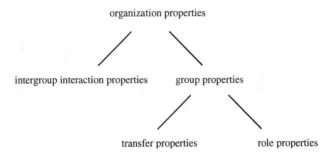

Fig. 1. Inter-level relations between dynamic properties

often parts of organizations can be used in other organizations. Thus, an organization design process can benefit substantially if reusable parts of organization models are maintained in a library and indexed in an adequate manner to retrieve relevant ones during the design process. The methodology for organization design, based on an extension of the AGR model, supports reuse of organization parts and, in particular, of groups. This will be addressed in subsequent sections.

4   Indexing Within the Library of Groups

The approach to reuse within the developed organization design methodology is inspired from the literature on reuse in software design [13]. The main steps of the approach that are related to the reuse of groups are the following:

1. Groups are characterized from an external perspective by abstract identifiers at different levels of abstraction.
2. The complete group specification (from an internal perspective) is stored in the library, and indexed with the identifiers obtained in 1.
3. An organization designer queries the library for a group based on certain information expressed in terms of the characterizing identifiers.
4. The library returns all groups that match the query, based on a matching function.
5. The organization designer reviews the returned groups and incorporates one of them possibly modifying it as necessary.

The manner in which (formal) specifications of the internal structure of groups are stored in the library is shown in Section 2. It is assumed that these groups are indexed by identifiers at different levels of abstractions according to multi-dimensional taxonomic structures, one taxonomy for each dimension that can be considered in the query. This section studies different methods of indexing groups. Section 5 shows how these indexes can be combined into a multi-dimensional taxonomy to allow flexible queries.

4.1   Indexing by Group Functionality, Output or Input

A first dimension to consider for indexing is group functionality. Such a functionality can be considered as a relation between input state properties and output state properties of a group. The simplest form of a relationship is that a certain input state property at a certain point in time leads to a certain output state property at some later time point. However, especially for ongoing processes, the relationships between input and output state properties can take the form of more complex temporal relationships, expressed by dynamic properties as discussed in Section 2. For simple primary functionality descriptions, there may be other secondary functionality descriptions involved, such as other constraints on how the group should carry out this primary functionality. Often, there are restrictions on the group's process that have to be satisfied. One form of constraints requires that a certain condition is maintained throughout the group enactment. For example, in our running example, a designer could additionally require that no role should announce a final price p for an item a, without getting the permission of the second role. This is a constraint that should be maintained at any time in the group. The temporal trace language TTL (see Section 2) can be used to specify such dynamic properties as part of a functionality description.

Example 5. Let the previously defined communications carry their meanings and let `communication_from_to(Role1, Role2, permit, announce_price)` mean that `Role1` gives a permission to `Role2` to announce the agreed price. The following TTL formulation then expresses the following property. If both Buyer and Seller inform the other for a desire on agreed price, then at a later time they will communicate each other the same agreed price. And if either the Buyer or the Seller announces the price to a third-party C, then that will be done with the other party's permission.

$\forall t$ [state(γ, t, output(Buyer)) $\models$ communication_from_to(Buyer, Seller, inform, desired_price_for(a))
&
state(γ, t, output(Seller)) $\models$ communication_from_to(Seller, Buyer, inform, desired_price_for(a))
$\Rightarrow$
$\exists t' \geq t \; \exists p$
state(γ, t', input(Buyer)) $\models$ communication_from_to(Seller, Buyer, inform, agreed_price_for(p, a)) &
state(γ, t', input(Seller)) $\models$ communication_from_to(Buyer, Seller, inform, agreed_price_for(p, a))]
&
$\forall t'' \; \forall C$ state(γ, t'', input(Buyer)) $\models$ communication_from_to(Buyer, C, inform, agreed_price_for(p, a))
$\Rightarrow \exists t''' \leq t''$
state(γ, t''', input(Buyer)) $\models$ communication_from_to(Seller, Buyer, permit, announce_price))
&
$\forall t'' \; \forall C$ state(γ, t'', input(Seller)) $\models$ communication_from_to(Seller, C, inform, agreed_price_for(p, a))
$\Rightarrow \exists t''' \leq t''$
state(γ, t''', input(Seller)) $\models$ communication_from_to(Buyer, Seller, permit, announce_ price))

Recall that the group properties as defined above from an internal viewpoint relate input properties to the output properties of roles within a group. One (most specific) way to identify a group is to use such a dynamic group property of a group as an identifier. The advantage of such a specific group property is that it captures a relevant part of the functionality of the group succinctly. The main disadvantage of its usage as an identifier, however, is that it contains too much internal information to sufficiently abstract the group. A designer in need of a group would have to know the roles in this group as well as the exact inputs and outputs of the roles to retrieve the group from the library. For example, if a designer had used the group property above to search for a group, then the designer would need to know that the group contains at least two roles of Seller and Buyer and their inputs and outputs. Since many designers would not know this much internal information about a group, searching a group through such group properties mighty only be useful for designers with high expertise.

Next, we study two opposite ways that the groups can be identified. On one extreme, we have designers who know precisely how the group they are looking for should behave from an external viewpoint, but do not know, and do not care for, the internal details of the group. For these designers, a group identifier is created that captures the externally observable functionality of the group in detail, but abstracts from the internal details of the group. More specifically, we start with the group property (specified from an internal viewpoint) considered above to derive from it a more abstract property (specified from an external viewpoint). Following the same example, the instantiation of a group would have carried the organization from a state of where participants declared interest to reach an agreed price to a state where they have reached the agreed price. Intuitively, this functionality can be specified in an abstract group identifier that captures the information on interest and agreed price in respective input and the output states of the group, but does not refer to any specific roles or information transfer inside the group. As an example consider the output state of this group; i.e., there is an agreed price. This output state (OS) or the input state (IS) can be defined using certain signatures Σin and Σout, and state properties Win and Wout, respectively. These signatures can be taken as copies or abstracted forms of the internal signatures related to some of the roles (see also Example 10 below). For simplicity we assume that the internal signatures for the roles are disjoint, so that there is a one-to-one correspondence between signatures used at group input or output states and some of the internal signatures. Given the group input and output signatures, the abstract group identifier relates group input states and group output states, and abstracts from specific role names.

Example 6. Recall the group property of Example 4 where the Buyer and Seller eventually agree on a price. The property here uses that of Example 4 as a basis but the specification is now done from an external point of view. The specification does not refer to the Buyer and Seller roles but to variable roles X and Y.

$\forall t$ [state(γ, t, input(G)) |= $\exists$ X, Y:ROLE communication_from_to(X, Y, inform, desired_price_for(a))
& communication_from_to(Y, X, inform, desired_price_for(a)))
$\Rightarrow \exists t' \geq t \; \exists p$
state(γ, t', output(G)) |= $\exists$ X, Y:ROLE communication_from_to(X, Y, inform, agreed_price_for(p, a)) &
communication_from_to(Y, X, inform, agreed_price_for(p, a))]

A group input state carries information obtained from outside the group, whereas a group output state carries information targeted for the outside of the group. In Example 8, the information on the input to group G, expresses that some X initiates a communication of a certain type to some Y. Similarly, the group output state carries information that results from a communication of some X and Y. Note that the X and Y in this dynamic property may be related to other roles (other than Buyer and Seller) in other parts of the organization, for example Standkeeper and Visitor. When incorporating the negotiation group, by a group interaction these other roles will be connected to the Buyer and Seller role. Not all descriptions of group functionality have the simple form that one input state property Win after some time will lead to an output state property Wout. It may very well be the case that a group is adaptive, in the sense that, depending on the amount of work it does, its functioning is improving over time. For such a group a dynamic property of the format 'exercise improves skill' can be expressed in TTL:

Example 7. In the following TTL expression, state($\gamma1$, t', input(G)) $\models$ has_work_level(v1) means that in trace $\gamma1$ at time t', at the input of the group, the group has work level v1. The TTL expression then means that for every pair of traces $\gamma1$ and $\gamma2$, if over a certain time interval a trace has a higher work level than a second trace, then after this time interval the first trace will perform with a higher quality level.

$\forall\gamma1, \gamma2, t$
[$\forall t' \leq t$ [state($\gamma1$, t', input(G)) $\models$ has_work_level(v1) & state($\gamma2$, t', input(G)) $\models$ has_work_level(v2) $\Rightarrow$
v1 $\leq$ v2] &
state($\gamma1$, t', output(G)) $\models$ has_quality_level(w1) & state($\gamma2$, t', output(G)) $\models$ has_quality_level(w2)
$\Rightarrow$ w1 $\leq$ w2]

Notice that this property, expressible in TTL, is more complex both in the temporal structure and in the fact that two possible traces are compared (which is not possible, for example, in standard temporal logics).

An abstract group identifier has the advantage of identifying a group with a group property (i.e., captures the functionality well) but also has the advantage of only capturing the externalized functionality of the group without referencing any internal roles or information flow.

On the other extreme, we have designers who have a vague idea of the group they are looking for. The queries that these designers pose will be far from capturing the input and output states or the functionality of the group they are searching for. For these designers their search can be characterized at best by more abstract identifiers, i.e., general keywords. These keywords can vary in terms of how specific they are. Obviously, general keywords can be associated with many groups, while more specialized keywords can prune down the possible set of candidate groups.

To accommodate both types of designers, a library structure is constructed that can be searched with identifiers at different levels of abstraction, the lowest level being specific group identifiers expressed as specifications of dynamic properties. The group library index is structured as a set of taxonomies (trees) of identifiers with isa relations between them. For more details of the generic approach behind this, see Section 5.1. The first tree contains identifiers at different levels of abstraction that describe functionality of the groups in the library. The root of the tree is the most general keyword for functionality. With each branching of the tree, the identifiers are specialized further. For example, in the middle of the tree an identifier such as reach_price_agreement can be used. We view the abstract group identifier (i.e., the dynamic group property specified from an external viewpoint) as the most specialized identifier for a group. Hence, the leaves of the tree correspond to individual abstract group identifiers.

The second tree contains the output information for the group. This may be useful for designers that have an idea of what output is to be used in the rest of the organization, but have no specific knowledge about functionalities. Again, at the root of this tree, the output state is described at the most general level. Going down the tree specializes the output. The leaves of the tree are the specific state properties based on output signatures that are also part of the abstract group identifier. The third tree is similar to the second tree, except that the nodes of the tree describe the inputs rather than the outputs.

Example 8. An example of an output state property is then that there is a price over which X and Y agree.

∃ X, Y:ROLE ∃p communication_from_to(X, Y, inform, agreed_price_for(p, a)) & communication_from_to(Y, X, inform, agreed_price_for(p, a))]

At the input a similar property is that X and Y inform each other about a desire to agree on a price.

∃ X, Y:ROLE communication_from_to(X, Y, inform, desired_price_for(a)) & communication_from_to(Y, X, inform, desired_price_for(a))

4.2 Indexing by Environment Assumptions

The previous section describes how a designer can formulate a query for a desired group and find a set of groups that she could choose from. However, in many cases the designer can have additional constraints on the group. This subsection and the following ones classify important additional (meta)data about groups. This metadata can be supplied to the designer with the group, allowing her to investigate the properties of interest in more depth.

The first type of additional information about a group is formed by assumptions on the environment, which guarantee conditions under which the group can function properly. The environment of a group within an organization is formed by the rest of the organization and by the external world in which the organization is embedded. Assumptions may guarantee, for example, the availability of resources in the external world, or that upon certain requests generated as output by the group, other parts of the organization will provide answers as input for the group. An example of an environment assumption is the following:

Example 9. Whenever a certain X has a request to a certain Y on a particular item (q), then outside the group a certain Y will somehow find this information and communicate it to an X.

∀t [∃ X, Y:ROLE state(γ, t, output(G)) |= communication_from_to(X, Y, request, q) ⇒
∃t'≥t ∃a
∃ X, Y:ROLE state(γ, t', input(G)) |= communication_from_to(Y, X, inform, answer_for(a, q))]

In the previous example the information is received from outside group G. Then, for this group to function correctly, it should be used in an environment where the environment can satisfy the necessary information. This information could be generated by another group in the organization or from some other sources in the external world.

Environment assumptions can be addressed using a tree of different levels of abstraction similar to the cases shown in Section 4.1. From that perspective, the environment assumption given in Example 11 constitutes a leaf of the tree. The leaves are the most specific descriptions of environment assumptions in the tree. The higher nodes of the tree would contain assumptions that are described in more general terms. Again here, the higher nodes in the tree are assumed to be generalizations of the lower nodes.

4.3 Indexing by Realization Constraints

The organization designer can also have constraints on how the organization will be realized. Most of these realization constraints are related to the allocation of agents to particular roles in the organization. That is, the designer can already have one or more agents that are going to take part in the organization. Obviously, an agent can play a role in the organization only if its properties are compatible with the properties of the role that it is going to play [4]. Hence, a designer's choice of a group can also depend on the agents that are available.

This section discusses the criteria that need to be fulfilled to allocate agents to roles for the AGR approach. These criteria are crucial for realizing the organization dynamics successfully. One of the advantages of an organization model is that it abstracts from the specific agents fulfilling the roles. This means that all dynamic properties of the organization remain the same, independent of the particular allocated agents. However, the behaviors of these agents have to fulfill the dynamic properties of the roles and their interactions. The organization model can be (re)used for an arbitrary allocation of agents to roles for which:

- for each role, the allocated agent's behavior satisfies the dynamic role properties,
- for each inter-group role interaction, one agent is allocated to both roles and its behavior satisfies the inter-group role interaction properties, and the communication between agents satisfies the respective transfer properties.

Given these requirements, a designer who already has a number of agents with particular behaviors can search the library with these agent behaviors. An agent behavior can be represented with a dynamic property, similar to the role properties, as shown in Example 12. Again, an agent behavior dynamic property is the most specific identifier and constitutes the leaves of a tree. On the other hand, a more general behavior description will appear on higher nodes of the tree.

Example 10. Let `communication_from_to(Role1, Role2, inform, desired_price_for(a))` denote that `Role1` is informing `Role2` that it is interested in agreeing on a price for item a and `communication_from_to(Role1, Role2, propose, price(p, a))` denote that `Role1` is proposing to `Role2` price p for item a. Then the following TTL formulation of an agent property means that whenever the agent A receives information of a desire for an agreed price from an agent B, then A will propose a price for the same item to B.

$\forall t$ [state(γ, t, input(A)) $\models$ communication_from_to(B, A, inform, desired_price_for(a))
$\Rightarrow \exists t' \geq t \, \exists p$ state(γ, t', output(A)) $\models$ communication_from_to(A, B , propose, price(p, a))

5   Querying the Library of Groups

Section 4 studies the different methods for indexing groups. This section develops a multi-dimensional library structure that combines the different indexing schemes as different dimensions. Using this multi-dimensional taxonomy, the designer can have interactions with the system to reformulate her queries. Hence, the system is interactive.

5.1 A Multi-dimensional Taxonomic Approach

For the general approach it is just assumed that a number of taxonomies (the different contextual dimensions incorporated; cf. [8]) are given, where the nodes of these trees are used as identifiers for indexing the groups. For simplicity they are assumed to have the form of trees. Within these trees branches are defined by an isa-relation

isa(n1, n2)   (or, in infix notation: n1 isa n2)

meaning that node n2 is a direct specialization of node n1 within one of the trees. Based on the indexing, each node n in one of the trees corresponds to a subset gr(n) of groups from the library, namely those indexed by node n. It is assumed that the different levels in the trees are abstraction levels: levels of specialization (going down) or generalization (going up). This means that if a group is indexed by a node n, then automatically it is considered that the nodes higher in the same tree apply to this group. This assumption implies that more specialized nodes correspond to smaller sets of groups:

isa(n1, n2) $\Rightarrow$ gr(n1) $\subseteq$ gr(n2)

Moreover, a set S of nodes from possible different trees corresponds to the intersection of the sets of groups corresponding to the single nodes:

gr(S) = $\bigcap_{n \in S}$ gr(n)

This general setup suggests two strategies to minimize the set of groups retrieved based on a query:

- within a tree, in the query try to use an identifier as low in the tree as possible (lower nodes provide smaller sets)
- use not just one node in a query but a set of nodes, taken from as many trees as possible (using more trees entails that the set of groups is made smaller since an intersection is made)

As designers may not be expected to express their queries in terms of nodes that are most appropriate, the system offers support to reformulate queries to more adequate ones. This is discussed in the next subsection.

5.2 Query Reformulation

First assume that the group library is queried using one identifier n. When this is the case, then the taxonomy of identifiers from which n is taken is used to aid the search. If the keyword searched matches one of the leaves of the tree, then the set of groups associated with the leaf node is returned to the designer. Otherwise - if the query is matched to a node that is not a leaf - then the tree can be used to generate options for the user to further articulate her query. That is, starting from the node that matched the query, the designer can be asked to refine her query by proposing the branches of the tree as options. The underlying idea here is that the designer may know more about her needs than what she could initially formulate in a query. Hence, by posing choices to the designer, her query can be rephrased more precisely. Repeating the selection process will narrow the set of possible groups that will be returned for the query. If this query reformulation leads to one of the leaf nodes, then again the groups associated with that leaf are returned. If the user gets stuck in choosing between two branches before reaching a leaf node, then all the groups below the current node are returned. When more identifiers are present, the same can be done for other trees as well. This leads to a set of nodes S from the different trees for which each member shows a node that is as specialized as possible within the tree for that node.

Next, the groups corresponding to S is returned to the designer, which is the intersection of the sets of groups for all members of S.

In a case that a query leads to an empty set of groups, a reverse process of query reformulation may be needed: instead of specializing the query, in interaction with the designer it is generalized until the set of groups becomes non-empty. Finally, if an adequate query is reached, it is up to the designer to manually inspect the returned groups to choose an adequate group for her needs. Once the designer retrieves a group from a library, she can use it as it is or modify it further. Once, the group structure and the properties are finalized, the organization designer integrates the group into the organization structure. For our methodology, this would mean constructing appropriate group interaction properties between the new group and related existing groups.

Example 11. A designer's query could involve the identifier *payment* (for the tree describing the functionality dimension) as well as *price* (for the tree describing the output dimension). Both of these queries are vague; many groups could be related to payment as well as many groups could output some sort of price. By specializing both identifiers, a more specific combination of identifiers is reached, yielding a smaller set of groups.

5.3 Matching Query Terms and Indexing Terms

Given an abstract group identifier as a query, one needs to define a matching function that will be used to compare the query to the entries in the library. One matching function is exact matching which requires the terms of the query and the library entry to be exactly the same. A more loose way of matching is done by allowing the terms of the library entry to be logically stronger than that of the query. In other words, if an identifier of a group entails the term used in the query, one might consider it matching in a broader sense. Notice that such entailments can also be represented within the tree: a stronger term that entails a given identifier node within a tree can be added in this tree as a branch under this node. This addition can be left implicit if trees are not explicitly represented at forehand but (relevant parts of it) are generated during the process of using it.

Example 12. A query for a negotiation group is formulated where the output state is that the buyer and seller have reached an agreed price. Consider a group entry (Negotiate and Register) where in addition to reaching an agreed price, as an output it is also provided that the buyer and seller also register the price with a third party. With exact matching, the Negotiate-and-Register group will not be matched to the query. However, using entailment the group will be matched.

6 Discussion

Artikis *et al.* develop a framework that specifies a society by social constraints, social roles, and social states [1]. Social constraints define valid actions, permitted or prohibited actions, and the enforcement policies for these actions. A social role is defined as a set of preconditions and a set of constraints. The preconditions specify the requirements for an agent to play that role whereas the constraints specify what the agent should do once it is appointed to that role. Similar to our realization constraints, a role assignment procedure is then used to assign agents to roles based on the preconditions of the role and the capabilities of the agents as well as assignment constraints. Artikis *et al.* do not discuss a methodology for reusing their societies.

Padgham and Winikoff develop Prometheus, an agent-based software development methodology [12]. This methodology is intended for non-experts and thus mostly defined informally. The methodology consists of system specification, architectural design, and detailed design phases. The system specification phase outlines the necessary functionality of the software. The architectural design phase divides the overall functionality into smaller tasks that will be carried out by different agents. Finally, the detailed design phase develops the individual agents that will carry out the tasks. Prometheus does not capture any functionality templates that can later be reused. In our approach, the abstraction of roles make it possible for different agents to play defined roles based on the realization constraints. More importantly, the abstraction of groups provides templates of functionality that can be stored in a library and be reused by other multiagent organizations.

Bussmann *et al.* identify a set of criteria to classify multiagent interaction protocols [2]. Once the appropriate fields of these criteria are correctly set, the protocols can be classified and later be retrieved. Contrary to the criteria chosen in our approach, Bussmann et al. primarily consider quantitative properties, such as the number of agents involved, the number and size of the commitments between agents, and so on. Further, they do no consider a taxonomy of semantic identifiers as we have done here.

Malone *et al.* develop a library of business processes to help designers to create new organizations or restructure their existing organizations [9]. The library stores processes in specialization hierarchies. A process entry includes the name and the description of the process as well as links to more general and more special processes. Similar to our approach, the process library is developed with human designers in mind. However, in our approach we formalize the groups as well as the queries to semi-automate the search. After some groups are retrieved from the library, then the designer can investigate them further and tailor one to her needs. The content and the size of Malone *et al.*'s process library is appealing for designing multiagent organizations. Our approach can benefit from starting with such a library and extending its entries with the formalized identifiers.

The formal approach presented in this paper provides a solid basis for a software environment supporting the interactive organization design process. Parts of this software environment are already available as separate components, in particular an editor to formally specify organization properties, group properties and role properties, and software to guide the query reformulation process, as initially developed in the ICEBERG project; for a survey of this project see [8]. In current research projects on organization modeling the software environment is being integrated and developed further.

References

1. Alexander Artikis, Jeremy Pitt, and Marek Sergot. Animated specifications of computational societies. In Proceedings of the 1st International Joint Conference on Autonomous Agents and MultiAgent Systems (AAMAS), pp. 1053-1061, 2002.

2. Stefan Bussmann, Nicholas R. Jennings, and Michael Wooldridge. Re-use of Interaction Protocols for Agent-based Control Applications. In: F. Giunchiglia et al. (eds.) Proceedings of the Workshop on Agent-Oriented Software Engineering (AOSE), Lecture Notes in Computer Science 2585, pp. 73-87, 2003.

3. Katleen M. Carley and Les Gasser. Computational Organization Theory in Multiagent Systems: A Modern Approach to Distributed Artificial Intelligence. Chapter 7. Gerhard Weiss, editor. MIT Press, 1999.

4. Mehdi Dastani, Virgina Dignum, and Frank Dignum. Role-Assignment in Open Agent Societies. In: Proceedings of the International Conference on Agents and MultiAgent Sysetms (AAMAS), pp.489-496, ACM Press, 2003.

5. Jacques Ferber and Olivier Gutknecht. A meta-model for the analysis and design of organizations in multi-agent systems. In: Proceedings of the Third International Conference on Multi-Agent Systems (ICMAS), IEEE Computer Society Press, pp. 128-135, 1998.

6. Catholijn M. Jonker and Jan Treur. Relating Structure and Dynamics in an Organisation Model. In: J.S. Sichman, F. Bousquet, and P. Davidson (eds.), Multi-Agent-Based Simulation II, Proc. of the Third International Workshop on Multi-Agent Based Simulation, MABS'02. Lecture Notes in AI, vol. 2581, pp. 50-69, Springer Verlag, 2003.

7. Catholijn M. Jonker and Jan Treur. Compositional Verification of Multi-Agent Systems: a Formal Analysis of Pro-activeness and Reactiveness. International Journal of Cooperative Information Systems, vol. 11, pp. 51-92, 2002.

8. Catholijn M. Jonker and A. M. Vollebregt. ICEBERG: Exploiting Context in Information Brokering Agents. In: M. Klusch, L. Kerschberg (eds.), Cooperative Information Agents IV, Proceedings of the Fourth International Workshop on Cooperative Information Agents (CIA), Lecture Notes in Artificial Intelligence 1860, pp. 27-38, Springer Verlag, 2000.

9. Thomas W. Malone *et al.* Tools for Inventing Organizations: Toward a Handbook of Organizational Processes. In: Management Science, Vol. 45, No. 3, March 1999.

10. K. Meinke, J.V. Tucker (eds.), Many-Sorted Logic and Its Applications. Wiley & Sons, 1993.

11. Hafedh Mili, Ali Mili, Sherif Yacoub, and Edward Addy. Reuse-Based Software Engineering: Techniques, Organizations, and Controls. Jon Wiley & Sons, 2002.

12. Lin Padgham and Michael Winikoff. Prometheus: A Methodoloogy for Developing Intelligent Agents. In: F. Giunchiglia et al. (eds.) Proceedings of the Workshop on Agent-Oriented Software Engineering (AOSE), Lecture Notes in Computer Science 2585, pp. 174-185, 2003.

13. Hans van Vliet. Software Engineering: Principles and Practice. John Wiley and Sons, 2000.

Author Index

Lecture Notes in Computer Science

For information about Vols. 1–3247

please contact your bookseller or Springer